UNBLOCKCHAIN

Wouldn't it be great if there is a book out there that can help me understanding the latest trending technology - Blockchain in a relaxed manner with tons of graphics, which is even more fun than a barrel full of monkeys?!

HENRIQUE CENTIEIRO

Unblockchain

First edition

By Henrique Centieiro

ISBN: 978-988-75671-0-3 (Paperback)
978-988-75671-1-0.(eBook)

"I am very glad that Henrique describes the true meaning of Blockchain technology and perhaps, also the reasons why the 5th Industrial Revolution will be ignited. Let's buckle up and brace for the upcoming waves of creative disruptions right after you have digested the book's rich yet insightful contents."

Emil Chan, Fintech Evangelist

"As someone who has worked with Henri for the last couple of years sharing the same passion and interest in blockchains/DLT, this book is very informative, insightful as well as a joy to read."

Timothy Shum, Tech Lead, HSBC

"The blockchain space is ever-evolving, and I am delighted to recommend Henrique's latest book as a must-have to those individuals looking to thrive in the new era of decentralisation!"

Lavine Hemlani, CEO, xccelerate.co

"We need a book like this in the blockchain industry. Very informative and fun to read too. Written by practitioner Henri, Unblockchain is a perfect book for anyone who wants to understand the fundamentals of blockchain technology and why it matters. Highly recommend."

Edmund To, Senior Technical Architect, ConsenSys

"Unblockchain is an invaluable source of information for anyone who seeks deep understanding of blockchain technology. It covers all major technical and economic aspects together with latest trends like NFTs and Ethereum PoS. Reading this book is easy, enjoyable and fun!"

Mikhail Miro, CEO, LOC Game

"This book couldn't have come at a more apt time. Henri does an amazing job demystifying the hype and myths about blockchain while still presenting a compelling case for the ubiquity of the technology. The book provides sufficient information to assist the reader in making the leap from novice to expert in a fun to read and easy to understand format. A must-read for any leader of a technology company expecting to navigate the complexity and nuance of the Industry 4.0 evolution."

Kwadwo Konadu Ansah-Antwi (PhD), CEO & Founder, Hessner Technologies Limited

"Great book to understand Blockchain basics, but also with the necessary technical insights to understand what Blockchain really is about. It's written in a simple to understand language and also an entertaining read."

Frank von Thun, CEO of VTC GROUP

Table of Contents (Summary)

Table of Contents (the real thing!)

Chapter 1

Tired of facing the same problems? You have heard a lot about blockchain, but what's exactly the difference is between blockchain and a traditional database? What is the difference between blockchain and DLT? This section will give you some foundational knowledge and show you the key concepts of the blockchain technology. You will also read about the blockchain benefits and what makes a good blockchain use case.

Chapter 2

Wait, are we talking about use cases again? Yes, but now let's look at some examples of the existing blockchain use cases in the market. We will cover only a few use cases as an example because to cover all the use cases I would have to write a 2000 pages book (probably more than the Atlas Shrugged and all the Lord of the Rings combined).

Chapter 3

This is getting pretty serious now! This section will clear out any confusion related to the technology. We are going to the blockchain bottom line and look at all the blockchain components here, and you will be one step closer to become a blockchain expert! Now serious, the objective is to get some key concepts right to navigate the blockchain technology.

Chapter 4

Consensus mechanisms, cryptography, prime numbers, random numbers, mathematics and hashing?! Don't worry, I promise this section will be more exciting than going to the dentist! You will learn and play around with some really cool stuff. After this chapter, you will be top 1% most blockchain knowledgeable people in the world.

Chapter 5

If you want something done right, it's better you do it yourself! This section is pretty much hands-on. You can do read-it-only, but it works best if you follow along by deploying your own node and play around with it. I'm sure this section will be a lot of fun!!

Forenote

Disclosure: views expressed are purely personal and do not reflect any organisation's views or thoughts the writer of this book may be affiliated or associated with.

The future is decentralized. After hundreds of years of relying on big institutions as middlemen, the internet and the blockchain are changing how people do businesses. These new technologies bring back the barter system, allowing people who don't know each other; who are in different parts of the world; who speak different languages; who may eventually not trust each other, to trade between each other confidently in the same system. The magic of the blockchain can connect people together in social business networks. Can Ethereum be the new Facebook for business?

Blockchain is definitely here to stay. In 2021, 12 years after the creation of Bitcoin, we finally see the mass adoption of blockchains and cryptocurrencies. Many big corporations are either buying cryptocurrencies or adopting blockchain technologies. Have you heard that Mastercard, Facebook, Paypal, Microstretagy, Square, Diginex, Telsa and many other big corporates are big time in crypto? And what about all the financial institutions that are experimenting or using blockchain solutions?

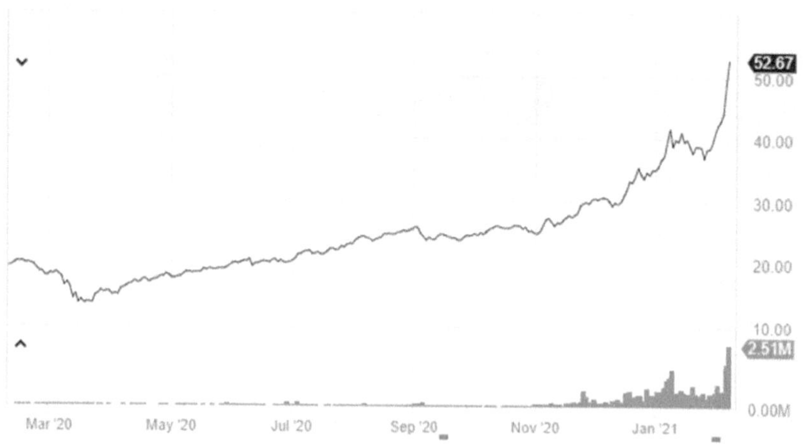

This chart belongs to Amplify Transformational Data Sharing ETF, ticker symbol BLOK. It's basically a blockchain ETF meaning that it's portfolio is made out of companies that are dealing with blockchain technology. The ETF had more than 150% return in one single year. Everybody knows that crypto (Bitcoin, Dogecoin, Ether, etc.) had amazing returns in 2020 and early 2021, but it's also important to look at the companies that are investing in blockchain technologies.

The growing demand for blockchain technology leads us to increase demand for blockchain jobs. Blockchain developers, software architects and project managers are among the most best well-paid jobs in the market with continuously growing demand. The blockchain space is, however, quite complex to navigate with many different blockchain technologies and different industries. Should I learn about public blockchains or private blockchains? Should I invest my time developing applications for cryptocurrencies or private business networks? Should I be learning about Dogecoin or Corda?

This book will guide you through the technologies that are used in both public and private blockchains. What are the use cases and what makes a good blockchain use case, how are blockchain business networks composed, the technologies used such as cryptography, hashing, public key infrastructure, how to deploy a node and much more.

Join me in this big leap to the blockchain world!

About the author

For a few years, I (Henrique, you can call me Henri) have been working in blockchain, project managing different blockchain projects from eCommerce to supply-chain and trade finance. Working as a Senior Project Manager for HSBC, I have successfully supported the implementation of blockchain and fintech solutions for trade finance and for the fintech industry. Experienced in Ethereum, Hyperledger Fabric, Corda and other technologies, I have also been providing blockchain training to different institutions and the fintech community and universities. With 15 years of experience in the financial industry (18 years to be exact if we start counting since the first forex and stock investments), I am extremely passionate about new technologies, cloud, fintech and AI's future, my girlfriend's silly jokes, dogs and underground hip-hop.

Introduction

The blockchain is a distributed database that is used to record data (assets, transactions, etc), has characteristics such as consensus, provenance, immutability, finality and the blocks of data are connected with hash functions and uses cryptography — Me 😎

This book will discuss blockchain protocols, how blockchains are architected, the main technology components such as cryptography, hashing, applications, and the constraints and limitations of this technology.

I will help you to understand when to use blockchain, the key concepts, the industry jargon, and a lot of additional information that will help you to interact with stakeholders in any blockchain project you may get involved.

Some parts of this book may be a bit technical, but any person with some basic IT experience will be able to follow along. No matter what's your background, after you finished reading this book, you will be able to get involved in any blockchain project.

Blockchain projects are bringing benefits in many industries, including substantial cost reductions, more efficiency, transparency and security, as well as the development of new business models and opportunities.

Bitcoin, also called "internet magic money", had a lot of hype and has drawn a lot of attention from the public. But is blockchain the same as Bitcoin?

Blockchain came about with the public's loss of confidence in the financial sector during the 2008 economic crisis. Bitcoin was the very first blockchain use case launched on Jan. 3rd, 2009 and was created by Satoshi Nakamoto. Nobody knows well who Satoshi Nakamoto is, and I could give my two cents, but that's a topic for a different book. The only thing I can say about that is that Craig Wright is not Satoshi Nakamoto.

However, blockchain is a much more broad concept that includes Bitcoin and many other cryptocurrencies, distributed ledgers, and thousands of potential applications.

Blockchain is now one of the core technologies in Fintech, and its applications go from Fintech to supply chain, trade finance, payments, insurance, settlement, buying drugs in dark web markets and much more.

Bitcoin currently has an average of 322 thousand transactions per day. More than 100 million Bitcoin wallets prove that Bitcoin (and perhaps blockchain) is getting more and more popular among the general public. It is also the oldest autonomous and decentralized system, running since 2009 without the need for intervention from central parties. It allows for the first time global real-time settlement (or almost real-time) where financial institutions take days.

Fun fact: back in 2014/2015 some people in Portugal wanted to send some transaction from Portugal to Brazil to buy/sell commodities, but bank transfers would take almost one week. The alternative was to contact Russian exchanges that would send a person from Russia to Portugal to sell Bitcoin to the customer, which was then sent to Brazil. Back then, this process was much faster than a normal bank transfer.

Blockchain, like any other innovation, didn't appear out of nowhere. Blockchain creation was inspired by a few existing technologies like cryptography, peer to peer networks and BitTorrent networks. Double-entry bookkeeping, digital cash concept - Hashcash from Adam Back, B Money from Wei Dai and Bit Gold from Nick Szabo and other projects from the cypherpunk community - also helped. Most of all, Bitcoin creation came from the wish to make the world more fair, democratic, and decentralized place when banks have failed to do so.

Blockchain is already changing the way we do business. It's slowly improving many business models, creating new business opportunities and changing the way we live even though most of us don't even notice it. Blockchain architecture naturally solves the multiparty trust issue in distributed bookkeeping, and there are hundreds of use cases, many of them considered quite successful.

We are going to take a look at why blockchain is considered so secure, what technologies are enabling blockchain, what kind of applications - financial and non-financial - can benefit from blockchain? What are the differences between Bitcoin, Ethereum, Hyperledger and Corda? How is blockchain secure, and how is data handled? How is hashing made? What's cryptography's role?

The introduction of Turing-complete programming languages and blockchains such as Ethereum marks the blockchain 2.0 era where almost anything can be developed on the top of a blockchain.

Blockchain characteristics allow business networks (different parts of a business or consortiums) to conduct transactions in completely different ways when compared to traditional, centralized legacy systems. This is why blockchain is disrupting so many industries. The industries that are currently benefiting the most from the blockchain are supply chain, banking and fintech, insurance, health, govtech, regtech, real estate, energy, retail, education, and don't forget the DeFi, fundraising and ICOs.

This book will help you to:

- Understand and apply shared ledgers and smart contracts to your business network

- Explore the blockchain technology in-depth

- Explore the blockchain architecture

- Deploy an Ethereum node

- Understand how to perform various activities in the Ethereum Blockchain using the command line interface

- Take it to the next level of the Dunning-Kruger curve

Hopefully this book is going to be a good step in your blockchain learning curve, bringing you more enlightenment that will help you going through the productivity slope with confidence.

Let's go down to the 🐰 hole?! Join me in the next chapter to get started!

Chapter 1

Blockchain - Why, What and How?

Let's start with a quiz:

Why do we need Blockchains or Decentralized Distributed Ledgers?

a) Because Bitcoin is the new gold

b) Because Dogecoin is going to the moon

c) Because blockchain is a distributed database that allows parties to transact in a trustless and seamless way

This one is hard to answer!

First of all, blockchain is NOT a complex technology. One of this book's objectives is to demystify the blockchain technology, and that's why I called it "Unblockchain". I'm tired of seeing people in the blockchain industry saying that it is a very complex technology when it is really just a database or a ledger that is replicated a number of times as has some additional mechanisms to ensure consensus immutability.

Straightforwardly, a blockchain is a distributed ledger or database that allows recording the state of an asset and allows a trustless relationship between parties that maybe don't know each other and allow to automate contractual agreements. How do we achieve this?

Being a decentralized system keeps the ledger in a peer-to-peer network where all the computers are connected and keep an updated copy of the ledger. All the nodes involved in a blockchain keep a full ledger and keep track of the balances or assets since the beginning. A node is basically a computer on the network, and the term comes from computer science. Nodes participate in peer-to-peer networks.

The ledger is shared across many peer nodes (from a few dozens to thousands) in such a way that each machine can verify the individual transaction and announce if the transactions are valid or not.

The magical book analogy:

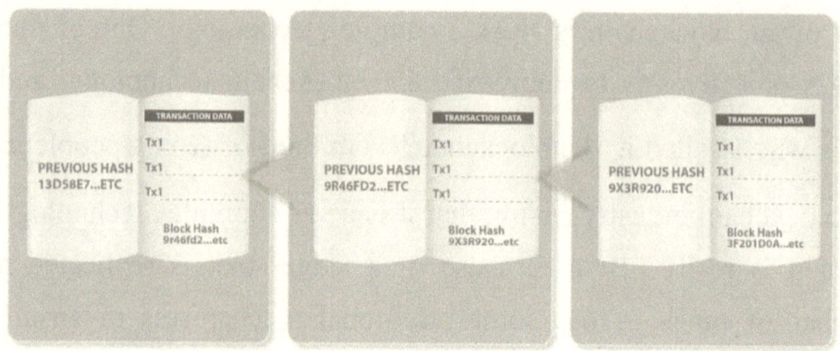

- Try to imagine an old paper book where each page refers to the previous page with a code

- The book is the blockchain, and each page is a block. Each line on the page is a blockchain transaction

- Because each page is numbered and refers to the previous page, it is easy to detect if a page was removed or changed

- Pages are numbered in a way that makes it easy to detect and prevent malicious activity

- Since pages are stacked on top of each other, it's tough to tamper with old pages

Decentralized or Distributed?

We see two terms being used frequently and interchangeably in the blockchain space: decentralized and distributed. What are the differences?

Distributed systems DO NOT equal to decentralized.

Distributed systems refer to a system that can store and process data in different locations; while the concept of decentralized usually refers to when there's not a single party that can make decision on how the system behaves or to change data that was distributed in the system. Therfore, decentralized means that there's no single point of authority that control or decide what the system should do.

There are however, distributed systems that are centralized in one single entity. Most big tech companies use distributed systems. Netflix, for example, uses AWS [i] distributed content delivery network, but the whole system is owned and controlled by Netflix and AWS. These entities have the power to perform any actions they wish to in the system.

Although the concept of distributing systems resembles blockchain, the concept is way older than blockchain, and they are widely used in computer networks. Another popular example of distributed systems would be file distributed systems such as the peer-to-peer network BitTorrent[ii.]

We can say that blockchains are distributed considering that the system is (again) distributed across many nodes. At the same time, blockchains (most of them) are also decentralized, which mean that they don't have a single point of authority or a single point of failure, and there's no single point of authority where decisions are made.

In a distributed system, two or more nodes work in a coordinated fashion (for example, synchronizing data). Although blockchain may have dozens, hundreds or thousands of nodes, the system is modelled in a way that the end users see it as a single logical system/application and a single source of truth.

In a blockchain, nodes are individual computers or servers in the distributed system. Usually, nodes can send and receive messages between each other and are connected in a peer-to-peer fashion.

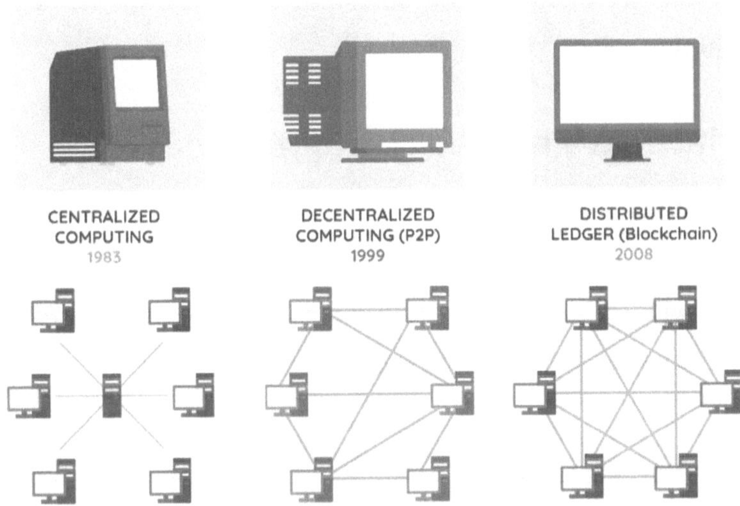

With no single party in control, a blockchain or distributed ledger is an open system where anyone can participate. The ledger is fully distributed across the network. Note, however, that in permissioned blockchains it is possible to design a blockchain so that data sharing is made on a need-to-know basis. In permissioned blockchain, we can give permission to only a set of parties in the blockchain network to read or write data.

Blockchain doesn't merely solve the data-sharing issues. It also solves the confidence and trust issues. In a peer-to-peer ecosystem, the individual user - not a third party - will decide what information is recorded in the blockchain and how it will be used. Blockchain allows users to manage their identities in a trustless way, i.e. without the need of trusting a centralized system. The blockchain system itself can be trusted. Confusing? No worries, I will explain everything.

So why do we need a Distributed Ledger Technology or DLT?

Until now, people need to trust a centralized party to be a trusted party where they can store and keep track of our money. The financial system is a good example of this. The bank basically keeps thousands of centralized ledgers and keeps track of all the balances of their customers. The bank is the only one responsible for the integrity, privacy and correctness of all the data, transactions and balances of their customers.

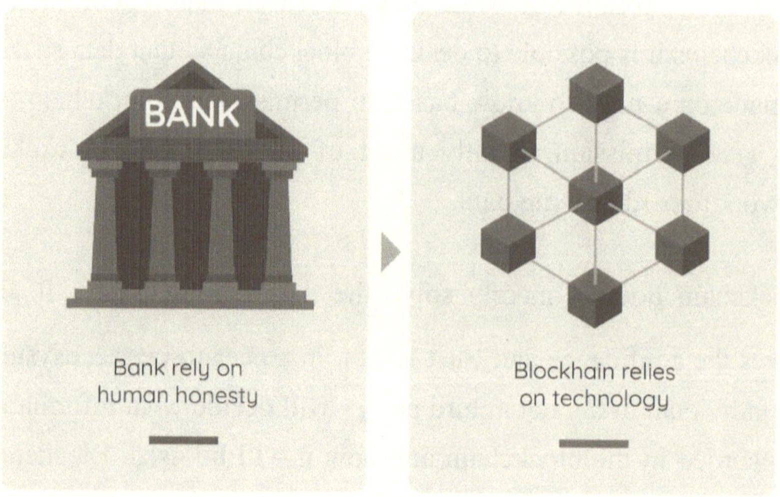

When Alice sends Bob $100, the bank checks if Alice has enough balance before sending the transaction, then updates the balance of both accounts, debiting $100 in Alice's ledger and crediting $100 in Bob's. Both trust the bank, and most of the times, this trust system works well. The bank also makes money by providing this service: charging fees and investing the depositors' money.

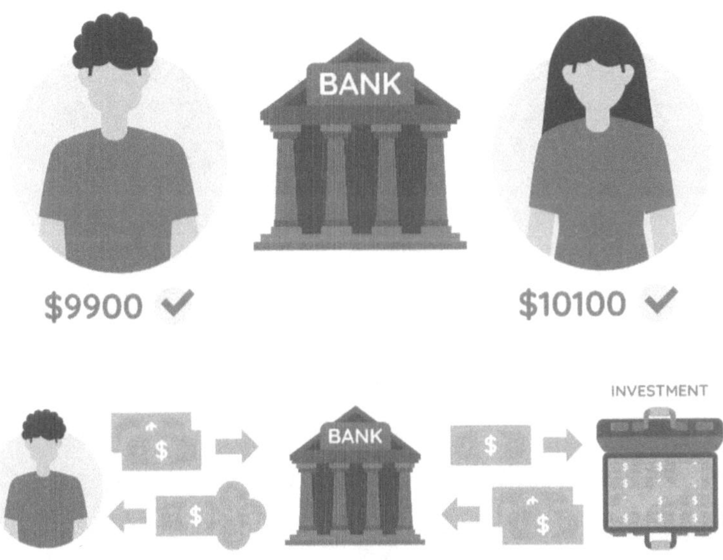

In the meantime, the bank may pay interest to the customers to attract more people to deposit their money.

Bank's original business has evolved and now provide hundreds of services other than providing deposit and lending facilities. Is it OK to trust a bank for all these services? Most of the times, we can indeed trust banks, but what about Lehman Brothers and all the banks that collapsed during the subprime crisis? The memory is still fresh on how banks lent to the 2008/2009 subprime crisis when hundreds of banks went bankrupt worldwide, hurting millions of depositors.

Although this book is not about the monetary system, the reality is that the whole monetary system is ran by central banks that have money printing machines (literally) and can keep interest rates artificially low, which results in boom-and-bust cycles. The crypto community continues to idealize that maybe, one day, blockchains will fix the system.

I understand why people trust so much in banks sometimes more than they trust Bitcoin and blockchain. Blockchains are invisible while bank buildings… Don't they look as they will last forever?

Blockchains such as Bitcoin could solve the monetary problem with a fixed and predictable supply of the currency.

But blockchains came to solve many other problems from supply chains, marketplaces, trade finance, decentralized finance and voting. Let's look at the global payments example: one of the big blockchain use cases.

- The middleman - usually banks or remittance companies - take fees for transferring money. Sometimes the fees are more than 10% of the amount transferred

- Most of the times, they have a minimum size for the transaction, which cuts the possibility for small transactions and micropayments

- Cross-boarder payment systems are not transparent in some countries

- Financial transactions are slow, and cross border wire transfers frequently take days to complete

- The sender and receiver have very little or no control over the transaction

- Lack of transparency in many financial instruments

- Slow processing time in most of the banking products

So as you see, we needed a system that could solve these big pain points. A system that could make people less dependent on big institutions serving as middlemen.

In 2009, Satoshi Nakamoto came up with a solution that would solve all this:

- Regulated (mathematically through algorithms) to maintain the supply of the asset

- No centralized authority control the creation of the asset

- Eliminate the need for intermediaries reducing the transaction costs

- Transparent and tamper-resistant blocking any possible manipulation or fraud

- Increasing transaction speeds from days to minutes and facilitating very fast ledger updates, no matter the geographical location

There are also some essential characteristics and advantages when referring to blockchain and cryptocurrencies. We will go deeper into this topic but let's take a high-level look at it:

- Decentralized: There is no centralized third party controlling the blockchain and its transactions, and there's no central management (exceptions may apply in permissioned/private blockchains)

- Anonymous (or pseudo-anonymous): according to the transaction information, it's no possible to obtain the user's real identity (exceptions may apply in permissioned/private blockchains)

- Secure: the blockchain security is ensured by the consensus mechanism and the very hard to break public-key cryptography

- Fast (relatively) and global: a blockchain can be accessed as long as there's an internet connection. Transactions can be completed in a few minutes.

- Cryptocurrencies are permissionless and public. Anyone in the world can use them, and the user's geographical location doesn't matter.

Why do we need Decentralized systems?

One word: trust.

As we know, banks and financial institutions charge fees for almost all the services provided. The services provided by financial institutions is no doubt important in creating a trust layer for people to transact and do business. But what if we can have a better, faster and cheaper way to do it?

When the modern baking system was created 500 years ago, the idea was revolutionary. The banks created during the Italian Renaissance were a technology disruption. Now blockchain is the new technology disruption challenging the old world.

If you send a wire transfer between banks in 2 different countries to support your parents, it's normal to pay up to $30 for a small transfer. At the same time, remittance companies such as MoneyGram, Western Union and UAE Exchange frequently charge more than 10% fee to people that want to send some savings back home. Many times, the people that most need essential financial services are the ones that pay the highest fees.

Do we really need these intermediaries? Or can we have a transparent system that allows transferring value without trusting a middleman?

Having a centralized party intermingling our transactions may have some advantages, but they naturally carry all these fees, which is part of the centralized business model.

There are other issues, such as privacy issues. The centralized party handling your money which can be a bank or even WeChat in China (the biggest chat and payment application in the world owned by Tencent) can look at your balance, transactions, how much money you have and your investments. They can share data with despotic governments, and they are seen as a giant honey pot target to cyber-criminals.

In recent years, government regulations force financial institutions to disclose customers funds. They have many times the power to freeze assets, which, unfortunately, may happen in an entirely arbitrary way in some countries.

Privacy issues related to data integrity and data security are also an issue these days, where cybersecurity is not always the main concern for the centralized party resulting in data leakages when hackers decide to take advantage of the centralized party vulnerabilities.

The 2017 Equifax attack exposed 143 million customers' personal data, including 209 000 Credit Card details, and the Ashley Madison data breach exposed (very!) private data of thousands of people using the dating website.

We could talk about thousands of examples related to privacy issues in the financial system too. Thousands of other data leakages or cyber-attacks happen every year to financial institutions, dating applications and literally every centralized service that handles significant amounts of personal data.

Centralized platforms also frequently use our personal data for Data Analytics and AI, which brings good outcomes and leverages Fintech technologies, enhancing our daily lives and bringing another risk vector.

There's no guarantee most of the times that the platform won't sell your data or use your data for other purposes, just like Cambridge Analytica was doing to manipulate Facebook users in the 2016 US elections allegedly. Cambridge Analytica scandal was luckily exposed by Brittany Kaiser, but what about all the other misuses of data that never reach the public knowledge?

This is one reason why some regulations such as GDPR were created, providing the users with more ownership over their personally identifiable data, aka PII data.

Another issue is that in many "centralized world" business processes, is that there are many databases or ledgers that need to sync to enable the business to happen. There are too many bottlenecks and unnecessary process redundancy in the existing systems. For instance, every time we need to open a bank account, subscribe to new insurance, buy a car, check-in at the airport, or buy a house, we need to provide specific subsets of data and repeat it over and over again.

Repeating this process requires time, produces inefficiencies and a big waste of paper.

The solution is to have a trusted distributed ledger where you can use to share your data on a permissioned and need to know basis according to the life events previously mentioned.

Introducing the Distributed Ledger Technology

Distributed Ledger Technology is the technology that finally brings trust to decentralized systems. It has a structure that resides across multiple computer devices or nodes. These nodes are usually spread across different locations.

Although distributed ledgers or distributed file systems already existed before the term blockchain was coined (for example distributed file systems and BitTorrent), Bitcoin was the first blockchain. Bitcoin marks a new era where existing technologies are put together to build a blockchain: peer-to-peer networks with timestamping transactions, cryptography and a consensus mechanism.

A DLT will require three components to work, and these three components are:

- a data model or data standards

- a common language and

- a protocol used to build the consensus system among the peers

These three elements, data standards, common language a common protocol, will allow all the nodes in the network to be connected seamlessly, talk the same language, and provide the user with a unified experience.

Most of the traditional ledgers and centralized systems don't share all these 3 components. Traditional ledgers may have different data standards, different languages and use diverse protocols.

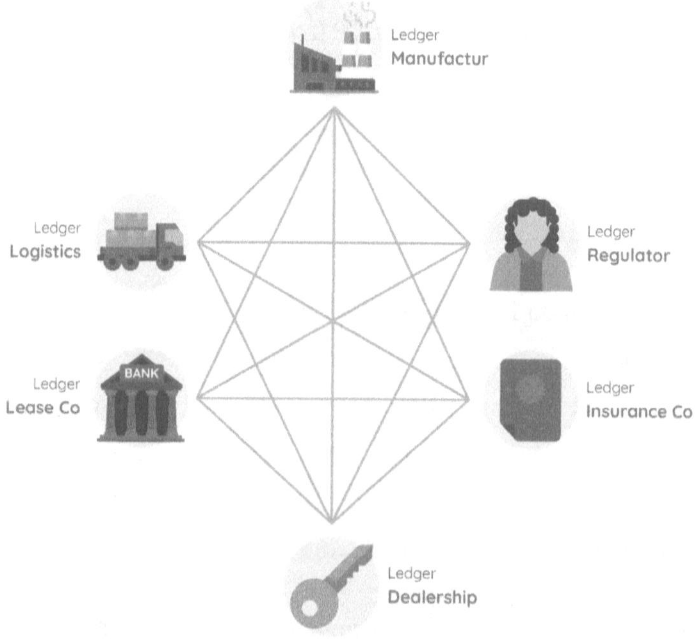

A basic example can be seen in this diagram which can be applied to the car industry.

In this example, different parties have different ledgers: the manufacturer, regulator, logistics company, lease company, dealership and even the scrap merchant. All these different ledgers are expensive to maintain, slow, vulnerable to fraud, mistakes, cyber-attacks, and it is simply inefficient.

It also needs many integrations, and systems may speak different languages. Most important, they are not synchronized, and there's no transparency whatsoever among the parties involved.

I gave the car industry example, but we could really have any business network that involves several parties.

The traditional process is hard to monitor, data is scattered, and it's just messy and problematic:

- It is expensive because it duplicates the effort to update the ledgers across the different parties in the business network

- Each participant keeps their ledger which is very asynchronous

- Very inefficient and vulnerable because of incidents like fraud, cyber-attacks on the ledgers. Additionally, mistakes are easy to happen

Blockchain can radically transform the process and make it much more efficient. In most blockchains, the technology enables parties that don't know each other and may even have conflicting interests to transact efficiently and faithfully.

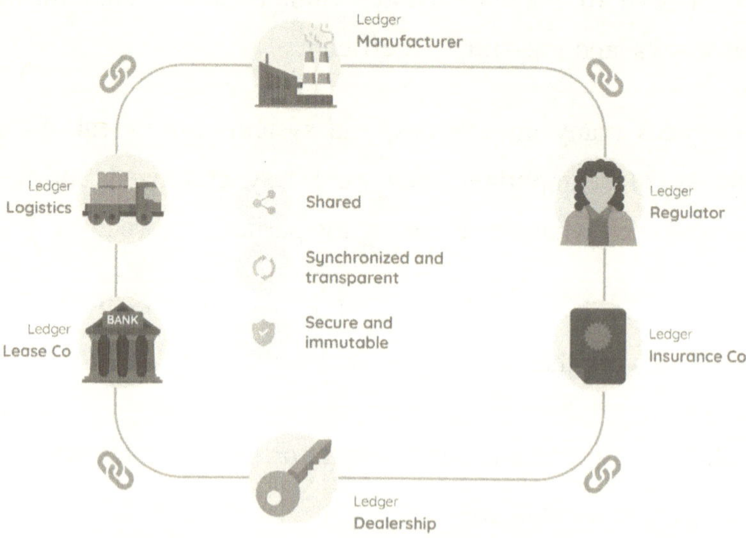

The diagram above shows a shared blockchain solution hypothetically enabled by a permissioned blockchain.

If all these parties adopt the same blockchain application, the data is shared across the different parties according to the blockchain's business logic and permissions. In other words, the business logic can be embedded in the blockchain via smart contracts representing the business flow between parties. The manufacturer may, for example, have the capacity to "write" new assets the cars - in the ledger, while the dealership can update the ownership of the assets in the ledger.

Compared to the legacy systems, blockchain can bring more security, improved availability and data integrity, reduce transaction times, saving costs and help to eliminate paper. Blockchain is also fully auditable and tamper-resistant.

Now you can see the reason why blockchain is such a great solution with many use cases.

Instead of keeping all the transactions in a single place like a bank or keeping one different ledger per participant like the example above, we can put all the transactions on the chain where everybody can get a copy and check/audit all the transactions.

This system brings transparency to what blockchain is known for. You can see it as a system where everyone has access to the same version of the data, and everyone agrees with what's considered the truth. Everyone is now sharing the same ledger.

Note that according to the way a blockchain is designed and architected, different parties may be able to see/verify the transactions but eventually not be able to modify them. In the example above, the regulator may have read-only capacity because regulators won't need to create new transactions but only to supervise the transactions that were created by the other participants. You can tailor made any new blockchain solution according to the business needs.

Financial institutions can get huge benefits from using blockchain. For example, global securities trading is complicated, inefficient and has prolonged settlement times. According to the European Central Bank, the settlement cost is 5 to 10 billion dollars, and the cost of reconciliation exceeds 20 billion dollars. Blockchain can help to lower these costs and change the transaction time to near real-time.

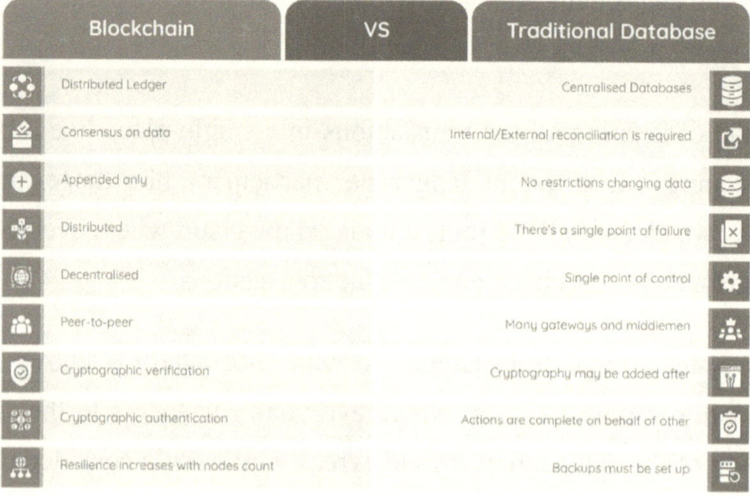

Besides business benefits, the blockchain can also bring other non-functional benefits such as high availability - blockchain is a very redundant database, i.e. replicated many times a thus, it is highly available. Blockchain can offer close to 100% or even 100% availability. This is typically seen in public blockchains such as Bitcoin and Ethereum, but private blockchains can also achieve amazing availability levels.

Blockchain may also bring many other advantages – fully synchronized databases, security, cost-saving, verifiability, auditability and awesomeness.

Blockchain provides participants with the capacity to share updates across the business network every time a transaction occurs in a peer-to-peer fashion. At the same time, participants see only the data in the ledger that is relevant to them according to the business logic through some cryptography capabilities.

Smart contracts can also be embedded in the blockchain code. They can automate any business logic, determining the conditions under which a transaction occurs or how assets are transferred between participants. The participants will agree on specific rules since they join the blockchain network — rules such as how transactions are verified and committed in the blockchain. This implicit agreement is achieved through a consensus mechanism which we will also discuss in this book.

In permissioned blockchains, participants can also agree to some kind of offline governance oversight. Most times, the offline governance models are brought by consortiums of companies or non-profit organizations.

When building a new blockchain, we need to talk about blockchain participants, not only to consider the business logic of the application but also some blockchain characteristics that are always present in any blockchain. Can all the participants on that business network accept these characteristics?

The main characteristics of blockchains are provenance, immutability, finality and consensus. Let's take a look at them:

- Provenance: each party knows where a transaction or asset comes from and how the ownership has changed over time

- Immutability: no participant can change a transaction once committed in the blockchain. If a transaction was a mistake, then a new transaction needs to be done – this gives us an excellent audit trail

- Finality: participants have one final and single place to determine the state of an asset or transaction

- Consensus: participants have a mechanism to agree on what a valid transaction looks like

From the very well known Bitcoin to JP Morgan's Quorum, every blockchain share these characteristics.

What makes a good blockchain use case?

The time when adding the word blockchain to a project just for the hype is gone. Even Kodak announced the "Kodakcoin" which caused the stock price to triple, but…is there a use case?

It's essential to build a logical decision tree to better understand if a blockchain fits your business's needs.

If your business case needs one or more of the points below, then it may be a candidate to explore blockchain technology:

- Multiple participants that need to have access to the data

- Need a common shared database

- Need to improve the transparency of data shared across different parties

- Need to have a synchronizes database across different parties

- Parties involved may have conflicting incentives

- Need an immutable database

- Rules of the business network can be established since the beginning

- Need an extremely redundant database

- Need to look cool in front of stakeholders ;) Nah

If your use case fits one or more of the points above, then blockchain may be the right solution. Maybe it's time to POC it!

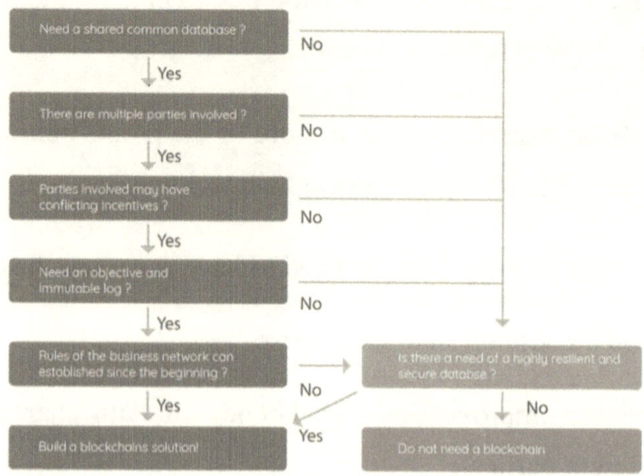

You can also use this blockchain decision tree to help with the decision.

Now that we have looked at the questions that make we need to ask to make a blockchain use case, we also need to look at the limitations. It's not everything sunshine and rainbows in the blockchain world.

Blockchains are still limited for some use cases, and they may not be suitable at all to be used as:

- Data warehousing

- Storing big files or large volumes of data

- To replace purely centralized databases

- When there's no need for a network or for sharing data

- When there's a need for a very high I/O (there is some latency)

- Just to look cool to investors or to the management

Stop reading this book, grab a pen and paper, and write down use cases that you think may be a good fit for blockchain. It can be related to your business, your company or something you would like to solve in your daily life. Does your business case pass the test? Is it a good candidate for blockchain technology?

Having a decentralized trust system

Except for some exceptions like blockchain consortiums, a single organization cannot own a decentralized system or a blockchain. Well, technically, a single organization can own a blockchain, but it wouldn't make sense to centralized something that is supposed to be decentralized.

v? In a centralized system like a bank, we trust that when we send $100 to the flower shop (yeah, I buy expensive flowers), the bank is going to update the account balance with that amount. What about a decentralized system?

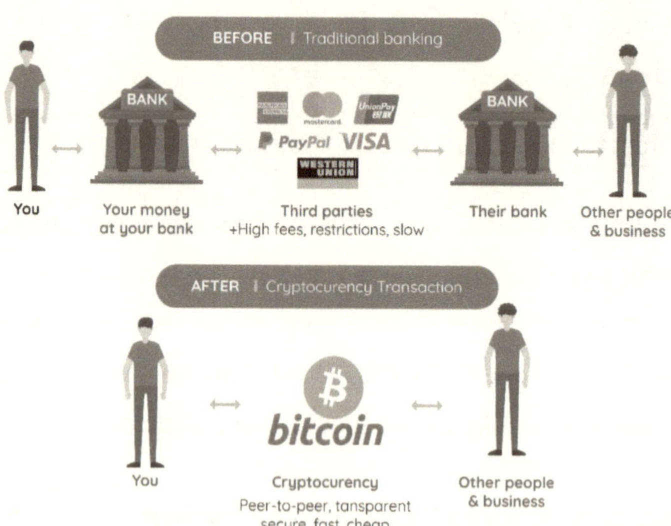

In a blockchain-based decentralized system, the account balance ledger is distributed across many nodes on the internet that agrees on the same information and allows anyone to check/verify the data, and all actions are transparent. For example, in the Bitcoin blockchain, thousands of nodes are synchronized and keep the ledger updated continuously.

When someone receives 0.1 Bitcoin, that transaction is broadcasted across thousands of nodes that run a consensus algorithm and will append that transaction to the ledger. Those records are shared across thousands of nodes, making it extremely difficult or almost impossible to corrupt or tamper with the data. Imagine the transaction is shared in this accounting book, but the accounting book is not in your accountant office only. It is instead in 100's or 1000's of accountants office ledgers. Very secure, right?

In the Bitcoin blockchain, if Alice wants to send 0.1 Bitcoin to Bob, the blockchain nodes can easily verify if Alice has that amount of Bitcoin because the ledger is distributed and replicated across many many nodes. They see that Alice has 0.1 BTC, indeed. When Alice sends the 0.1 Bitcoin to Bob, the ledger is updated, and the update is shared across all the nodes.

If Alice wants to send 0.1 Bitcoin, but she doesn't own Bitcoin, she cannot merely hack or bribe a few nodes to change the ledger because the majority has to agree. She would need to bribe or hack thousands of nodes. Subsequently, it extremely difficult to hack or change existing data in a blockchain.

With a blockchain, you can simply trust the system.

Security, Integrity and Privacy Issues of a Decentralized System

It is very difficult for any party in a blockchain system to modify a already committed transaction. This is why blockchain is the perfect technology when coordination and trust among parties are required. If you don't trust 100% your counterparties, having an immutable ledger of records is excellent to have a trusted source of data.

Blockchain is even more useful when the different parties may have some conflicting interests or have some complex coordination between them. In these cases, a distributed ledger, where everyone can see what's happening and have access to exactly the same data, can really help.

When deciding whether to use a blockchain for a business, we need to consider specific requirements without which a blockchain it's not a blockchain. Alongside the blockchain decision tree that we previously saw, we also need to consider that blockchain will also be offering:

- A shared ledger where records are append-only and shared across the business network

- Transactions are secured, encrypted and protected through cryptography which may bring design constraints

- Privacy where only permissioned participants (on permissioned blockchains) have visibility over the data and can verify transactions

- The trust system where transactions are accepted in the ledger according to specific predefined rules cannot be changed frequently

- Smart contracts that are used to include the business terms may have security flaws

To start, let's go through the very basics of what is blockchain. As you progress in the book, we will go deeper and deeper to understand the blockchain's different layers. Let's peel one more layer out of this onion.

Important also to say that decentralization is not really a blockchain catachrestic. All blockchains are distributed, and resilience increases with node count. Coincidently or not, more nodes also mean more decentralization. However, decentralization is NOT necessary to have a fully functional blockchain system. When we are talking about enterprise solutions, it may be good to have a certain degree of centralization in order to have well-defined governance rules. Still, for example, 20 nodes may, in many cases, may be already considered fairly decentralized when comparing to traditional centralized databases.

Blockchain Benefits

Most of the world's prominent financial institutions are developing or already working with some sort of blockchain technology. These blockchain technologies bring benefits such as transparency, immutability, cost reduction and traceability, crucial for some use cases.

Although blockchain was created may years ago in 2009 and enterprises started to explore it around 2015, it still far from becoming a mainstream technology. Many financial institutions continue exploring business cases by developing blockchain pilots and Proof of Concept (PoC) projects. However, a few banks and financial institutions are already using it, as we will see a bit further.

We have talked about cost reduction and transparency, but what are the practical and non-functional benefits that blockchain may bring for a business?

In most use cases where enterprises are adopting blockchain, multiple benefits can be achieved:

- Blockchain can save time and speed up transactions that traditionally take hours or days to a few seconds or minutes (blockchains still have speed limitations and it cannot speed up transactions that need to be done in milliseconds like the ones processed by Visa)

- Blockchain reduces risks related to fraud, tampering and cybercrime

- Blockchain can reduce costs, especially costs related to intermediaries

- Improves discoverability, especially when everyone can see who are the participants in a specific network and trade with them (for example a trading platform connecting buyers and sellers of goods or commodities)

- Improves network effects in business networks - the more participants a network has, the better the network's value and the capacity to conduct business in the network grows. For example, a trade finance application has more value when more banks and corporates join the network. Before the blockchain, trade finance networks are very limited or inexistent. You can see a telephone as a good example of network effects: more people have a telephone, more useful a telephone is

- Automate processes through coding the blockchain or creating smart contracts that run the business logic on the same shared ledger for every participant

- Trusted record keeping - no party can modify or delete any ledger record without the other participants' consensus. Consensus ensures the immutability of the data in the blockchain.

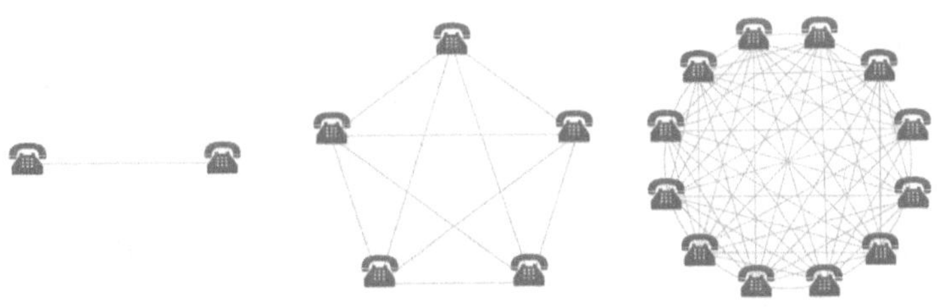

Did you play with walkie-talkies when you were a kid? Walkie-talkies are way older than mobile phones. You could have some fun with it, but they were usually limited to 2 devices, and you could only speak with one friend (or one communication channel). There were no network effects. However, mobile phones, for example, became the first mobile communication device to allow network effects. You can talk with any person in the world that owns a mobile phone, and there are literally billions of them.

In the same way, you can transact with any person or business that is on the same blockchain network as you are.

Network effect brings value to the telephone network, to a social media network or to a blockchain. Blockchain can bring network effects to parties that otherwise would be siloed.

Consensus and truth

How trusted can a blockchain record-keeping be? Can we say in "Bitcoin we trust" as much as we used to say in "US dollar we trust"? Can we trust Jerome more than we trust Satoshi? Let's see how trust comes to the blockchain.

In most of the blockchains, it is impossible to modify or delete data considering that it's impossible to make all the participants agree to the change unless the change is according to the consensus mechanism. Confusing? Continue reading!

A consensus mechanism is a way in which a majority of the participants in the blockchain agree on a value or piece of data.

I can't make the blockchain network participants agree that I own 1000 Bitcoin when I don't own it. Blockchains work like this because of their consensus mechanism. The majority in the network has to agree on the state of the blockchain. Practically speaking, if I wanted to create a fake amount of Bitcoin for myself, I would have to gain control, hack or bribe at least 50% of the Bitcoin network. It would costs billions of dollars and huge amounts of resources, making it practically unfeasible.

Blockchain will not betray you.

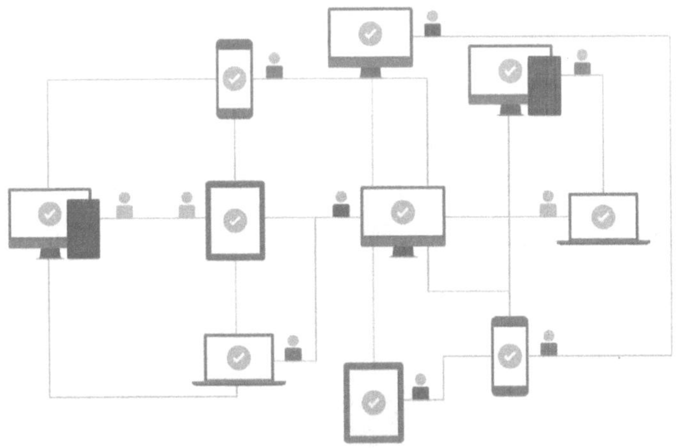

In smaller permissioned blockchains with fewer nodes, it could be easier to change the records. However, in permissioned blockchains, the users are identified with their real name or legal entity name, often linking them to legal agreements.

Another example of how far a consensus mechanism can be stretched in a blockchain is the DAO hack in 2016.

After the hack where 11 million Ether were stolen, half of the Ethereum miners accepted to restore the stolen funds. In contrast, the other half didn't accept to restore it because it would require to change a record already in the blockchain, which according to many it was not in accordance with the philosophy on how a blockchain should work. The result was the hard-fork that divided the Ethereum blockchain into two: Ethereum and Ethereum Classic. The blockchain cannot simply be changed without everyone agreeing.

Disintermediation

In some cases, blockchain allows removing the middleman or mediator or the trusted third party that helps others to carry business. There are many examples of intermediation, but the financial industry is the most significant example. With a blockchain, it is possible to remove that middleman that is often the intermediary.

We can now track and audit records with the blockchain consensus algorithms.

How do we verify, for example, a university degree for an employee that we are hiring? The traditional way is to hire a background check agency. That agency will call the university to check the degree. There are, however, some limitations: how do we know if the university computer wasn't hacked? If we call the university, how do we know that we are not talking with someone who was bribed to provide fake information?

It is very hard to verify certain kinds of information with 100% accuracy in traditional centralised systems, bringing additional risks. How can we verify that the university degree without having to trust an email sent by the university? How do we know if the person replying to the email is to be trusted?

We can use blockchain as a trustless system and solve all these problems.

Confidentiality

Although blockchain is an open and decentralized system, enterprise blockchain systems are private and confidential due to encryption. Many technologies can restrict data sharing based on the users' public key or permissions set by the blockchain system. Blockchains such as Hyperledger Fabric, Corda and Ethereum Enterprise offer privacy and confidentiality features that allow only certain parties to access data using a Certificate Authority (CA) server. A blockchain/DLT can be developed so that data is shared on a need-to-know basis only.

Important also to add that most of the public blockchains like Bitcoin and pseudonymous. Pseudonymous means that the Bitcoin address is identified with a number, but this number of not linked to a real-world identity.

Robustness and Availability

Blockchains offer extreme fault tolerance due to inbuilt redundancy and decentralization. If some of the nodes on the blockchain are down, it will not affect the data availability, and blockchain application can always be used. There are no risks of having data being erased. Disaster recovery in the blockchain is excellent, and robustness increases with node count.

Centralized databases are sometimes replicated across 2 or 3 different datacenters to ensure high-availability and disaster recovery. But what if you have a blockchain database replicated 20 or 2000 times? Blockchain can achieve extremely high availability and disaster recovery capabilities.

Bitcoin is probably the only IT system in the world that never had any downtime and was never hacked in more than 10 years. These characteristics are very good for critical systems. You could nuke some of the biggest Bitcoin mining farms, these big warehouses full of Bitcoin miners, at it wouldn't affect a single bit the Bitcoin performance.

Verifiable and Auditable

Any records and transactions are openly verified in the blockchain by the parties that have access to it. Of course, it is possible to have the encryption layer on the top of the records, which allows auditing the blockchain data integrity without actually having access to the data in many cases (see hashing section of the book). One of the blockchain's magic is that it is possible to confirm that certain data is valid without seeing the data.

For example, any person can look, audit and trace all the transaction in the Bitcoin or Ethereum blockchain by using one of the many "blockchain explorers" available on the internet. These "blockchain explorers" are websites that work as a window to the blockchain.

If you want to audit a blockchain at a deeper level, you can become a full node of that blockchain. A full node will download and validate the entire ledger. We are going to do this later in the book.

Imagine that you can download a bank's entire database with all the accounts of all the customers. It requires a wild imagination in the banking world to think about this, but it's precisely what happens in the blockchain world.

It is also easier to audit any transaction trail when required. This can be especially interesting when we are talking about regulated activities such as insurance and the financial industry. For example, through Regtech [iii] technologies and blockchain, it is possible to allow the regulator to audit the data without any external third parties involved.

The blockchain hype

Blockchain is undoubtedly a very cool technology. It has many great use cases and can disrupt some industries like payments, trade finance, supply chain, fund-raising, and a few others. Blockchain, however, is not the solution for everything. Between 2016 and 2018, there was a phase where it seemed that blockchain was the Panacea remedy for all diseases.

Some projects didn't have much to do with blockchain, but they could raise millions of dollars riding the blockchain hype through ICOs - Initial Coin Offers. Now the market is more mature, and there are solid use cases, live projects and recognized security patterns in the IT industry.

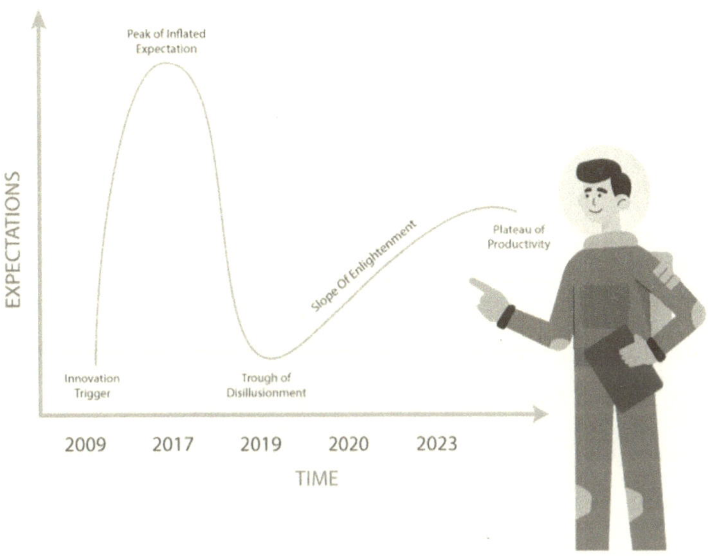

The Blockchain industry was also a victim of how the Dunning-Kruger effect and the self-proclaimed "crypto-experts". When an individual is learning a new topic, he may think of himself as an expert after the first initial stages of learning, only to realize some time after (at least if he wise enough) that he was not an expert at all. There's an ocean of learning to do to really become an expert in the matter. This is why every time I see someone calling themselves "Blockchain expert" or "Blockchain guru", I suspect that they don't know much about the topic.

Chapter 2

Blockchain use cases

Some of the most common use cases are trade finance, remittances, payments, digital identity, supply chain, and multiple types of smart contracts for dApps [iv]. We saw some blockchain characteristics and benefits to having into account. A blockchain use case should fit this category of projects that can benefit from those characteristics, not to have them as a constraint or bottleneck.

Everybody knows already about Bitcoin and cryptocurrencies and how they are used to send value from A to B, so now I think we should focus on other industry use cases and other blockchains too!

Let's see some of these use cases in detail:

Trade finance is one of those industries where widely adopted blockchain applications are already a reality. From supply chain traceability, PO financing, open account [v], Bills of Lading [vi], Letters of Credit, all these are digitized in the blockchain.

Trade Finance is one of the best examples of blockchain use in Banking. Most of the Trade Finance products didn't change much over the last 50 years. They continue to use a lot of paper sent via courier, phone calls and emails. Let's look at the benefits of blockchain for Trade Finance and why it is causing such an impact in this industry and could cause a similar impact in other sectors:

- **Traceability** - The ability to track and trade assets allow parties to know where goods are and reduce risks

- **Transparency** - increase commercial transparency. All the parties involved in a trade can, at any point in time, check the status of the transaction

- **Auditability** - parties can audit the blockchain, which has an audit trail for the trades. The immutability feature creates data provenance, which plays an essential role in the auditability of the blockchain.

- **Security** - transactions are verified in the network, and the parties involved can securely share data with the best industry-grade cryptography and encryption mechanisms

- **Collaboration** - blockchain can allow different parties to come together in business networks to collaborate and to create network effect and economies of scale. Allowing for collaboration creates more value and user-centric applications

- **Efficiency** - creating a distributed ledger across different participants reduces a lot of work-related do synchronize all the data. Additionally, trade finance blockchains applications work in pair with trade digitization, digitizing and streamlining the paperwork related to trade and also reducing the time to complete a transaction from a few days to a few hours

- **Better working capital** - efficiency and reducing the time to complete a transaction benefits the working capital of the companies involved

PO Financing - (Purchase Order Financing) example

PO financing and invoice financing is one of the big blockchain use cases for trade finance.

A PO – Purchase Order – is a document issued by a buyer to a seller, and it has a description of the goods that a buyer wants to buy and respective offer.

There are different parties involved in PO financing: a seller, a buyer and a bank. PO financing is a form of short term financing where the objective is to have the bank lending money for a short period to the supplier/manufacturer to allow enough time for the buyer to pay the invoice. The issue is that the banks often reject PO financing because of the risks involved. There are risks related to the track record/risk of the buyer. Will the buyer pay for the goods? There is the risk related to PO fraud, where the supplier can fake or tamper the PO and other frauds like duplicate financing, where the supplier presents the same PO to multiple banks simultaneously.

How to solve these risks? Blockchain!

A PO Financing blockchain application allows different banks to have a node participating in the network. PO data is then synchronized across all the participants allowing everyone in that PO transaction to have access to the same data, and it will allow the creation of audit trails for other banks.

For example, they can share only the hashes of the transactions between them, allowing them to trace and audit the transactions. Hashes are pre-image resistant, i.e. can't be reverse engineered, offering a good level of data protection.

When the PO is presented, data is stored in the bank node. Then, the PO hash is shared across the network to the other banks. This way, the banks in the network know if the same PO is presented simultaneously because the PO's hash would be the same. The mechanism allows the banks to compare POs without actually sharing the details in the PO.

In this same PO application and hashing mechanism, it is possible to verify that the buyers' identity exists, verifying the KYC hash of this buyer, allowing the bank to check that the buyer actually exists and has a good track record.

So you see that in this use case, blockchain enables the banks to share data without having to worry about breaching data regulations and data privacy. All the parties can use the blockchain data as a trusted source of information to make better credit decisions and reduce risks for everyone.

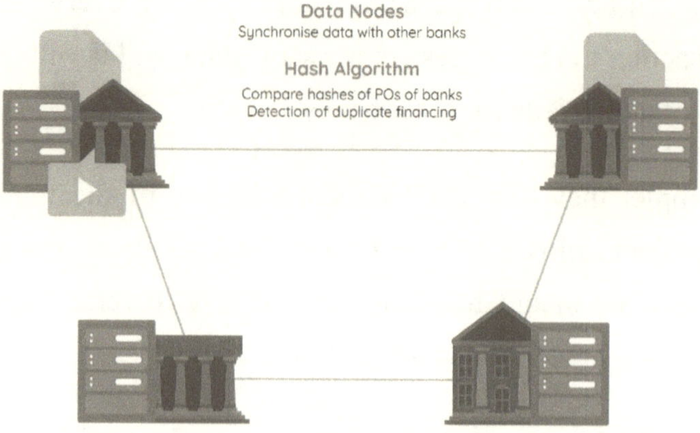

There is a multitude of supply chain applications using blockchain. Supply chain financing, supply chain traceability is one of the most useful use cases with use cases to improve product sustainability and fair trade – traceability of diamonds, coffee, palm oil, tuna and other products.

Blockchain is also useful in fighting counterfeit products and luxury goods. Embedding an identifier of the product in the blockchain (NFT's or Non-Fungible Tokens, for example, is useful in this case).

Projects like the Walmart/IBM Food Trust and Circular improve many products' traceability, which helps prevent the spreading of foodborne diseases. Better traceability can help save lives by quickly allowing track/trace and discard produce from affected farms.

All Walmart suppliers for fresh leafy greens are currently required to use the Food Trust blockchain to record their products in the supply chain, as we will see in a bit.

Diamond Supply Chain

Track and tracing diamonds - De Beer's, the biggest diamond company in the world, has implemented a blockchain application - The De Beer's TrustChain - to track and trace diamonds for authenticity and ensure that they are not "blood diamonds". Chow Tai Fook, the jewellery company in Hong Kong, is also using blockchain. Chow Tai Fook's T MARK are blockchain-secured diamonds with digital diamond grading reports.

A GIA grading report recorded in a blockchain application.

These applications record the diamond supply chain and ownership in the blockchain. The buyer of the diamond can check its source and previous owners.

Blockchain plays a vital role in tracking high-value assets that may be associated with illegal activities. How cool it is if you buy a diamond ring for your fiancé and it comes with a digital certificate in the blockchain?!

IBM food trust and food traceability projects

Wallmart partnered with IBM to build the IBM food trust. This food safety application creates an ecosystem of producers, suppliers, manufacturers, distributors, and retailers that feed the product's supply chain application.

IBM food trust is a permissioned, permanent, shared record of food system data that allows at any time to audit and check the provenance of any product. Why is this important? Some well-known cases of salmonella outbreaks in the USA resulted in people getting sick, some dead and millions of dollars of losses for the industry. From peanut butter to lettuce and spinach, it was extremely hard to trace the salmonella contaminations, which resulted in nationwide withdrawals of all the lettuce and all the spinach and peanut butter to avoid more people getting sick. The problem was that a few years ago, Walmart, for example, would take approximately 7 days to trace a batch of lettuce back to the farmer. With Food Trust, it is possible to trace the product's origin in a few seconds only.

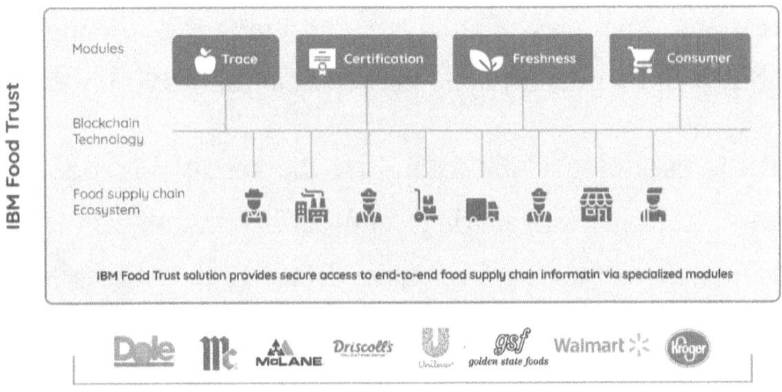

Early Adopters

Walmart looked at blockchain as a good fit for a decentralized food ecosystem. To develop the application, they partnered with IBM and developed the application using Hyperledger Fabric.

According to Karl Bedwell, Senior Director at Walmart Technology, "IBM brought Hyperledger Fabric to us. We looked into Ethereum, Burrow project and others. Ultimately, we decided to go with Hyperledger Fabric because it met most of our needs for a blockchain technology. We felt that it best met our needs. It is an enterprise-grade blockchain technology, and it is permissioned."

The IBM Food Trust platform is currently offered as BaaS – Blockchain as a Service by IBM Cloud.

Digitizing supply chain ecosystems

As you see, blockchains have multiple use cases in the supply chain. It provides a digitally permanent, immutable, auditable, that shows the provenance of any product.

Applications such as TradeLens provide end-to-end product traceability and digitization, no matter what industry they are from.

TradeLens uses blockchain to digitize the supply chain ecosystem, enabling information sharing and collaboration in a single application across the supply chain. Maersk, the biggest shipping company in the world, is one of the main TradeLens partners. Each participant in the supply chain can have full visibility of the goods' progress through the blockchain.

Shipping documents used to be shared either via courier, email, fax, smoke signals and EDI - Electronic Data Interchange, a 50-year-old technology.

Tradelens is changing this. One single application can track all the critical data related to the supply chain of goods, digitizing them all in the blockchain. The application also allows the integration with APIs vii so that manufacturers and others in the supply chain can be seamlessly involved in the big immutable and transparent record.

One of the first big partners of TradeLens was Modern Terminals, the Hong Kong, the company that operates the local port. In this case, ports like Modern Terminals, feed data related to the containers' status into TradeLens. This data comes from the port's TOS - Terminal Operating System and many RFID [viii] that monitor cargo movements.

Other entities such as customs, wholesalers, transportation companies and banks are also involved in the TradeLens supply chain.

Other applications such as Provenance or Skuchain are also interesting examples of blockchain applications for supply chain tracking. Provenance is an application that gathers product information during the product journey, and Skuchain, an application that gathers data and tracks inventory across multiple supply chain tiers, enhancing control over production schedules and the origin and quality of raw materials.

Contour – Letters on Credit on the blockchain

Contour has a special place in my heart. Contour is a letter of credit application developed by a consortium of 8 banks. Its objective is to connect the 4 parties in the Letter of Credit process seamlessly: buyer, seller, issuing bank and nominated bank.

Why is this important? Letters of Credit are an important product in Trade Finance. They facilitate trade between companies that are usually located in different countries. However, the Letter of Credit is usually slow and cumbersome. The process hasn't changed much over the last 50 years, but that was until blockchain has arrived.

Contour uses Corda DLT to connect the Letter of Credit participants' nodes and allow them to share data on a need-to-know basis. Transactions are fully transparent, and the time to complete a transaction can be reduced from 2 weeks to a couple of days or less.

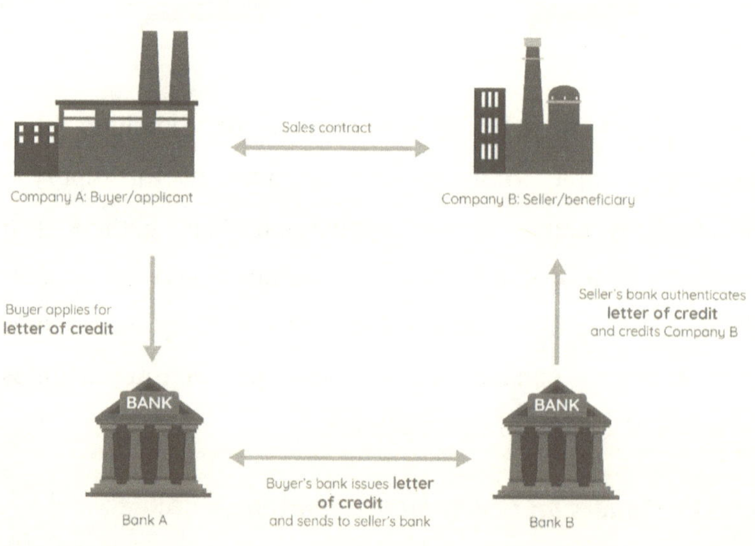

Contour and other trade finance applications not only bring full visibility and auditability over the transactions but also save a lot of paper by digitizing all the documents into the blockchain.

Since Contour launched its commercialization version in February 2021, corporates and banks are joining the network, leveraging the potential network effects that may help companies worldwide transact with each other.

Smart Contracts

Smart Contracts enable to code events. Smart contracts are self-automated computer programs that can execute terms of a contract. They need to run in a Virtual Machine such as EVM - Ethereum Virtual Machine. EVM is a Turing-complete decentralized platform that runs smart contracts without the possibility of downtime, censorship, third party interference or fraud. Smart contracts can be developed in multiple public and private blockchains. Later we will read more how Smart Contracts work.

Smart contracts are really the enablers of any automation on a blockchain, bringing business logic to any use case, and there's a multitude of them. Anything that you can imagine requires different participants or different business parties. This is just a high-level list:

a. *Distributed cloud storage*

SIA, Storj, FileCoin. These are blockchain applications that allow users to rent their storage capacity in their computers. You can see it as a decentralized Dropbox

b. *Property deals*

Shelter Zoom, a New York-based tech company that develops software for property management, developed a real estate platform that uses blockchain technology to simplify the end-to-end real estate process. Buyers and sellers can submit their offers in the blockchain application and streamline the property transaction.

c. *Paying salaries on the blockchain*

BitWage is a (big) payroll provider allowing companies to pay their workers in Bitcoin or other crypto-assets such as stablecoins like USD coin (USDC). Bitwage can drastically cut fees related to bank transfers and allow payments to be processed faster compared to traditional banks. Stablecoin usage to pay salaries is getting more and more popular because it removes the risks related to volatility when compared to cryptocurrencies like Bitcoin. It is also a great alternative to perform payments to countries where local currencies suffer from massive inflation and depreciation like the Venezuelan Bolivar or Argentinian Peso. In these markets, the use of crypto-payments helps to provide more stability to the local communities.

d. *Electronic Voting*

Blockchain seems to be the ideal technology for online voting - or at least a better method than the postal voting we saw as a huge mess during the 2020 presidential. Blockchain, employing cryptography, appended only records, auditability and immutability are ideal to register ballots information to be transmitted over the internet as an alternative to postal voting.

West Virginia, Utah, and Denver County already allowed in the past military staff abroad to vote using blockchain through their mobile phones. However, some security specialists are not so confident about online or mobile phone voting, considering that the users' device or the computers in the election office may be infected with malware or suffer DDoS attacks that would disrupt the service and potentially change the results of the elections.

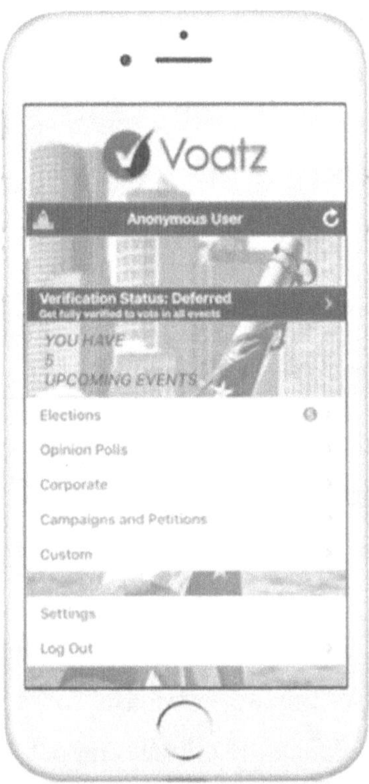

Voatz uses MFA - Multi Factor Authentication - fingerprint and facial recognition for pre-registered users on the top of a robust blockchain. The app encrypts all personally identifiable data and voting results on the blockchain.

Estonia is a role model for electronic voting. The Estonian electronic voting system has been in place for more than 10 years, reaching more than 50% of the population.

e. *Carbon credit trading*

Blockchain can create a more efficient, transparent and fast system to exchange carbon credits, the certificates that incentivize reducing greenhouse gas emissions.

Issuance of Carbon Credits under the cap-and-trade agreements have the objective to set limits to companies' carbon dioxide emissions.

Poseidon is an application that helps analyze and track carbon footprint in any product or service and then process the carbon credits in fractions down to the product sold at the point of sale. This way, the buyer is able to know what's the exact carbon footprint of that ice create that he is buying. Companies use this to purchase more carbon credits and effectively rebalance the climate impact of the product.

Blockchain helps to integrate a ledger connected to the points of sale. It allows the storage of the carbon credits details and makes it and available in the blockchain immutable ledger. Ben and Jerry's is one of the early adopters of blockchain for carbon credit tracking.

Other projects such as Infinite Earth REDD+ Carbon Credits also use blockchain to help companies offset their carbon emissions by planting trees that will help offset those emissions or other programs that help protect biodiversity and forests.

f. DeFi

This wouldn't be a blockchain book if we don't talk about DeFi but I will keep it really short because this topic deserves a whole book. DeFi deserves a bible!

DeFi stands for Decentralized Finance and it's trying to get of the middle-man in the finance market. DeFi applicarions allow any person to take up a loan, use collaterals, make term deposits to get interest in return, staking money into a pool to provide liquidity in the market and get interest in return… well, it provides a complex financial ecosystem that lives in the Ethereum blockchain.

Insurance can be automated with Smart Contracts.

- Remittances. Reducing fees and facilitating cross-border payments.

- Securities trade and settlement.

- Decentralized exchanges.

- and many more. This is not an exhaustive list, but we could even talk about a blockchain that tracks dog chip IDs

Crypto collectibles and non-fungible tokens

This topic should be totally part of the use cases section, but it kinda deserves a section only for itself given the rising importance of Cryptokitties. No kidding!

Fungibility classifies assets as identical based on their specification, properties and value inherent. An asset is fungible if one unit of the asset is substantially equivalent to another unit of the same asset, having the same quality and can be substituted for each other at any given place or time. Fiat currency is a relatable fungible asset because a $20 bill in New York is the same as $20 in Texas. Fungibility of assets is also evident in how value can be retained in divisibility e.g. two $10 bills have the same value as one $20 bill. In the crypto space, it is believed that cryptocurrencies are fungible e.g. BTC has a supply of 21 million identical coins, and a BTC can be substituted for another BTC in whole or in fractional Satoshis while retaining its value.

Non-fungible assets are unique and special because they differ in value and properties. Units of non-fungible assets can not be valued as another unit of the same asset, i.e. they are not mutually interchangeable. They are often rare and scarce, hence, they tend to be highly valued by collectors.

Collectibles are items that are sought after because they are considered to be worth of value to the collectors. Oftentimes, they can be exchanged for money much more than the items are originally worth. In the traditional world, these items are often unique, limited in supply and/or rare. Once they are collected, their value increases because of demand, e.g. stamps, antique furniture, comic books, posters, art etc. With the advent of computers, virtual collectibles have become quite popular in the last decades e.g. in-game collectibles are highly valued in the gaming space and other valuable items in their own digital ecosystem. When these rare items are embedded into the crypto ecosystem, they become non-fungible tokens (NFT).

What are Crypto Collectibles?

A crypto-collectible is a cryptographically unique, non-fungible digital asset created on the blockchain in form of a token. It is often referred to as Non-Fungible Token (NFT). These tokens are not interchangeable and each token cannot be divided into smaller units. A non-fungible token uniquely stores information about an asset in its smart contract on the blockchain.

History of NFT

The collectibles market has grown massively in the last century with a global estimate reaching hundreds of million dollars. Crypto collectibles came into existence in the early days of Bitcoin with the creation of Colored Coins. In 2012, Colored coins were made of small denominations of a Bitcoin and used to represent various assets on the blockchain. After which came a series of other NFTs which didn't gain much popularity until Cryptokitties hit mainstream in 2017. Cryptokitties is a game built on the Ethereum network that allows players to collect, breed, and exchange cute virtual cats. It uses the ERC-721 NFT token standard and is notorious for creating a congestion on the Ethereum network due to the high volume of activities of the users.

NFT's stand for non-fungible tokens and are a whole new world

Why is this Cryptokittie worth 1 million dollars? Because it's a unique piece of art! That's right, this, and many other NFTs have a big demand in the market, increasing their value.

NFT's are tokens that have fungibility, meaning that each token is unique and irreplaceable. They generally use the Ethereum ERC-721 standard that was introduced in the Ethereum network in January 2018 and revolutionized an entire industry.

Now, even Christies entering the NFT's market by organizing its first NFT-based auction in February 2021. Ethereum's NFT market has the potential to totally disrupt the art market and the way things are owned.

An NFT represents the ownership of an item. It's true that I can copy/paste any image to my computer but the ownership of that item will always be linked to someone in the Ethereum blockchain.

Application of NFT

Tokenisation of non-fungible assets has created endless possibilities for blockchain asset digitisation. Blockchain offers the collectible market much more security and digital scarcity, especially to ensure assets' authenticity and eliminate counterfeiting. NFTs are popular in the gaming ecosystem but besides gaming, NFTs can be used to digitise anything considered to be of worth.

Decentralised applications (Dapps) on the blockchain use NFTs for investment purposes, digital identities, virtual assets, fine art, trading cards etc. Since the explosion of NFTs in the cryptospace in 2017 coincidentally aided by the ICO boom, there has been a significant growth in the crypto-collectible market with over a hundred successful NFT projects. Here are a few popular ones:

Decentraland - a virtual reality platform that is wholly owned by users, powered by the Ethereum blockchain. Users can create, experience, and monetise content and applications.

Binance Collectibles - created in 2018 as a series of holiday-themed NFTs to serve as prizes for a festive engagement campaign during the season of giving.

MyCryptons - digital collectibles of public figures, ranging from Head of States to celebrities like Oprah Winfrey, can be collected and sold.

SuperRare - a blockchain project that is creating NFT that enables digital artists to link an image or a GIF they've created to a token.

Nifty - a marketplace to buy and sell NFTs that represent artwork or limited edition items created by artists, brands and content creators.

Creating an NFT

Tokenising an asset has been made easy with smart contracts on the blockchain. The most popular and widest implemented approach standard is the ETH-721, and there are numerous Dapps in the crypto space that have ready-to-use templates and tools accessible for the creation of NFTs without coding expertise. Another token standard that can be used to create NFT like the ERC1155.

NFTs are becoming popular in use as it offers a non-restricted use of blockchain technology in the most unique and futuristic approach. Virtual assets such as tweets, digital art and domain names are being tokenised, and this is made possible because the transfer of ownership and authentication of assets are secure on the blockchain. Although like blockchain technology NFT is considered to be in its infancy with a need for improvement. One of the challenges it faces is the cost of token transfer as NFTs are immensely gas heavy (i.e. fees paid to the network may sometimes be high).

Defining DeFi: What Is Decentralized Finance?

A completely democratized access to financial services sounds good, given the fact that billions of people worldwide remain unbanked. This is a huge problem, and its root cause is the largely centralized structure of the institutions that make up our traditional financial system.

DeFi is a great trustless alternative that offers the users greater control over their money. Financial instruments like loans, insurance, and derivatives that are presently controlled by big organizations will witness these middlemen's elimination.

The anonymity that blockchains ensure will also enable faster borrowing and lending of money without any need for trust in the form of KYC or credit scores.

In simple terms, DeFi can be defined simply as an open or decentralized financial system that's devoid of a centralized setup in which powers are in the hands of a few powerful organizations such as exchanges or banks, with the help of blockchain technology and smart contracts.

Thanks to DeFi, existing financial instruments (like loans, savings, trading, etc.) can now be accessed in a decentralized, trustless manner by anyone, anywhere in the world. This enables financial processes and workflows to be more streamlined in terms of speed, cost and accessibility.

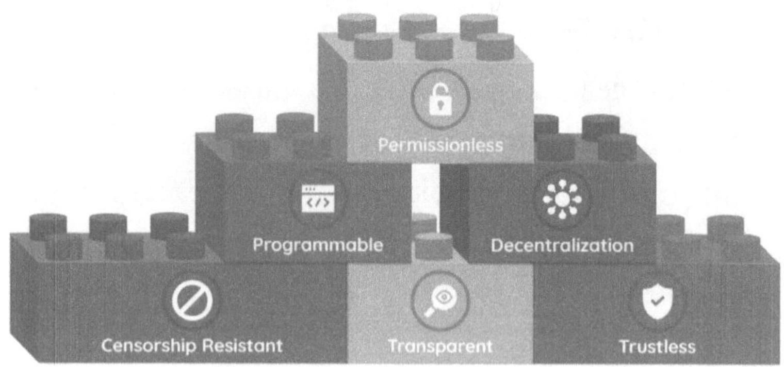

Properties of Decentralized Finance (DeFi)

Here are three prerequisites financial solutions must satisfy to be truly decentralized.

Interoperability

Interoperability simply means cross-communication. In this case, it means different blockchains' ability to communicate with each other or see, access, and share information across blockchain networks without intermediary intervention. Central exchanges currently play this role.

Interoperability isn't just a good feature, but it is incredibly critical in the DeFi space due to various blockchain networks' ability to communicate with each other. This then creates an ecosystem in which several different dApps are able to "borrow" various functions by integrating with other dApps. Transparency is also an advantage of interoperability.

Composability

DeFi apps are open source, and, as such, anyone can view or use the code as the basis to develop new applications. This concept is known as composability i.e. something existing can be used to create a new product using different arrangements or combinations.

Lego is a great example of composability. You can use parts from existing projects and then change the bricks' sequence to make something completely different each time. These apps can then be used together to create more complex and efficient financial products.

Programmability

Programmability is basically the ability to automate processes; it is what makes smart contracts, well, "smart". Since smart contracts are essentially pieces of code, the automation level that can be integrated depends on how sophisticated the program is.

Ethereum is considered the best option for building decentralized finance solutions because of its flexibility. Thanks to Solidity, the programming language used to build and deploy smart contracts on the Ethereum blockchain.

The sad truth, however, is that only a few DeFi solutions meet all three points. This is partly due to the fragmented state of the current blockchain landscape, making interoperability and composability difficult to achieve.

As such, most decentralized finance solutions are left with the third prerequisite (i.e., programmability), achieved through smart contracts — and nothing more.

Smart Contracts

When carrying out business deals, one sometimes needs to rely upon middlemen to exchange products or services for money also has to give a share to them. Digital smart contracts are programs based on blockchains that automate the exchange process, and the contract can be programmed to switch the assets only when certain conditions are met. And the ownership of the assets cannot be challenged or disputed since the transactions are recorded on the public blockchain.

The most prominent smart contract platform at the moment is Ethereum. The main reason behind this is the programmability of Ethereum using Solidity, which is the programming language specifically used for implementing smart contracts.

Ethereum is also the most popular platform which has nurtured a really good ecosystem consisting of thousands of developers who keep it updated. It also has the most significant amount of value locked in smart contracts. This highly flexible nature of Ethereum is what makes it an excellent choice for building decentralized applications.

DeFi apps are typically open-source, and hence anyone can view or use the code as the basis to develop new applications. These apps can then be used together to create more complex and efficient financial products.

Various Use Cases of Decentralized Finance

DeFi has several uses, all aimed at improving the traditional financial landscape. The most popular ones have been listed below.

Borrowing

The borrowing activity in DeFi is over-collateralized, meaning that you exchange an asset, in this case, cryptocurrency in exchange for money locked up in a smart contract called the collateralized debt position CDP. But the money received in turn is less than the true value of the collateral

Hence, if the collateral falls' value, the crypto that is exchanged can be liquidated to make up for the fall in value. But the perk of this system is that it is really fast, and almost anyone can easily borrow money, unlike bank loans.

Lending

Rather than keeping crypto assets static, people lend them to earn interests. One of the most popular platforms for this is Compound. It is an algorithmic, autonomous interest rate protocol that makes it possible for people to earn interest on their cryptocurrency by lending it to other users.

Stablecoins

Since cryptocurrencies are notorious for being very unstable, an alternative to this was developed, called stablecoins. These coins minimize the volatility and are tied to existing assets outside of the crypto world, such as the US dollar or precious materials.

However, most of the stablecoins are backed by fiat currencies. This makes them centralized since they're run and controlled by the central authorities that issue the currencies. Some of them include Tether (USDT), TrueUSD (TUSD), and USD Coin (USDC).

One example of a decentralized stablecoin is Dai, which is backed by Ethereum and pegged to the US dollar.

Decentralized Exchanges

Decentralized exchanges (DEXes) are alternatives to centralized crypto exchanges. These allow the exchange to crypto to take place in a decentralized or permissionless manner, and the users do not have to risk giving up the custody of their coins.

What the Future Holds for DeFi

Although DeFi looks promising and has several advantages over traditional finance, it's a nascent concept that's still in early development and, hence, has several drawbacks included.

As it stands, the potential for DeFi adoption among everyday users is massive. If DeFi continues its steady growth, then it will transform the finance industry as we know it, most likely for the better.

Blockchain in Fintech

If cash is king, Fintech is the kingslayer!

The Fintech industry is riding the ABCD technologies wave - AI, Blockchain, Cloud and Data Analytics. Blockchain and Distributed Ledger technology are probably among these technologies the most disruptive. They are building new ways of doing business, sharing data, new ways of trusting and creating business networks.

Fintech is widely using blockchains to improve services such as cross-border payments, securities trading, regulatory compliance, insurance, asset tracking, trade finance and post-trade settlement.

Blockchains allow entries and transactions to be seen real-time across the ledgers of different participants, reducing the time for clearance and settlement from a few days to almost real-time.

A report from Accenture in 2017 claimed that DLT could dramatically reduce infrastructure costs for banks: "Blockchain technology could reduce infrastructure costs for eight of the world's 10 largest investment banks by an average of 30%, translating to $8 billion to $12 billion in annual cost savings for those banks".

So, should financial institutions jus adopt blockchain straight away? Well, banks face significant regulatory challenges when adopting blockchain. It is a lengthy and cumbersome process for banks which slows down the adoption of blockchain. Also, banks need strong use cases for blockchain use, and the question asked within any bank's IT departments is, "why can't we do this in a normal database?".

Financial institutions can benefit from some cost reduction, and I do believe that blockchain can also bring them ROI by providing a better user experience to customers through blockchain applications.

Payments clearance and settlement is a big use case in Fintech, both for cross-border payments and for settlement of securities such as stocks and bonds. This is a big pain point for the industry and a substantial source of inefficiencies, locking away billions of dollars due to slow transaction processing. This happens because each participant maintains their own ledger and must communicate to update the ledgers and where they are in the process. As a result, the settlements usually take a few days which is outrageous considering that we are in the XXI century.

Because blockchain shares data almost real-time (it may take a few seconds, which is already very good when compared to hours or days), it eliminates the need for manual conciliation and all the slow legacy systems.

Payments is another big Fintech use case where blockchain is coming big. In payments, J.P. Morgan has created one of the biggest private blockchain payment networks until now - Liink - formerly known as IIN - Interbank Information Network. Using a proprietary blockchain called Onyx, Liink enables entities - banks and corporates - to securely make payments and share data in a peer-to-peer fashion. Being in a peer-to-peer network in a permissioned blockchain, participants go through a vetting process before they join the network making it more secure for the participants.

According to the founder John Hunter, "We created Liink understanding the vast complexities of the global banking system. Through leveraging distributed ledger technology, we have created a more open and efficient network of information sharing, comprised of many of the largest financial institutions in the world."

The blockchain application also allows integrating APIs so that banks and corporates can connect them to their existing backend systems.

Mastercard announced in 2017 the Mastercard blockchain, which enables business and banks to make cross-border payments using not only the account-based and card-based system but also a new blockchain-based payment system.

The Mastercard blockchain can bring more privacy - transaction details are only shared on a need-to-know basis on the blockchain, flexibility - partners can use the blockchain APIs in addition to the existing Mastercard APIs. Also, scalability - the Mastercard blockchain can process many transaction and network effects - the company has already 22 thousand financial institutions moving funds.

KlickEx, a Polynesian payments system for low-value electronic fx transactions, also introduced a blockchain to enable peer-to-peer payments, serving around 1 million users every day across eight countries in the Pacific region. For KlickEx, blockchain helped solve a pain point related to batch payments: the exchanges could process the payments between 90 to 200 seconds. Although it may seem fast, it was not fast enough, and it would require the exchange to use batch processing, slowing down the payments even more because payments received would often outpace payments issued without the batching. This could lead payments to take many hours to be processed. With the implementation of blockchain, KlickEx was able to reduce payment processing to seconds. Using the IBM cloud blockchain platform, they can now use an account-based system that can process up to 8 million payments per day nearly real-time, rather than in batches.

Due to its decentralization, eliminating the trust issue, tamper-resistance, safety and reliability characteristics, blockchain technology has been used in lots of fields, including financial services, credit and ownership management, trade management, cloud storage, user-generated content, copyright protection, advertising and even gaming. In these cases, blockchain either solves multiparty trust problems in the transaction or reduces traditional industries' costs and risks.

There are many more potential use cases, but we should proceed from the blockchain's characteristics to find the right application scenario and use case. We also need to consider the blockchain application's objectives and the boundaries and limitations of blockchain technology.

What are some of the barriers to blockchain adoption?

The main barrier to blockchain adoption is the lack of knowledge about it.

Just like any other new technology, organizations may face challenges when adopting a blockchain. These adoption barriers may be seen as constraints that need to be addressed and explored to improve the way the organization is innovating. For example, suppose a bank is implementing a new blockchain product and needs approval from the local regulator just like he would need to implement any other application but blockchain will probably raise additional concerns. In that case, he just might leverage this engagement with the regulator to lay down some additional bricks to built better innovation products in the future.

The cost barrier. The need to replicate data across many nodes will likely increase the costs of maintaining this data compared to a centralized solution. A centralized database is only replicated for HA/DR purposes (High Availability and Disaster Recovery). The redundancy used for HA/DR aims to ensure that the system is highly available, i.e. that it offers an SLA [ix] that is according to the business requirements. A critical system like a payment system may be required, for example, to be available 99.9% of the time. To ensure this, the system will require a certain level of redundancy by duplicating the databases. For instance, suppose one of the databases is not working because of a power shortage, or because it was hacked or simply because the system is being updated. In these cases the system will automatically read for the replicated database.

On the other hand, a blockchain system is highly redundant by nature. Blockchains are very redundant, and the data is replicated across all the nodes in the blockchain (although some blockchains like Corda and Hyperledger may not have this level of redundancy). Replicating the same data so many times increases costs related to the database storage and bandwidth.

We can probably say that the Bitcoin or Ethereum database has the best SLA ever because it is updated literally 100% of the time and is 100% reliable. Always.

Bitcoin's fantastic level of reliability can be achieved only because the Bitcoin database/ledger is replicated thousands of times which is expensive to maintain. Not all blockchain applications need such a redundancy level off course, but even permissioned blockchains will have higher storage costs than a single centralized database.

Another factor to consider for the costs when using blockchain is that usually, one entity owns one node compared to a centralized database. If we look at the car merchant example that we have discussed before, adopting a blockchain in more likely to reduce costs considering reducing frictions and manual work.

When deciding whether to use a permissioned or permissionless blockchain, the cost consideration also needs to be brought to the table. Public blockchains such as Ethereum can run applications (or dApps for decentralized applications), but fees, gas fees, are paid every time a smart contract is executed or a new transaction in the network. Depending on how frequent these transactions are, the transaction amount and who is paying, the costs related to transaction fees in public blockchains need to be considered because they can become quite substantial.

Latency and scalability: again, the need of replicating the data across many nodes brings scalability challenges because all the transactions need to be broadcasted and recorded in all the nodes, which may be a bottleneck in regards to the number of transactions. All blockchains have consensus mechanisms that will ensure that all the nodes are synchronized. When the blockchain needs to be updated with a very large number of transactions, i.e. thousands of transactions per second, the blockchain starts to throttle and will get slow. Bitcoin may be the most secure and decentralized blockchain, but it comes with a price: it can only handle a maximum of 7 transactions per second (tho the Lightning Network can handle more transactions). Other less decentralized public blockchains such as EOS can handle around 1000 transactions per second.

If we are able to compromise decentralization and security, we can get the blockchain system to handle much more transactions. A permissioned blockchain only with a couple of nodes, for example, would be able to handle a huge number of transactions, but a blockchain with a couple of nodes is not a very meaningful blockchain, and it will not bring the benefits that blockchain has like security, decentralization, immutability, network effects, etc.

Regulations and compliance: Financial institutions and banks may be hesitant to adopt blockchain because it's complex to explain to regulators how data is shared across the blockchain participants. Industries like banking and insurance are more traditional because they have a big fiduciary responsibility. They basically must be traditional. The regulators in these industries are also more risk-averse, and in many countries, regulatory frameworks are lagging many years behind.

Blockchains bring new models of data sharing that may make regulatory institutions confused. Can we use a blockchain to store a hash of private/confidential data? Common sense would say yes because hash algorithms used in blockchains are pre-image resistant, meaning that it's impossible to convert the hash into its input data. However, sometimes, some regulators see the world with a "one size fits all" lens and will not accept any data shared in a public manner, even if it is a hash that is impossible to crack.

When engaging with regulators, it will be essential to clarify where the blockchain data is stored (on-premise data center or cloud provider), in which countries (in some countries, data cannot be stored cross borders) and how the data is transferred from party to party.

Engaging with regulators may be a lengthy process, but it is improving in some countries via regulatory sandboxes and a common understanding between financial institutions and regulators.

Different parties need to join forces, especially in a private blockchain. To build meaningful blockchain solutions, the participants on a business network need t agree to come together, work on the solution and join the new application. For instance, a trade finance blockchain application is much more useful if a decent number of banks join the application. If one entity builds a trade finance application without the banks' involvement, it will be very hard to create network effects and attract customers. This would be like building a telephone line where only one person manages and owns the telephone. Not very useful, right?

To overcome the barriers to blockchain adoption, we need to have the entire organization on board. It often means the innovation team, IT teams, cybersecurity, compliance, management, finance, and more, to make sure the barriers and blockers are overcome. Oh, and to decide on blockchain applications, organizations cannot use the HiPPO decision method: Highest Paid Person's Opinion.

Chapter 3

The blockchain technology deep dive

Let's now start the most exciting part of the book, leaving the theory behind and start diving into the technology! We are now going to look closely at the technology components and how do they work.

Let's start with the basics by asking what blockchain is. Yeah, I know, we have been talking about blockchain, but now, I want you to wear the geek suit and see this more from the technology perspective. Don't skip this part! It's essential to make everything clear and consolidate knowledge!

What is Blockchain?

Although there are a few definitions for blockchain, it all comes down to one thing: blockchain is a decentralized database-like system that is very transparent to all the nodes in the network. Participants in the blockchain have a consensus mechanism to agree on what should be included in the blockchain and how it should be included.

So blockchain is a decentralized protocol that distributes a database across a number of nodes, establishing a consensus mechanism for past and current transactions where blocks represent the data structure.

Blockchain characteristics

Decentralized: blockchains do not depend on a central authority, and there's no centralized point of control. Instead, it depends on a consensus mechanism for the participants to agree on what's true

Transparent: Anyone in the blockchain can see and audit the transactions in the blockchain

Immutable: Once settled in the blockchain, data and transactions cannot be altered unless agreed upon by the consensus mechanism

Encrypted: blockchain protocol relies on cryptography algorithms that are used to sign transactions, verify transaction validity and to keep the data in the blockchain immutable and secure

What are blockchains used for?

In this book, I talk about some of the blockchain applications. Although blockchain is not the solution for everything (definitely not for big workloads or centralized databases), there are hundreds of possible use cases. I could write a 2000 page book about all the multiple use cases, but that would be way too boring. However, we can lay down the key technologies behind blockchain and help create a framework to understand what makes a blockchain use case.

To talk about blockchain use cases is a bit like to talk about databases use cases. Databases have a vast number of use cases, and so blockchain has. However, when comparing with traditional databases, blockchains can bring more transparency, reliability, fast transactions (when compared to multiple centralized databases) and much more. Blockchains can enforce contracts the so-called Smart Contracts (we will later see what this is), which can replicate almost any real-life contract in an automated way.

Bitcoin initially introduced blockchain in late 2008 when the Bitcoin whitepaper was released. The first blockchain allowed for the first time for simple transactions to be carried in a totally decentralized manner. Later, Ethereum and other blockchains 2.0

brought the possibility of embedding code into the blockchain – the Smart Contracts – that are automatically self-executed in the blockchain Turing-complete system.

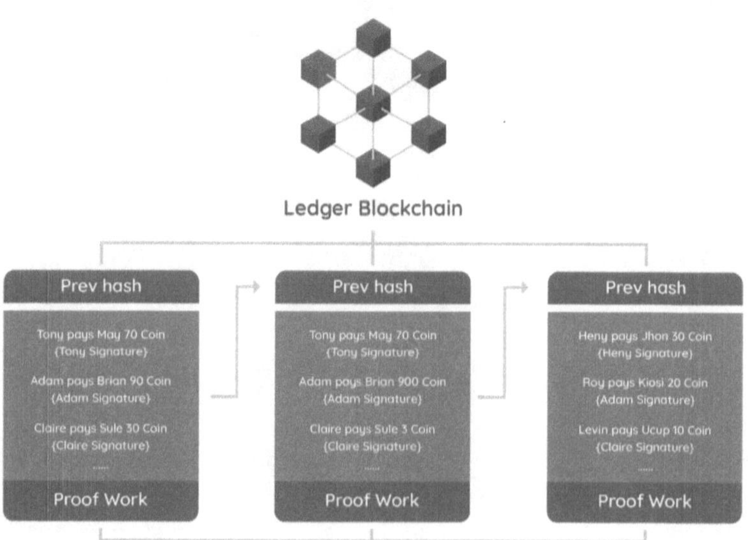

We already discussed that a blockchain is a distributed and immutable database, but how can this be achieved?

Each block in the blockchain is linked to the previous block through a hashing mechanism. Each block contains the hash of the data in the previous block, creating a chain of blocks that are linked between each other. It is not possible to change the block's order or change any data because if a block is changed, the hash of the block will change, marking it as invalid. This is from where the blockchain immutability comes from. Any change would be automatically invalidated because it wouldn't match the hash.

In theory, it is possible to change the data or block history, but you would have to acquire consensus, aka 51% attack, which is generally very hard to achieve.

We saw that each block contains the previous block hash in the block header (including the previous block transaction). The block also contains the transactions included in the block. Transactions can be either financial transactions or events, i.e. a transaction doesn't necessarily need to transfer value. It can rather be a transfer of and asset or simply a transfer of data.

All the blockchain participants agree on common rules on how a block is included in the blockchain. Each blockchain may have a different consensus mechanism defining how blocks are included. Still, you have probably heard of Proof of Work, Proof of Stake, Delegated Proof of Stake and PBFT – Practical Byzantine Fault-Tolerant. We will detail later how these cool consensus mechanisms work.

Types of blockchain

There are different blockchain types, and they have different use cases -public blockchains and private blockchains.

Public blockchains such as Bitcoin, Ethereum and many more allow anyone to participate with a node contributing to the consensus mechanism or issue transactions.

Public blockchains are also typically known as permissionless, considering that anyone can join without needing a permission or membership certificate. These blockchains are, in nature completely decentralized with no ownership or centralized governance. Users/nodes in public blockchains have access to all the data and uphold a ledger copy, except in some DLT cases. In most public blockchains, they reach consensus through proof of work or proof of stake consensus mechanisms. For example, we will later in the book deploy an Ethereum node and synchronize with the blockchain, which is something any person can do.

Public blockchains usually have a significant number of participants, and they basically rely on these participants to run nodes that will keep the blockchain resilient against attacks. In public blockchains, the network security and resiliency increase with node count. The bigger a blockchain is, the harder it is to be successfully attacked. The consensus mechanism used also includes some incentives for the nodes, also known as miners, to maintain the blockchain and validate transactions. Bitcoin, for example, incentivizes miners rewarding them with 6.25 BTC (as per 2021), every time a miner creates a new block. This way, people have an incentive to contribute to the network.

One of the big advantages of public blockchains is that they are also very secure precisely because they have a lot of nodes participating. If a blockchain has ten nodes only, a hacker needs to control at least 6 of the nodes to control the network, which may not be very difficult. However, if a blockchain has 100 000 nodes (which is the Bitcoin case), a hacker would have to gain control of more than 50% of the network nodes, which would be practically impossible, unless the hacker can spend billions of dollars in equipment and electricity. Really not worth it.

Thanks to the decentralized nature, encryption and consensus mechanism, participants are incentivized to keep the ledger trustworthy. Bitcoin and most of the major cryptocurrencies are probably the most secure IT systems in the world.

Public blockchains are not a paradise, though. There are also some disadvantages: the slow processing time and latency – a transaction may need a few minutes to be settled – low throughput and sometimes the transaction cost.

Public blockchain	Private blockchain
Anyone can join, read, write and download the ledger	Usually permission-based participation
Anyone can see the data	Only members case see the data
Decentralized	Less decentralized
Pseudonymous	Users identity is known
Proof of Work or Proof of Stake consensus	PBFT, RAFT or Proof of Elapsed Time consensus

So as we can see, in public blockchains, anyone can join a public blockchain, download the entire ledger, read historical transactions, write new transactions (but never change existing transactions) and participate as a node/miner. Public blockchains are totally transparent, and anyone can see everything and contribute to the consensus.

On the other hand, private blockchains are usually permissioned, which means that participants need to get permission to participate. Private blockchains typically have a smaller number of participants. These participants can be a group of people, companies or organizations who share some kind of business process. Usually, private blockchains are by invitation blockchains, and the participants are connected to their real-world identity – name, company name, etc.

In public blockchains, users are pseudonymous. They are not linked to a real-world identity, whereas the user's identification is not nameless in private blockchains.

Private blockchain technologies such as Hyperledger Fabric, Quorum, Multichain and Corda, allow different kinds of configurations so that participants may have different permissions and capabilities in the blockchain. Private blockchains are usually more scalable when comparing to public blockchains, allowing high throughput, fast transaction speed and low latency. Private blockchains generally have a smaller number of users; thus, it's easier to broadcast the data among them and reach consensus. Some private blockchains allow up to thousands of transactions per second.

One of the main disadvantages of private blockchains is that they tend to be more centralized and miss decentralization advantages. More centralization may allow better throughput, better governance and comply with regulations, but it comes at the cost of additional security concerns. Considering a smaller number of nodes are involved, it is easier for a lousy node to manipulate or try to take advantage of the system.

Semi-private blockchains are blockchains can also be kinda hybrid, meaning that they are partially private and partially public. On the public side of hybrid networks, anyone can join (for example, write new transactions), while some functions may remain private (for example, a validating node). EOS can be seen as a semi-private blockchain where validating nodes, known as block producers on EOS blockchain, are 21 selected nodes. Users have access to the network and can issue transactions in a public manner. On the EOS case, a delegated proof of stake mechanism is used to nominated the 21 block producer nodes that will forge the blocks. We will later read more about EOS delegated proof of stake consensus mechanism.

Side-chains

Side-chains are blockchains connected to the main blockchain, where assets or transactions can be carried in the side-chain and later be recorded in the main-chain. Assets can also eventually be transferred from side-chain to main-chain and vice-versa, and users can send assets to the side-chain so that they can be used there. A good example of a side-chain is the Bitcoin Lightning Network, where Bitcoins can be transacted in a much faster way.

Blockchain on the top of blockchains? What kind of witchcraft is this?

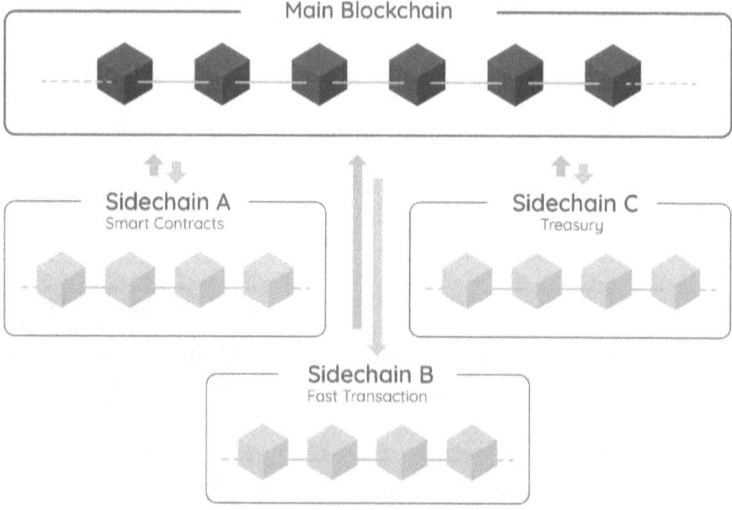

A blockchain can have multiple side-chains for different purposes connected to it, and they can be independently managed.

Side-chains can also allow the seamless transfer of assets between chains or allow Cross-cryptocurrency exchange in some cases.

The Lightning Network is connected to the Bitcoin blockchain a records the balances in the main-chain. Private blockchains can also have side-chains that record an asset related to the main-chain or a side chain that process payments, expanding the blockchain's functionalities.

Bitcoin Lightning Network is considered a "Tier 2" payment system that runs on Bitcoin's blockchain. It's designed to improve transaction speed between all contributing nodes, and it's a recommended solution to the lack of scalability that has been an issue with processing bitcoin transactions.

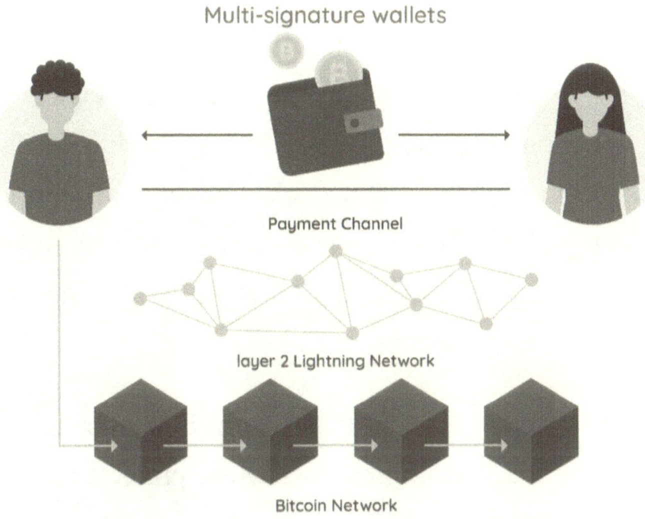

Lightning Network adds another layer to the Bitcoin blockchain and allows users to create payment channels between the two parties at this additional layer. These channels can exist as long as you need, and once established between two parties transacting, the transaction will happen almost instantly, and the fees will be very low or none at all.

As we have already discussed before, Bitcoin can only manage roughly seven transactions every second. It was enough at first, but the system got overwhelmed as the network users get larger and larger over the years. As a result, transaction processing takes a longer time, and transaction fees are sometimes unreasonable.

If Bitcoin wants to become a full-fledged alternative to the existing payment system, it must be able to be a high-performance network and remove the scaling bottlenecks. Currently, Bitcoin is not even close.

The lightning Network seems to be the right answer to the scalability question. Lightning Network is an additional layer of connectivity built on top of the blockchain that dramatically improves performance. This allows Bitcoin to process millions of transactions per second with nearly zero fees, opening up more opportunities than traditional money.

Other side-chain examples are Plasma for Ethereum and Liquid Network, also in the Bitcoin network. Other projects also address blockchain interoperability by building sidechains. Some examples are Polkadot and Cosmos. By the way, don't you love the crypto projects name?

What other applications do you thing can leverage the use of sidechains? Can we connect other blockchains together to allow a blockchain super connector?

Permissioned blockchain

Let's now take a look at permissioned blockchains. We have already talked about private blockchains, and although most private blockchains are also permissioned, private and permissioned are not synonyms and to keep this book accurate, it's better to make a clear distinction.

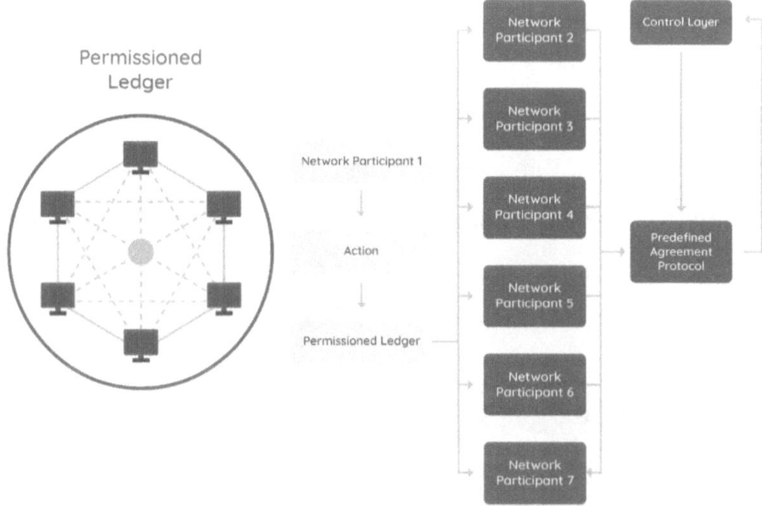

Imagine a party (yes, a party with music and booze) that is open to everyone and any person can go to the party and see who is there. This is a public permissionless blockchain.

Now imagine that the party is restricted to 21 VIP party-animals, but this party is being broadcasted over the internet. This is a public permissioned blockchain, i.e. only those 21 people have permission to be at the party.

The third example is a secrete party. A "Eyes Wide Shut" party. It's a by invitation only party, and it's not broadcasted anywhere. It's one of those semi-secrete parties in a mansion where only the invited people knows what's going on inside. This is the private permissioned blockchain.

While privacy refers to who can see the data, permission refers to the blockchain's control layer to control the participants' actions. Permissioned ledgers can eventually be public but at the same time have a set of rules on who and how participants can participate. Enterprise Ethereum and Hyperledger Fabric make good examples of permissioned blockchains. They also have a more centralized governance model, having a consortium, a foundation or a company behind it.

Distributed Ledgers

Distributed ledgers are often confused with blockchains. They can be private or public, sharing data often on a need-to-know basis among participants. Each participant keeps their own copy of the ledger or a copy of the subset of data shared with him. These records of data are not placed in blocks. They are instead recorded and hashed continuously, each node updating individually.

Distributed ledger may have membership/doorman nodes - to control/vote who can be a member in the network – and notary nodes that approve and notarize the data in the ledgers. When the notary nodes reach a consensus of approval over a transaction, the participants can update their own ledger with the new transaction.

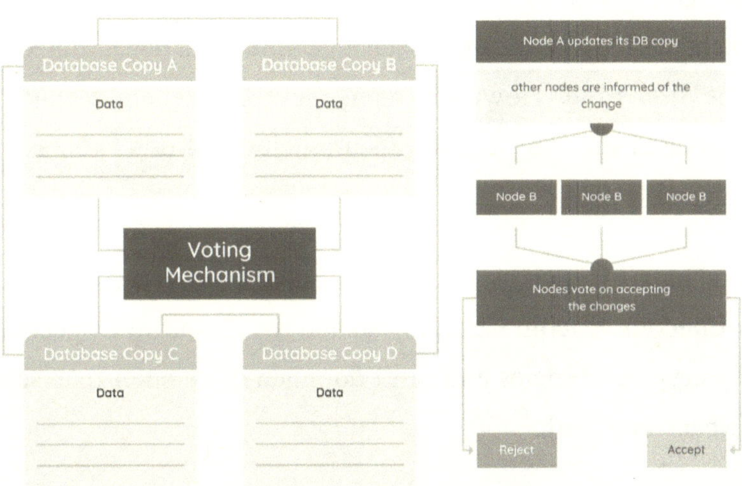

Instead of recording the transactions and data blocks, they are broadcasted to the notary, which manages a voting mechanism and a consensus. If the data pass the checks, it's then broadcasted and recorded to certain nodes according to the business logic. The data is time-stamped, and a hash is recorded for immutability and data provenance purposes, but it is not distributed across all the nodes in the distributed ledger. Only a few specific nodes, the notary nodes, keep the hashes and the time-stamps.

Corda is the most well-known example of a DTL and, if we really want to be accurate, we shouldn't call it a blockchain considering the lack of blocks and that information is only shared on a need-to-know basis.

Blockchain VS Cryptocurrencies

Blockchain started as a cryptocurrency – Bitcoin. We can see these blockchains 1.0 as a mean to exchange value in a decentralized way for the first time. However, many new blockchain technologies were created that are not cryptocurrencies and don't represent an exchangeable asset.

Blockchains 1.0 such as Bitcoin and bitcoin forks, cryptocurrencies such Litecoin, Bitcoin Cash, Zcash and my favourite Dogecoin, are purely cryptocurrencies and can't do much more other than sending value back and forth.

Blockchain 2.0 started to allow scripting functionality, i.e. smart contracts, embedding business logic and function as a data storage for many many use cases. Some of these blockchain 2.0s are not cryptocurrencies.

Cryptocurrencies are blockchains that, due to their nature and use case, also need a "coin". These "coins" are used not only to exchange value between users or store value, but they also have another critical functionality: cryptocurrency are public and usually permissionless blockchains that need people to join as a node to keep the network running. People can have "coins" as an incentive to contribute with nodes/miners that will keep the network validating transactions.

Blockchain 2.0 doesn't store only data related to cryptocurrency transactions. It stores any data. The so-called blockchain protocols can also be included in the blockchain 2.0. They allow scripting functions, creating smart contracts and running decentralized applications.

Blockchain components

Let's look at some of the components that make a blockchain a blockchain. In this section, we will start with addresses – i.e., what is a blockchain address, transactions and transaction fees, blocks, how are blocks formed, smart contracts and much more. Although we had already looked at these concepts at a high-level, we will now look at it more from a technical perspective. In the end, this book objective's is to make you a blockchain pundit, right?

This is going to get more technical, but please bear with me. Okay?

Addresses

In a blockchain, addresses are unique identifiers associated with an entity, a wallet or a smart contract. They are usually composed of an alphanumeric string with between 26 and 35 characters. In the Bitcoin case, the address is a 160-bit hash of the public key generated from the ECDSA private key.

The address and the public key can be shared with anyone with no security restrictions. On the other hand, the private key cannot be shared and should be kept secure (unless you want to lose all your money).

In most blockchains, the address derives from the public key, and there are 3 simple steps to create an address:

1- Creating a private key (ECDSA)

2- Take the public key from the private key (Public Key Infrastructure always have private/public key pairs)

3- Hash the public key to generate the address

Although we are going to take a deep dive on ECDSA keys later in this book, let's take a look at how to do this in the command line. Depending on the blockchain, the address generation may be slightly more complex, but this is pretty much how it rolls.

Start doing the nerd stuff by opening your command line. To open the command line on your computer, click the Windows icon and type "cmd" and hit enter. If you are a Mac user, you can either open your Applications folder, then open Utilities and double-click on Terminal, or press Command - spacebar to launch Spotlight and type "Terminal,".

Then, the following command will create a new RSA key pair. After generating the key pair, you can run the SHA256 hashing algorithm to generate an address.

ssh-keygen

sha256sum publickey.pub

```
C:\Users\henri
λ ssh-keygen
Generating public/private rsa key pair.
Enter file in which to save the key (C:\Users\henri/.ssh/id_rsa): address1
Enter passphrase (empty for no passphrase):
Enter same passphrase again:
Your identification has been saved in address1.
Your public key has been saved in address1.pub.
The key fingerprint is:
SHA256:G9wpd7tS9+5mKUZogqWXD7pEZI51rroLH7SqBmYnM94 henri@Crazy-motherfucker
The key's randomart image is:
+---[RSA 2048]----+
|                 |
|                 |
|      + .        |
|     *.oo .      |
|    o oS.= o     |
|.* .. oo.X +.o.  |
|= *. o o+ =.o. ..|
| o E+ +.  .. + .+|
|.... =o..  .o .=o|
+----[SHA256]-----+

C:\Users\henri
λ sha256sum address1.pub
648de3bb9ac5df0bd0ef8ad99d75ad6b8d789c1e6ea7f29d6bab5f7125fccb5a *address1.pub
```

The long hash

97e75487c0afc7c54e7d0a463bafd6a099a55c4cac8d1130ce1db5714ee

bad7a is an unique address! It's almost impossible to generate the same address.

Oh, you may also be asking what's that randomart image. This is a graphical representation of the key that you have generated. Your private key will have always the same randomart image. The idea is that humans can easily identify if there's a change in the image, while it would be harder to identify a change in a long hexadecimal string. You can easily see that the previous randomart kinda look like a tree. However, if you check your RSA key and it looks like a dong, you know something is wrong!

Transaction

In the blockchain, a transaction is an event. Transactions don't necessarily mean a transfer of value. It can be an event or a message or some data sent from Alice to Bob. In blockchains like Bitcoin, however, transactions indeed refer to a transfer of value in the form of cryptocurrency. These transfers occur from one address to another.

In most blockchains, a transaction will include the value, a message, sender, receiver, the block to where it belongs, a timestamp and hash of all the transaction data together. Transactions are then packed together into blocks. The only exemption are DLT technologies or hashgraphs where transactions are hashed sequentially and not stored in blocks.

Transaction fee

Validating nodes in a blockchain, also known as miners, need to perform some work in order to include the transactions in the blockchain. Thus, they need to have an incentive to do this work, and this incentive can be paid in the form of transaction fees.

The transaction fees don't depend on how big is the transaction in terms of amount. No matter if you are transferring $100 or $100 000 000 worth of Bitcoin, the transaction fee would be similar. In a blockchain, what influences the transaction fee is the size of the transaction in bytes, not the size in value. A Bitcoin transaction size is on average 500 bytes, and the user pays a transaction fee according to the size and according to how fast he desires the transaction to be included in the blockchain. Miners choose the transactions from a transaction memory pool, prioritizing the ones that pay the highest fees. Consequently, if a user wants his transaction to be included in the next block, he would have to pay a higher fee to "bribe" the miner pick up the transaction first.

You can the blocks in the blockchain as trucks. Or trains with limited capacity. Each truck can take 1000kg of cargo. The driver is a greedy dog and tries to maximize the reward for each truck. The price of each package that you send will depend on the weight of the package. If your package is heavier, you will need to pay the truck driver more money to make sure your package is included in the next truck. Yeah, this is how blockchain works too. Continue reading, I will talk about this again in a few pages.

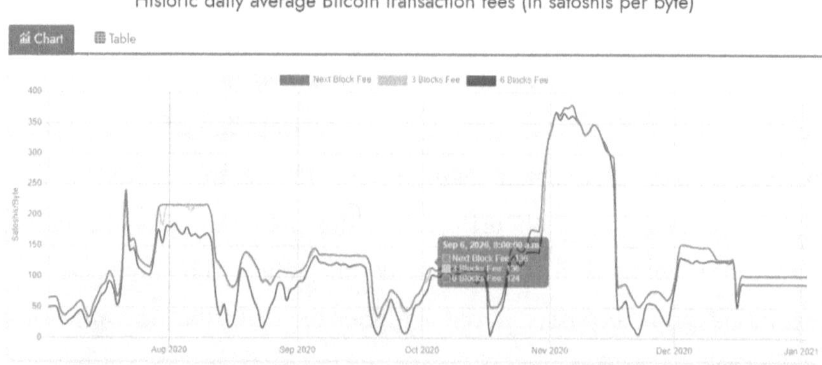

Source https://privacypros.io/tools/bitcoin-fee-estimator/

In Bitcoin, transaction fees are measured in Satoshi/Byte, where a Satoshi corresponds to 0.00000001 Bitcoin.

In January 2021, the average transaction fee to include a transaction in the next block (within 10 minutes) is 90 Satoshi/Byte:

90 satoshi/Byte * 500 Bytes = 45 000 satoshi = 0.00045 BTC

which as per March 2021 BTC/USD rate is approximately 13 USD.

Note that the miners will sooner or later pick up transactions with low fees, but they may take up to a few hours to be included in the blockchain. If you pay a really low few, it may even take a few days for a miner to pick up the transaction.

In the blockchain, transaction fees are also an important feature to avoid network spamming or DoS – Denial of Service Attacks. In this kind of attack, the attacker would flood the network with dummy transactions to exhaust the blockchain resources and clog the entire network. DoS or DDoS attacks usually don't happen in blockchains such as Bitcoin because the fees would make the attack extremely expensive and infeasible.

Turing Complete

Some blockchains like Ethereum or Hyperledger Fabric use Turing complete programming languages meaning that developers use to create smart-contracts that can do pretty much anything, from simple to more complex functions. Turing complete means that it is computationally universal, being able to perform any real-world general-purpose function.

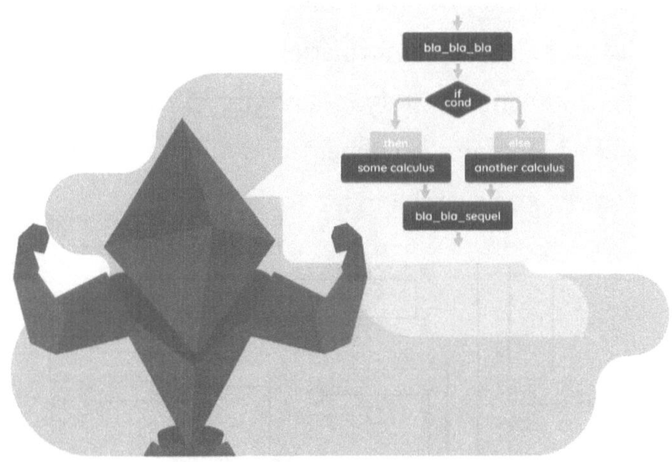

For example, the Ethereum Virtual Machine is a Turing complete decentralized virtual machine, meaning that it can replicate any possible computing logic or function. This computing logic in Ethereum is made via smart contracts, and they can be written in the Solidity programming language (although they can be written in other languages too).

Block

A block in the blockchain is usually composed of the block hash, the previous block hash, time-stamp, nonce, a Merkle root and/or a number of transactions. Once a block mined, broadcasted and accepted by the other nodes in the blockchain, it can no longer be modified or deleted. Each block contains the hash of the previous block, forming a chain between them.

Block Explorer

A block explorer is a user interface for users to look at the blockchain. It is a tool, often a web-based app, the allows users to view and explore all the information in a blockchain, including transactions, transaction history, addresses, blocks, etc.. Behind the scenes, the block explorer is connected to a full node with the entire ledger and works as a search engine for that ledger.

Block 664015 ⓘ

Hash	00000000000000000000dd3de88b3faef969b5c20b368b4430dda2259f99ef887
Confirmations	1
Timestamp	2021-01-02 00:00
Height	664015
Miner	Unknown
Number of Transactions	1,905
Difficulty	18,599,593,048,299.49
Merkle root	998382dcd35385ccb7c4c784af7f59ebf85da3968720b610d1f05b2ee2863225
Version	0x20000000
Bits	386,867,735
Weight	3,993,521 WU
Size	1,316,444 bytes
Nonce	2,107,244,866
Transaction Volume	7400.98639448 BTC
Block Reward	6.25000000 BTC
Fee Reward	0.73989728 BTC

Source https://www.blockchain.com/explorer

There's an online block explorer for any major public blockchain, but we can see here an example of what information is shown in a Bitcoin block explorer. In this image, you can see the full structure of a block:

Hash: a SHA-256 hash of the data in the block.

Block height: it represents how many blocks were mined between the current block and the genesis block. Approximately 144 new Bitcoin blocks are mined every day.

Time-stamp: the exact time when the block was mined.

Previous block hash: although not shown in this image, every block also contains the previous block's hash.

The number of transactions: corresponds to the number of transactions included in that specific block. Each block has a size limit – for example, 1MB, 1.3MB or 8MB – and the number of transactions that a block can include is a constraint to the block size. You can see the block size as the truck size. A small truck can carry 1000kg of cargo, while a big truck can handle 8000kg of cargo. In the same way, a bigger block can include more transactions.

Block reward: the Bitcoin block reward is at the moment 6.25 BTC. This is the miners' reward as an incentive for them to contribute to the network and create blocks. The block reward started at 50. BTC per block in 2009, and it's halved every four years or, to be more accurate, the halving occurs every 210,000 blocks. Because of the halving, the block reward will get to zero in 2140.

The reward is contained in each block's Coinbase transaction, which is a unique transaction created to pay the block reward. For the block in this example, the 6.25 BTC reward would be equivalent to approximately USD 184 000.00. Not bad, huh?!

Fun fact (especially for the ones who did it): back in 2009 you could mine bitcoin blocks with your personal computer. If you have mined one single block, the 50 BTC reward would in 2021 be worth 2.3 Million dollars.

Fee reward: in addition to the block reward, fees are also paid to the miners. For example, in this block, the miners were paid approximately 0.7398 BTC, around USD 22 000.00.

Merkle root: the Merkle room comes from the Merkle tree, and it's the hash of all the transactions in the block, organized in a tree. If any data in any transaction in the Merkle tree changes, the Merkle root would also change.

Number of transactions: how many transactions were included in the block.

Transaction volume: how much BTC was transacted in the block. In the example that we are looking at, approximately 7401 Bitcoins were transacted which is around USD 217 589 400.00 in the block above (in only 10 minutes!).

Nonce, difficulty and bits are related to mining, and we will have fun looking at it later in another chapter.

As you see, there's a lot of information in a block explorer, and any person can also check the transactions included in each block in a completely open and transparent way.

As an example, let's take a look at the coinbase transaction included in the first block ever in the Bitcoin blockchain – the genesis block!

Details ⓘ

Hash	4a5e1e4baab89f3a32518a88c31bc87f618f76673e2cc77ab2127b7afdeda33b
Status	Confirmed
Received Time	2009-01-04 02:15
Size	204 bytes
Weight	816
Included in Block	0
Confirmations	664,080
Total Input	0.00000000 BTC
Total Output	50.00000000 BTC
Fees	0.00000000 BTC
Fee per byte	0.000 sat/B
Fee per weight unit	0.000 sat/WU
Value when transacted	$0.00

Details of the Coinbase transaction in the Bitcoin genesis block

This was the first transaction ever. As you can see, there are no fees paid, and the block has more than 600 thousand confirmations which means that already more than 600 thousand blocks were mined on the top of this block. This block is well inside the blockchain onion. It also contains a pretty cool hidden message that you can check by yourself too!

The input of the transaction has the following HEX Sigscript:
5468652054696d65732030332f4a616e2f3230303920436686
16e63656c6c6f72206f6e206272696e6b206f66207365636f
6e64206261696c6f757420666f722062616e6b73

You can convert this HEX message to ASCII text in your command line by typing the following:

echo
5468652054696d65732030332f4a616e2f323030303920436861 6616
e63656c6c6f72206f6e206272696e6b206f66207365636f6e64
206261696c6f757420666f722062616e6b73 | xxd -r -p

```
C:\Users\henri
λ echo 5468652054696d65732030332f4a616e2f32303039204368616e63656c6c6f72206f6e20627
2696e6b206f66207365636f6e64206261696c6f757420666f722062616e6b73 | xxd -r -p
The Times 03/Jan/2009 Chancellor on brink of second bailout for banks
```

Converting HEX to ASCII in the command line

This message was the headline of the London Times on the 3rd of January of 2009. Quite a special meaning for Bitcoin. This headline represents the failure of an entire financial system in 2009which fueled the interest in Bitcoin, blockchain and decentralized systems.

The London Times in the 3rd of January of 2009

Smart Contracts

A smart contract is a piece of a computer program that can execute a contractual agreement between two parties. Smart contracts can pretty much execute any contractual condition or functions. They are Turing-complete, meaning that they use programming languages with conditional statements and conditional branching. These are the programming languages that have "if, then, else" and they can replicate any computer logic.

Smart contracts are autonomously executed, meaning that there's no need for third-party intervention to execute once deployed, and their execution cannot be stopped. Smart contracts can self-enforced the rules they were written/coded in the smart contract. For example, you can program a smart contract to work as an escrow and settlement service, where the smart contract can receive funds from Alice and release the funds to Bob once Bob sends asset D to Alize. In a smart contract, code is the law. You can also program a smart contract to lock $1000 worth of cryptocurrency and only unlock it in the year 2030. Once this contract is deployed, there's nothing you can do to change it and the money will be locked in this vault until 2030 no matter what. Anything that you program in a smart contract will later self-execute.

Smart contracts are deployed in a blockchain such as Ethereum where they are executed in the EVM – Ethereum Virtual Machine. Many other blockchains, including private blockchains, feature smart contracts.

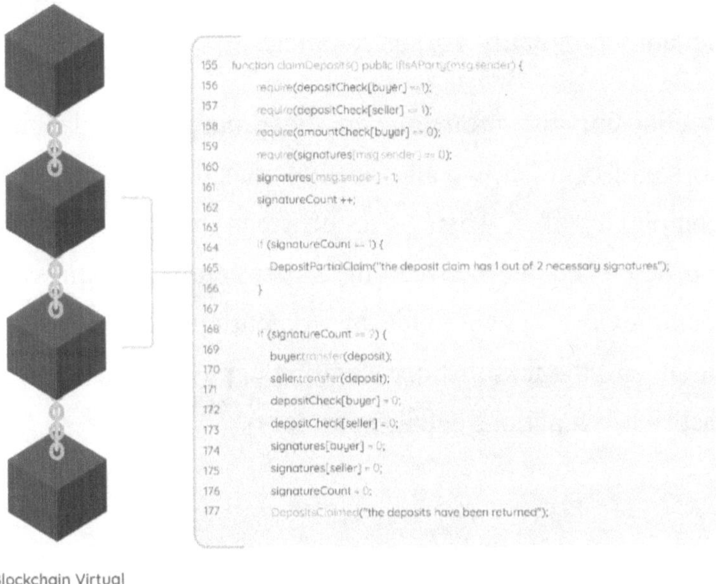

Blockchain Virtual Machine

Illustration of a section of an escrow smart contract in the blockchain

Some of the characteristics of the smart contracts are:

- Smart contracts are self-executed

- Smart contracts are turing-complete

- Parties remain pseudonymous

- Smart contracts are transparent and fully auditable

- Smart contracts are immutable

Side note: Turing completeness is more an idealization. In reality, computers and virtual machines are limited by finite memory and computing capacity. Additionally, smart contracts in the blockchain require fees to be executed. Smart contracts are thus limited and consequently not totally Turing-complete.

When choosing the protocol and the programming language to write a smart contract, we also need to consider the expressiveness and complexity of it. There is an efficient frontier, and trade-offs need to be considered between the smart contract's expressiveness and complexity. The amount of computing power required to execute it, and the fees that one's willing to pay to execute the smart contract (more functions equals more fees).

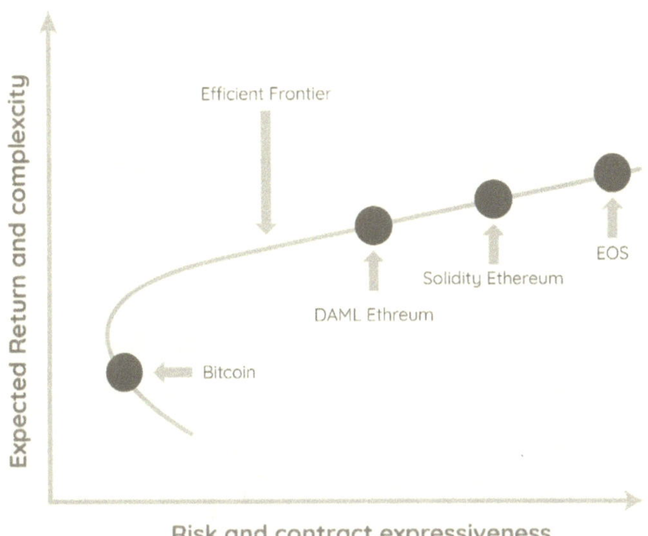

The Nobel Laureate Harry Markowitz introduced the Efficient Frontier theory in 1952, and it's widely used in modern portfolio theory to efficiently create optimal investment portfolios. The efficient frontier shows the highest expected return for a defined level of risk. I think it's pretty cool if we apply it to the Turing-completeness of blockchains.

Different blockchains and programming languages present different return/complexity levels and correlate with certain risk and contract expressiveness levels. More loose programming languages may allow for more complexity. Still, they may be less easy to reason about, developers make more mistakes, are prone to more bugs, and the blockchain capacity also limits them in terms of computing power, throughput, and fees that are feasible to pay.

In Ethereum, developers can use a programming language called Solidity or Kotlin and C++. DAML is, however, a more safe way to program smart contracts. These smart contracts can achieve different levels of complexity, considering that Ethereum is Turing-complete.

Although possible, building extremely complex smart contracts is not advised because the execution of more complex smart contracts requires more gas (the fee that is paid in Ether to execute smart contracts). The smart contracts are executed by the Ethereum nodes (any person can have an Ethereum node because it is a permissionless network), and these nodes run EVM Ethereum Virtual Machine. The users' gas fees reward the nodes for transaction execution and executing functions in the smart contracts.

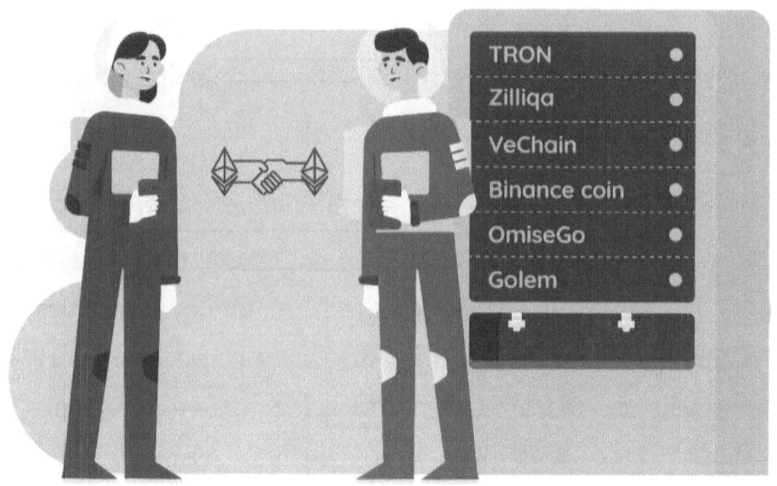

Each Ethereum smart contract has an address used to interact with it, including interacting with other smart contracts, which expands the automation capabilities.

Smart contracts allow for the first time in the history of IT the creation of dApps that offer come new advantages:

- Enhanced security: improved dApps security with the public key cryptography and the blockchain consensus mechanism, which ensures the correct execution of smart contracts

- Autonomy: dApps are developed on the top of smart contracts (the app logic), and these smart contracts run in a decentralized way in the blockchain. dApps can run automatically and autonomously without the need for third-party intervention

- Traceable: transactions or any events of the dApp are traceable considering that the information (related to the smart contracts) is stored in the blockchain (note that a dApp may also have off-chain information)

- Stability: because smart contracts are distributed across many nodes in the blockchain with redundancy, the dApps will continue to run smoothly even if some nodes fail.

Other permissionless blockchains allow smart contract creation and execution. Other than Ethereum, blockchains like Cardano, Tron, Lisk, Stellar, Monax, RSK and Counterparty also allow smart contract scripting and can be a decent alternative to Ethereum.

Some of these blockchains use the same programming languages used by Ethereum since their creation was inspired by it. Oh, and don't forget private/permissioned blockchains. The Hyperledger blockchains, Corda, and others also allow smart contracts.

Oracles

Oracles are third party sources of data that are considered trusted. Oracles can derive information from external sources into the ledger. An oracle could be the price of a stock through Bloomberg that is fed into a smart contract to execute a trade or the price of beef from CME Group and fed into a blockchain that is tracking a beef supply chain marketplace.

Other examples of this off-chain data source could be ERP software connecting to the blockchain or IoT devices used to track goods.

These oracles help to create smart contracts that bridge between the blockchain and the outside world. Oracles may be agreed upon contractual agreements where it is agreed that a certain source of information from the outside is relevant to execute smart contracts or on-chain transactions.

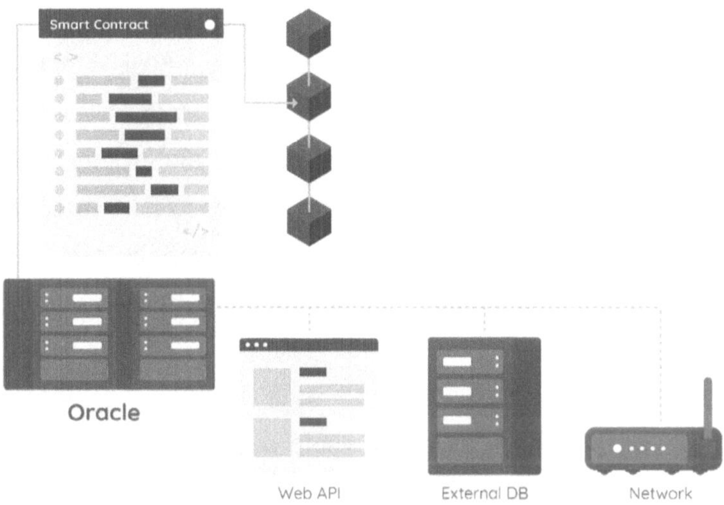

Other oracle data sources can also be a database, a device, an IoT source or RFID. They feed information to smart contracts because smart contracts are unable to access external information by themselves. An example of an interaction between a smart contract and an oracle could be a smart contract that automatically performs a payment when a product leaves a shop. The product is equipped with an RFID sensor, and as soon as it leaves the doors of the shop, the smart contract will be triggered to perform a payment.

Now you may be wondering: what if the oracle sends inaccurate information to the blockchain?

This is a very good question, indeed—the garbage in - garbage out problem. If you send inaccurate information to the blockchain, the data will stay there, and it will not be possible to change it due to blockchain immutability. However, at least you can audit that data and understand who and how that data went there.

Imagine this: a blockchain application pays insurance automatically to farmers if it doesn't rain for more than 45 days. This blockchain is connected to an oracle that provides the weather data: the local weather station. There is a little problem, tho: the brother of the gal that works there is a big farmer, and she decides to fake some weather data so that he can receive insurance. This can be an issue, but blockchain will allow us to audit every action, anytime.

Consensus

Consensus mechanisms deserve a whole book, but here I'm going to try to go straight to the point. Consensus mechanism is an algorithm that defines the rules for the multiple nodes on a blockchain to agree on how the blockchain should look and what constitutes valid data in the blockchain. Consensus is the set of rules that defines how nodes agree on the state of the blockchain. All the blockchains have a minimum threshold of how many nodes need to agree in order to reach consensus.

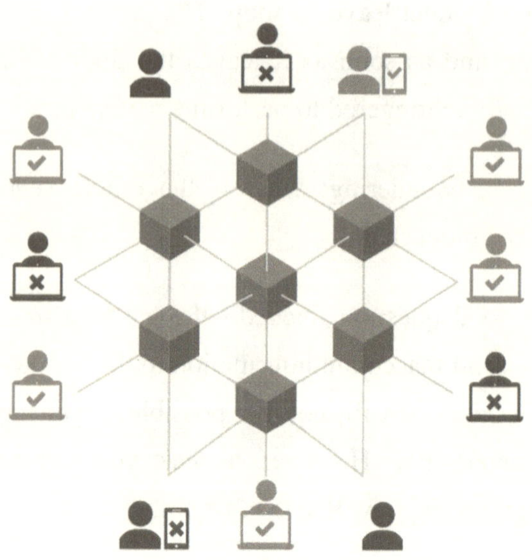

This is called the fault tolerance percentage, and it corresponds to how much power an attacker would have to accumulate in order to create a separate chain or gain control over the main blockchain. In Bitcoin and most of the public/permissionless blockchains, this percentage is 50%. In permissioned blockchains, this percentage is lower. PBFTx blockchains, the fault tolerance is 33%, and Ripple can tolerate the Byzantine Problem in 20% of the nodes.

Confirmations

A confirmation happens when the entire network has processed the transaction, settling the data in the blockchain. Once a transaction is confirmed, it's considered immutable. For the transaction to be confirmed, it's not enough that the two transacting nodes agree with the transaction. Consensus will need to be reached within the validating nodes in order to consider the transaction final. In Bitcoin, for example, the transaction needs to be mined in a block. This is why when dealing with big Bitcoin payments, one always needs to wait for at least one confirmation, i.e. to wait for the transaction to be included in a block. Otherwise, the transaction can eventually be reversed.

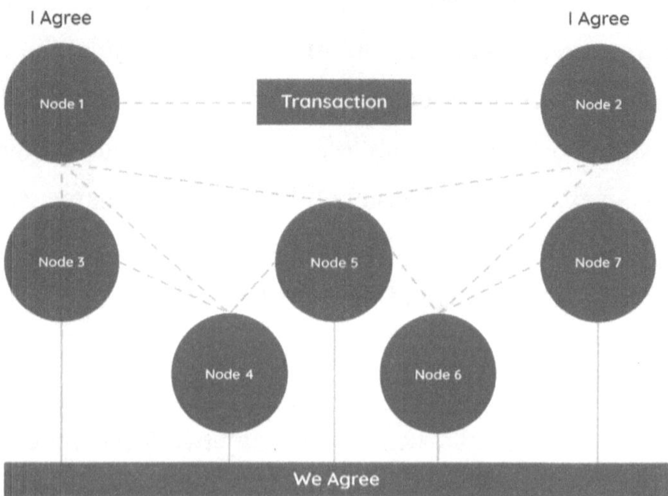

Never forget, in a blockchain, a transaction is considered complete not when it's sent but when it's recorded on the blockchain. Thus, the importance of waiting for at least one confirmation when you are receiving a transaction from someone.

For example, someone may send you a transaction with a very low fee (for example, 1 satoshi/byte). Simultaneously, the sender will send the same amount of Bitcoin to himself with a higher transaction fee. The receiver may see in his wallet that a payment was initiated to his wallet, but it still has zero confirmations. It will be more likely in this case that the transaction with the higher fee is cleared first, and you will actually never receive the Bitcoin amount. However, if you have one or more confirmations, it means that the transactions were included in a block and permanently registered on the blockchain.

Why do some exchanges or vendors require 6 confirmations? Just to be extra secure. If you are receiving a small payment, 1 confirmation is totally enough. However, a $10 000 000 worth of Bitcoin (or another cryptocurrency) deserve additional precautions. Say the sender is also a big Bitcoin miner, and he is able to forge some blocks, putting his fake transaction in 1 or 2 blocks that later will not be validated by the other nodes in the blockchain and will become "orphan" blocks. We will look at orphan blocks later.

Cryptocurrency

Cryptocurrencies are digital currencies. They rely on the blockchain, but they shouldn't be confused with blockchain. What I mean is that cryptocurrencies always sit on the top of a blockchain, but not all blockchains have a cryptocurrency (Hyperledger blockchains, Corda and other enterprise blockchains are some of the examples of blockchains without cryptocurrency).

Cryptocurrencies leverage blockchain's cryptography and encryption features, and the first and most famous is Bitcoin with a trillion-dollar market cap. Other cryptocurrencies are:

Dogecoin – Dog's favorite cryptocurrency

Ether – Ethereum cryptocurrency

USDT – Tether cryptocurrency

XRP – Ripple cryptocurrency

ADA – Cardano cryptocurrency

XMR – Monero cryptocurrency

And many, many more! Each one of these cryptocurrencies has specific features and are utilized in different ways. Bitcoin can be used to make payments and to be used as a store of value. Ether can be used for the same purposes as Bitcoin, but it is also used to pay the fees related to Ethereum smart contract execution. USDT is a stablecoin, pegged to the USD. XMR is an anonymous cryptocurrency designed with advanced cryptography that ensures the total anonymity of the users. Even Dogecoin has good use cases: its transaction fees are very low, meaning that it is an excellent cryptocurrency to send microtransactions.

Hash Functions

Hash functions are the heart of blockchain technology. Hash functions take any input value of any size and create an output of a fixed length. No matter how big is the input, the output always has the same size. If there's any change in the input value, the output automatically changes.

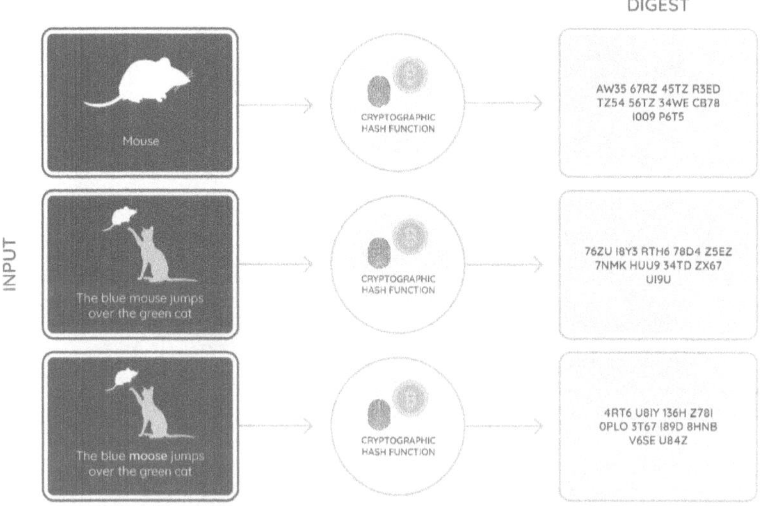

Anything can be hashed. Blockchain transactions, the Complete Works of William Shakespeare, an image or a document, the hash output is always the same size and has specific characteristics. The SHA-256, SHA-3 and Keccak are widely used in several blockchains, and it produces a hash (output) of size 256 bits (32 bytes).

Let's take a look at the hash functions characteristics:

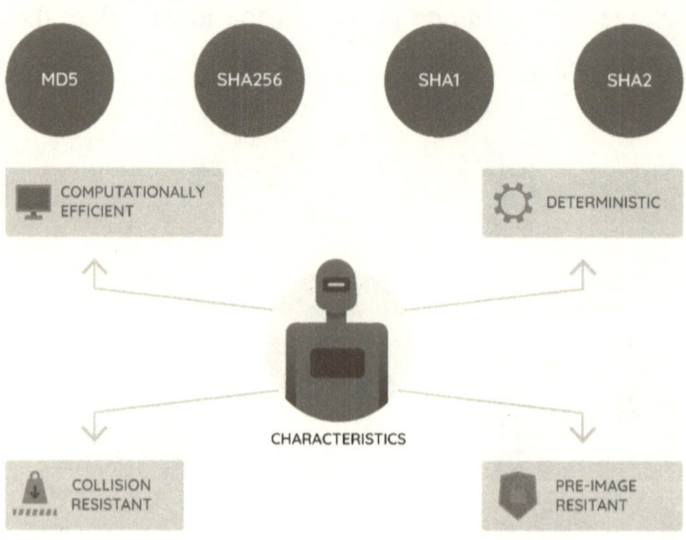

Computational efficient: it doesn't require many computational resources to compute or verify a hash.

Deterministic: the output of a hash will always be the same as long as the input is the same. If I hash a specific cat photo 1000000 times, the output will always be the same. However, if I change one single pixel in that cat photo, the output (the hash string) will be totally different.

```
C:\Users\henri
λ echo The blue mouse jumps over the green cat > mouse.txt

C:\Users\henri
λ sha256sum mouse.txt
da19c4cdd1db41899c12a11b4009b84c7042383966b776304f20ab95515d0d49 *mouse.txt

C:\Users\henri
λ echo The blue moose jumps over the green cat > mouse.txt

C:\Users\henri
λ sha256sum mouse.txt
ca3c1761164961d4e398605ea948b6cff6533332520dbf569502a585aaeb31e8 *mouse.txt
```

In this screenshot, we check what's the SHA256 hash output of a sentence. You can see that changing a single letter in the sentence totally changes the hash output.

Collision resistant: it is extremely unlikely to have the same hash output for two different inputs. SHA256 has 2^256 results which is a very^{very} large number:

2^256 =
115792089237316195423570985008687907853269984665640394575840079131296399936

That's a 75 digit number! There is 1 in over 115 quattuorvigintillion chances of finding a collision. God created the universe only 435196800000000000 seconds ago when the Big Bang happened.

Pre-image resistant: it is impossible to convert the output of a hash to the input.

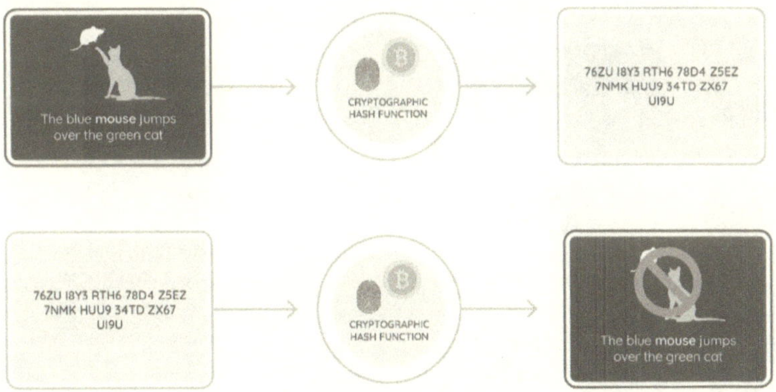

The output of a hash doesn't reveal anything about the input. It is currently impossible to discover what's was the input of a certain hash output. Even a quantum computer would find this task very hard.

Digesting what hashes are, hashes are the output returned by hash functions. No matter how big is the file or text, or transaction fed into a hash function, the output will always have a fixed length. If the input changes by a single letter, the output hash will be different.

dApp (or DAPP)

A dApp is an application that outsources part of its logic in the blockchain. dApps resource to smart contracts for some of its logic, but they are not 100% hosted and decentralized in the blockchain.

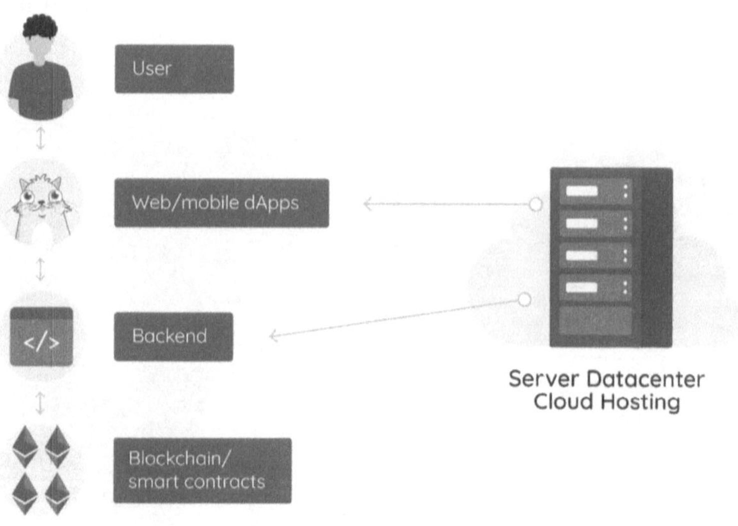

Most of the dApps are hosted in a traditional datacenter or on a cloud provider, while the business logic relies on smart contracts on the blockchain.

The web/mobile app and the backend will be hosted in a cloud provider, while the smart contracts are on the blockchain.

Similar to dApps, a DAO – Decentralized Autonomous Organization – is an organization that works almost like a company but has all the rules written on the blockchain.

Difficulty

The difficulty represents how hard it is to find the hash needed to mine a new block in the blockchain in a proof of work blockchain. The difficulty represents the number of possibilities/combinations for the miners to guess the hash. Greater the difficulty, more work the miners need to perform in order to guess the hash and create a new block. The difficulty is adjusted in the Bitcoin blockchain so that new blocks are created on average every 10 minutes. If more miners join the Bitcoin network, thus contributing with more hash power, the difficulty will increase and adjust so that the miners discover the hash on average every 10 minutes.

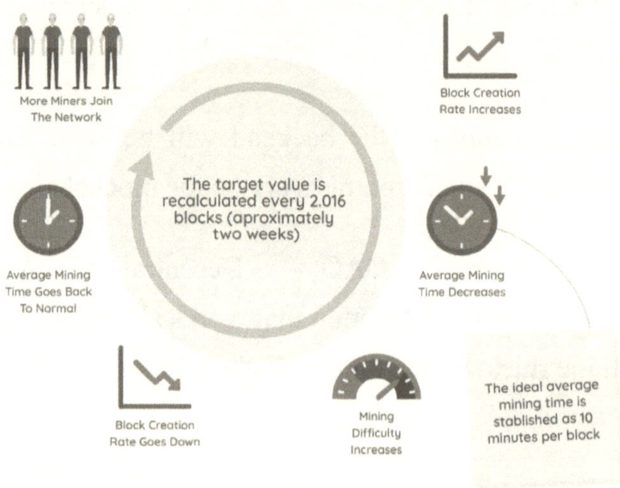

The mining difficulty is adjusted every 2016 blocks, which is approximately two weeks considering an average of 10 minutes per block. Bitcoin algorithm provides this adjustment very easily. If the previous 2016 blocks took more or less than two weeks to find, the difficulty is increased or decreased in the proportion of the amount of time difference to the two weeks.

Digital signatures

Digital signatures are very hard to forge when comparing with traditional handwritten signatures. Digital signatures are used to sign a message, transaction or document that the sender is sending. Depending on the algorithm used, it is usually composed of a hash of [private key + transaction + time-stamp + magic number]

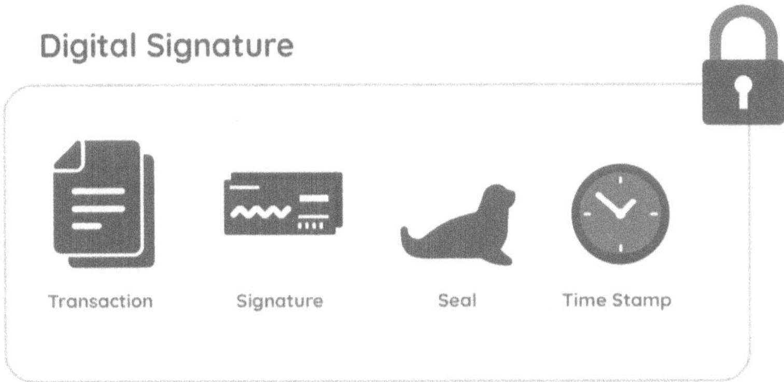

In this image, you can see the elements that compose a digital signature, making it unique.

We will later see in detail how to digitally sign a transaction with ECSDA.

Multi-Signature

Multi-signature is a security feature that requires signatures of multiple pre-defined entities in order to issue a transaction. It's considered more secure than a single signature, and it's an essential feature in some cryptocurrency wallets and custodian services.

A multi-signature wallet would require, for example, 2 out of 3 keys to make a transaction. This will align with the organization's compliance, risk management and governance.

A single signature wallet may put at risk the funds stored in that wallet, especially when we are talking about big organizations.

In 2019 the CEO of the largest Canadian crypto exchange mysteriously disappeared or died, and with him, the key for the wallet with $190 million also died. Multi-signature wallets can be used to make sure funds are safe, and there's no single point of failure.

Double spending

Double spending is a type of attack where the attacker attempts to duplicate a transaction. In this attack, the attacker tries to spend the same coins twice, sending it, for example, to a recipient and himself at the same time. Blockchains try to prevent this by time-stamping the transactions and including them in a block. Attackers may try to mine the block that contains the duplicated transaction to increase the probability of tricking the receiver that that transaction was sent.

This kind of attack is more common in proof of work blockchains where the attacker can exploit the intermediate time between two transactions' initiation and confirmation.

Before the second transaction is mined to be invalid (because there is a conflicting first transaction), the attacker already got the first transaction output resulting in double-spending. In this type of attack, the attacker would send the same transaction to a vendors BTC address and a colluding wallet that the attacker himself control. Then, if his transaction gets mined first, he manages to keep the BTC for himself. For this reason, anyone receiving BTC should wait at least for one confirmation, i.e. wait for the transaction to be included in a block. This way, you can make sure that the transaction is settled.

In reality, double-spending attacks require the attacker to gain more than 51% of the network in order to be successful, which is very hard or impossible to happen in any of the major public blockchains. However, the attacker may trick the receiver for a short period of time, and that's why it is important to wait for a few block confirmations in order to ensure that the transaction was settled in the network.

In 2020, a group of three men stole around $30 000 from Bitcoin ATMs in Hong Kong. The group targeted Bitcoin ATMs that didn't require the confirmations. These Bitcoin ATMs accepted transactions with zero confirmations, meaning that a client could send Bitcoin and immediately get cash for that transaction. This loophole was easily exploited by the thieves. They have sent Bitcoin to the ATM with a very low transaction fee – 1satoshi/byte – and then sent the amount to a different wallet controlled by them using a higher fee. Because of the low fee, the first transaction never got confirmed on the blockchain, and the second transaction is confirmed, leaving the first transaction invalid. The thieves got the cash and kept the Bitcoin.

Ethereum

Ethereum is the first blockchain 2.0, allowing smart contract scripting in the Turing-complete EVM – Ethereum Virtual Machine, with a programming language called Solidity. You can see Ethereum as a huge distributed computer with a massive amount of computing power, capable of executing anything. It also has a native cryptocurrency called Ether. Smart contracts can be deployed in the Ethereum blockchain, blocks are smaller and produced more often when compared to Bitcoin – the average block size is 20 kb to 30kb. Ethereum is also well known to be the main issuance platform for the many tokens in the market and home to most DeFi applications and many other dApps.

EVM

Ethereum Virtual Machine is the world biggest distributed computing platform, a network of nodes that run the Ethereum software. Any person can deploy an Ethereum node/miner. We will actually learn how to do it later in this book.

Testnet

A testnet is a network that mimics the main network, but it's made for testing and not production. It may also be called UAT network or staging network. It allows developers to do tests in an environment that is similar to the production environment. It can be seen as a development environment for the blockchain. Developers need to test applications and smart contracts before moving to production i.e. the main network. Ethereum has different testnets: Gorli, Kovan, Rinkeby and Ropsten. Can you guess what these names have in common?

Fork

A fork is what you use to eat food. Oh wait, in this case, we are talking about blockchain. A fork is an update to the blockchain. Forks may happen because of changes in the protocol. In blockchains, updates can never be retroactive.

Soft Fork

A soft fork is one of those plastic forks…. Kidding   a soft fork is a backward compatible fork meaning that the updates are compatible with the previous version or with nodes that are still running the old version. These updates only represent a soft fork as long as they continue to respect the protocol rules.

- Soft fork is backward compatible

- After the soft fork, nodes running the previous version can still interact and add new blocks as long as they comply with the rules

Hard Fork

A hard fork is an update that it's not backwards compatible. Nodes that update to the new protocol will no longer be compatible with the previous version and will create a new fork of the blockchain. Nodes that update to the new protocol cannot process transactions in the previous protocol.

- Hard fork has no backward compatibility

- All nodes must upgrade to the new version, or the blockchain will break into two

- Nodes that do not accept the upgrade will not be compatible with the nodes that do

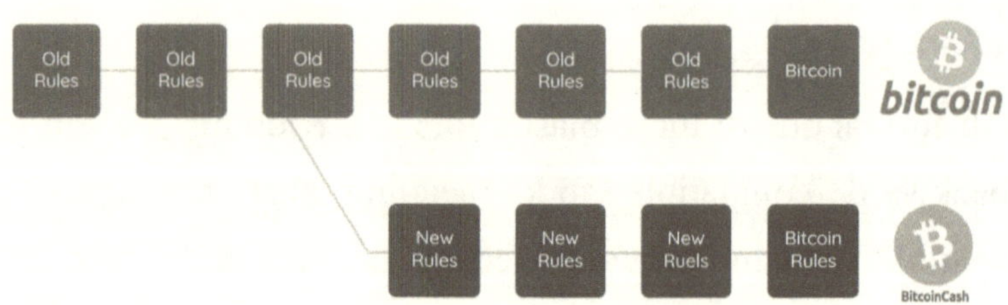

For example, Bitcoin has frequent updates that represent soft forks, and they are called BIP – Bitcoin Improvement Proposal. In 2017 however, there was a hard fork when some developers decided to propose to increase the Bitcoin block size from 1 MB to 8 MB. The nodes that continued to run the previous version continued running the Bitcoin protocol. The nodes that adopted the changes increasing the block size to 8 MB created a separate blockchain called Bitcoin Cash. This fork created two distinct blockchains: Bitcoin and a new blockchain, Bitcoin Cash.

Forks and the 51% attack

A 51% attack happens when a person or a group tries to gain control of the network by acquiring more than 50% of the network's computing power.

To understand well how a 51% attack happens, we need to look at some assumptions. We know that:

1. There's no centralized authority in the blockchain

2. Miners track transaction validity

3. Miners append new transactions to the blockchain and broadcast new blocks to the blockchain miners/nodes

4. Miners follow the longest chain rule

5. According to the Consensus mechanism in place, the consensus among miner is reached with 51% or more of the miners

6. 51% attacks would happen only in permissionless blockchains. For Permissioned blockchains this is not a concern because the consensus mechanism is different, the participants' identities are known in the network, and the governance of the network would also protect it

The 51% attack happens when the bad actors gain 51% of the blockchain mining power, and it's one of the most well-known blockchain security flaws.

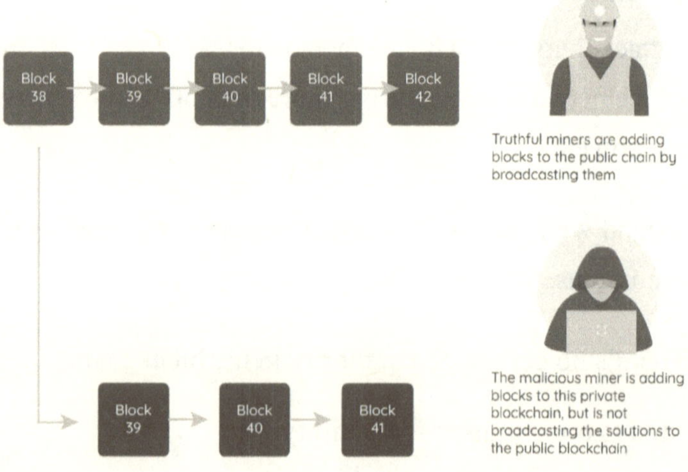

The percentage may vary from blockchain to blockchain, but in the Bitcoin example, if a bad actor can gain 51% of the mining power or hashrate, he can gain control of the consensus mechanism and eventually try to rewrite transactions. Once the attacker gains control of the consensus in the blockchain, he can start monopolizing the block mining and work on his own version of the blockchain. He would be able to perform double-spending, reverse transactions and prevent the other miners from confirming transactions.

The resiliency to the 51% attacks grows when the number of miners grows, but smaller proof of work blockchains may be exposed. In 2018, some cryptocurrencies were victims of 51% attacks: Verge, Zencash and Ethereum Classic, for example, were some of the victims. The attackers profited more than 20 million USD with these attacks.

It is, however, very expensive to carry these attacks. Just to try a 51% attack on the Bitcoin blockchain network would cost more than 25 million USD in equipment and more than 15 million USD in electricity per day. It is also essential to bring to the equation how often that specific blockchain adjusts the difficulty. In the Bitcoin blockchain, for example, every 2016 blocks (around 2 weeks considering that each block is mined on average every 10 minutes), the entire blockchain uses some clever mathematics to decide how "difficult" it should be for the next 2016 blocks in order to continue having one new block mined every 10 minutes, based on how fast blocks were found, averaged out over the last 2016 blocks.

This would be an advantage for the 51% attacker, considering that the difficulty of mining a new block would remain the same for two weeks for the attacker. However, some blockchains adjust the difficulty much faster and also DigiShield has been added to many blockchains including Bitcoin Cash, Ethereum, Zcash, Dogecoin,

Startcoin and many more. DigiShield allows the mining difficulty to be adjusted every block, increasing or decreasing it according to the needs and reducing 51% attacks' feasibility.

It is also important to say that even if an attacker pulls a successful 51% attack, most of the miners will shift the computing power by leaving the attacker out of the network. This means that even if someone succeeds in making a 51% attack, he won't have control of the network for a long as most of the miners would shift the computing power and leave the attacker alone.

The Bitcoin SV 51% attack on Bitcoin Cash

In November 2018, Craig Write, and a group of Bitcoin SV supporters wanted to create a hard fork through a 51% attack on the Bitcoin Cash network. They wanted to increase the block limit from 32 MB to 128 MB, launching a competing version of the protocol with the larger block size.

Although both chains can cleanly split in a hard fork, Bitcoin SV supporters wanted Bitcoin SV to emerge as the only survivor.

For this, Bitcoin SV planned to take over Bitcoin Cash hash power and totally wipe out the protocol in a hostile manner, putting together enough resources to create a 51% attack. With this attack, they could, in theory, discourage miners to mine in the Bitcoin Cash network and switch to Bitcoin SV by giving them additional rewards by mining empty blocks.

Many prominent people in the Bitcoin community joined the war on Bitcoin Cash side including Jihan Wu, Bitmain's co-founder (the biggest computer chip and ASIC company for Bitcoin mining) and Roger Ver, the Bitcoin Cash co-founder. In response to the hash war and to prevent the 51% attack that would kill the Bitcoin Cash blockchain, Bitmain allocated for a period of time 90 000 Antminer S9 devices to the network. Bitcoin SV received support from a couple of mining pools but didn't gather enough support for the and lost the 51% attack.

Bitcoin Cash VS Bitcoin SV hash rate. Source: www.bitinfocharts.com

The war led to millions of dollars of losses in both chains (approximately $20 million), and Bitcoin SV eventually announced their split from the Bitcoin Cash network, giving up on the hostile takeover.

This is an interesting case study on how blockchain governance conflicts may lead to a community-led 51% attack.

Hash rate

Hash rate is the number of computing hashes that a hardware can perform. Different hardware has different hash rates. From CPUs to GPUs or ASIC chips - application-specific integrated circuit – miners, try to have the most efficient hardware in order to have the best hash rate possible, which will increase their probability of mining a block in the blockchain and receive the rewards for it.

Mining

Mining is the method that is used in the blockchain to group transactions into a block, append this block to the blockchain and broadcast the new block to the network. Mining ensures the consensus mechanism is maintained and keeps the blockchain decentralized.

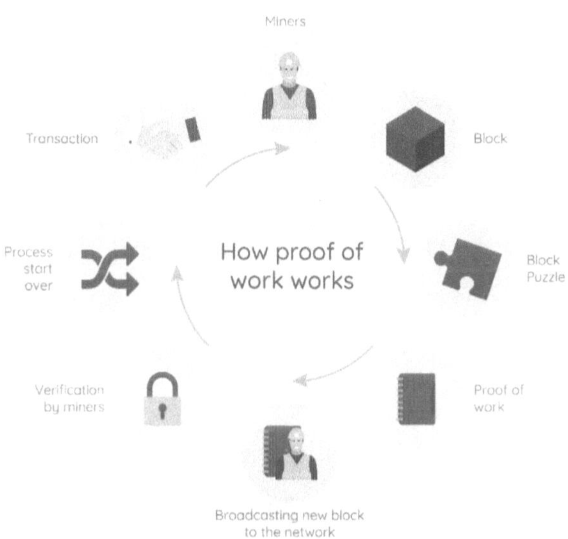

We are going to see in-dept how mining works later in this book.

Wallets

A wallet is used to store a private and public key. It is basically a piece of software that stores the private/public keys and allows the users to sign transactions in order to send a transaction, and allows users to receive transactions using their public key or wallet address.

An example of a Bitcoin wallet, in this case, a paper wallet. The perfect wedding gift.

There are different kinds of wallets, and they have different security levels: online wallets, mobile/desktop wallets, cold storage wallets or hardware wallets, and paper wallets are the most common wallets.

There are also a number of additional ways to secure private keys such as paper wallets, cold storage and multi-signature wallets to keep the private keys offline and secure. These wallets are less susceptible to theft because they can be stored offline. On the other hand, a hot wallet is a wallet that has the private keys stored online and thus more susceptible to be hacked and stolen.

Hardware wallets such as Trezor and Ledger are considered the most secure ways to store private keys.

There's a saying in the Bitcoin community: "You keys, your wallet. Not your keys, not your wallet."

Public keys

Public keys are generated from the user's private key (PKI infrastructure). They can be shared with anyone, and they are used by the recipient of a transaction to check that a certain transaction was signed by the user that sign it. The public key allows the recipient B to validate that a transaction was signed by the user's A private key, without needing user B to see A's private key.

Let's have some fun by creating a private key and generating a public key from the private key!

```
C:\Blockchainapp
λ openssl genrsa -out rsa.private 1024
Generating RSA private key, 1024 bit long modulus (2 primes)
........+++++
.................................................................+++++
e is 65537 (0x010001)

C:\Blockchainapp
λ cat rsa.private
-----BEGIN RSA PRIVATE KEY-----
MIICXgIBAAKBgQDgqMqSvOqcp9gHYV8jVD3ogRtMqk6QAzrwqUVIqX6Mzl68dPCO
uLYbgbScbM4IhzwvMiTiXLfRBkh0ocd96Rns3rtRa3hrvcSoxpRUPjQsVAHojQ2o
bxcHQGyq3TKjUeEOB8ekvIDB/S7T3dZ/cWf6x2/OtCWq7HM9d3f3PwMn4QIDAQAB
AoGBAKMxOWV6IZqGOeCylJ9fNFFOZ3w7QjJOhmQHMbLknG7AAgU3lP63omE8yOvQ
BaIgSlGmRTDBVS1bOQqv8e++gfs3rR8nckoYhryLamcBu109Q07RBppwxt8JOk1H
5cTlBhNGtLJ05OUqAjNNEShdS89Anbr9oRc3u0SyB7HP4LABAkEA/RbakqkV7+TV
YCgfLgIrPiW1AL1l2vn3ABY4l4pUDdtdJzCfu9Yw1YXq0kHBzQQC80IHTAm5glTh
CzwjWKRTQQJBAOM+O+ggwKk0y3vPJohY/FbObIEnKxUUbaLQQ9IGf0hD5Vt0XyGZ
9ggN721Gx/8pTAFoqhTVSgqnswwB0P+TzKECQQCCX6N4qWGDkn3YatK1ALkF6qaz
Gt29T8bNZKUCa1+hQ79Y0NN4D35YgAPXC8ips8dRSFI5+Uh2uwKypugOYZgBAkEA
wqVkGwky/bzDL2HY16GhQ5m9R0ONm5jL8FIERbpa/ENsClI7ykRegbeuBiRC20U8
XViRlxa7PTU4IGjN5J1tAQJAMrac4/fPq09l2upIKaFStwLJqyALmSjClqWFN4bj
jlPN3lm/zySdbnGJMi3InirrfXxdNPtY+hnFgo6Kphho9A==
-----END RSA PRIVATE KEY-----

C:\Blockchainapp
λ openssl rsa -in rsa.private -out rsa.public -pubout -outform PEM
writing RSA key

C:\Blockchainapp
λ cat rsa.public
-----BEGIN PUBLIC KEY-----
MIGfMA0GCSqGSIb3DQEBAQUAA4GNADCBiQKBgQDgqMqSvOqcp9gHYV8jVD3ogRtM
qk6QAzrwqUVIqX6Mzl68dPCOuLYbgbScbM4IhzwvMiTiXLfRBkh0ocd96Rns3rtR
a3hrvcSoxpRUPjQsVAHojQ2obxcHQGyq3TKjUeEOB8ekvIDB/S7T3dZ/cWf6x2/O
tCWq7HM9d3f3PwMn4QIDAQAB
-----END PUBLIC KEY-----
```

Here you can see some simple steps on how to create a private key and a public key from your computer. These private/public keys won't have any use in a blockchain, but they illustrate how a private/public key pair is created.

To generate the private key, open the command line, navigate to a folder and type the following:

```
openssl genrsa -out rsa.private 1024
```

Then press enter. The private key was generated. You can check the private key file with the ls command or cat the file to see the content.

To generate the public key, type the following command:

```
openssl rsa -in rsa.private -out rsa.public -pubout -outform PEM
```

We will see later in the book the mathematics behind creating these RSA keys. This kind of asymmetric encryption has multiple uses outside of the blockchain world: from having secure access to HTTPS websites to use TLS communications. RSA asymmetric encryption is also used every time we make payments online or using secure messenger apps.

CPU Mining, GPU Mining and ASIC Mining

CPU, GPU and ASIC mining respond in different ways to the different blockchain algorithms. Some algorithms are more easily mined (i.e. have a better hash rate) with CPU – more general-purpose – GPU – more resource-intensive for simple computations and better for memory intensive algorithms – or ASIC – designed for specific purposes. ASIC miners, although very efficient, they also have some disadvantages. Some blockchains developers have been trying to update the protocols in order to make them ASIC resistant, i.e. not possible to mine using ASIC devices. When this happens, the ASIC miners are rendered useless because they were designed with a specific algorithm in mind and can't perform any other task. Some blockchain developers believe that ASIC devices may increase centralization.

Note that this applies only to proof of work blockchains and not permissioned blockchains.

Mining algorithms

Proof of work blockchains has mining algorithms or cryptographic hash functions that takes a block as an input and creates a small output just like we saw before. The hash function is designed so that the miner has to keep hashing blocks until he brutes the desired output. To complete this task, the miner needs to try this same task millions or billions of times, requiring hardware, electricity and time.

For Bitcoin, the mining hash function is SHA256 and Bitcoin applies a double-SHA256 process for increased security. Ethereum uses Ethash or Dagger-Hashimoto Keccak. Different proof of work blockchains use different algorithms, but the most well known are:

SHA256 – 256 bit "Secure Hashing Algorithm" can be mined by general-purpose CPUs, and it's used by cryptocurrencies such as Bitcoin, Bytecoin, Peercoin, Namecoin and a few more. SHA256 is a very easy function, i.e. it is a simple boolean operation and 32-bit addition. Simple functions like this can be implemented in digital logic in ASIC chips, creating very efficient mining hardware.

Ethash – Ethash is Ethereum's proof of work mining algorithm. Because it's more memory intensive, GPUs offer a more efficient hash rate. ASIC miners were also developed to mine Ethash. Some of the blockchains using this algorithm, including Etehreum and Ethereum Classic.

X11 – Dash developers created the X11 algorithm, and it's considered one of the safest. ASIC miners were also developed for X11 mining. Some of the cryptocurrencies using it are Dash, Karmacoin and MonetaryUnit.

Scrypt – Scrypt is also one widely used mining algorithm. It's faster than the SHA256, and the leading blockchains using it are Dogecoin, Litecoin, Potcoin, MidasCoin and Gulden.

Cryptonight – this is another proof of work algorithm with a cool name. It was designed to be more efficient with CPU mining. The cryptocurrencies using it are Monero, Dashcoin, DigitalNote, Bytecoin, among others.

Chapter 4

Blockchain Architecture

This section of the book will look at some of the most important and coolest components of blockchain technologies: the blocks, consensus mechanisms, and cryptography. These components without which blockchain couldn't exist are tightly linked together to make blockchain secure. Let's break down that cryptography jargon that people in the blockchain industry love to talk BS.

Firstly, let's look at how a block is structured in the blockchain and then, we take a deeper look at some of the block's components. This is the first Bitcoin block mined in 2021. It was mined 13 minutes after New Year's Eve. Although we will be looking at a Bitcoin block, most of the blockchains follow very similar principles and have very similar data and fields in their blocks. The Bitcoin block is an excellent place to start studying block architecture.

Block height: 663852
Block size: 1,346,857 bytes
Block hash: 0000000000000000000092f5f21cd6db1d3d74252d6e343bd7a0fcac448ef01a5
Header:
Version: 0x20a00000
Timestamp: 2021-01-01 00:13
Bits: 386,867,735
Difficulty: 18,599,593,048,299.49
Nonce: 2,082,724,677
hashPrevBlock: 0000000000000000000059d6c6ef39775d01feec638c693b881cacc0546e7a249
hashMerkleRoot: 956c3cdc34c804e47ff344fc19077a3122ea87413cb133c038c92ef9b08d2d2d
Number of transactions: 2,907
Block reward: 6.25 BTC
Transactions:
Tx hash: 4b65af0b601df3eb6e7237f44218b9d951ef6dcd2bd7ab45744c3ec80556bcce
1.82428143 BTC from 1CUTyyxgbKvtCdoYmceQJCZLXCde5akiX2
To: 1CUTyyxgbKvtCdoYmceQJCZLXCde5akiX2
Fee: 0.00200000 BTC (775.194 sat/B - 193.798 sat/WU - 258 bytes)
Tx 2, Tx 3, Tx 4 …

You can also check this block or any other block by yourself by visiting one of the many block explorers available online.

Now let's look at the different parts in a Bitcoin block:

Block height: also know as block number, it's basically the number of the block in the blockchain chain, meaning that there were 663852 blocks mined until this block.

Block size: well, the block size is the block size. In this case, the block is around 1.34 MB, and it includes the block header and the transaction information.

Block hash: the block hash is the output of the block's header data hashed through SHA-256 function.

Version: it gives information about the version of the blockchain.

hashMerckeRoot: the Merkle Root is like a fingerprint of all the transactions in the block. It comes from the Merkle Tree. They are widely used in cryptography, and it was used before blockchains were invented. Merkle Trees were named after Ralph Merkle in 1979. They are a basic method to verify that data shared was not changed, damaged or altered.

The Merkle Tree is also a lightweight way to verify the validity of the data in a blockchain. For example, if you are using a Bitcoin wallet on your mobile phone, your wallet doesn't need to download all the blockchain transactions to validate them. The Merkle Tree with it's Merkle Root will do the work of validating all the previous transactions.

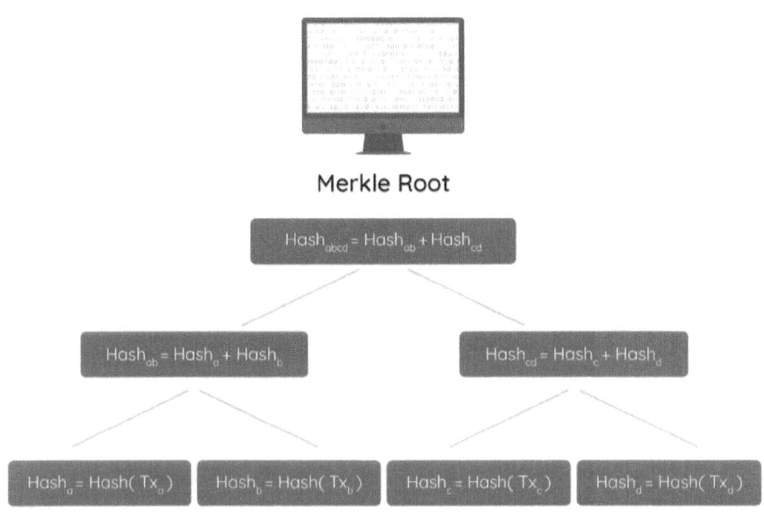

Structure of the Merkle Tree: The Merkle Tree result or Merkle Root is built recursively, i.e. it results from the hash of the leaves in the Merkle Tree, which in turn correspond to transactions.

The Merkle Root is solved by hashing individual transactions, which are called leaves. Additional pairs of leaves are hashed to create additional leaf nodes that may correspond to transactions in the blockchain network.

Although a Merkle Tree can be created from a big number of transactions, the Merkle Root always corresponds to a 32-bytes string or 256-bit (SHA256 hashing algorithm for instance, always outputs a fixed length of 32-bytes, regardless of the size of the input). This way, we can use something as small as 32-bytes to verify that a number of transactions – perhaps thousands – are immutable.

Number of transactions: the number of transactions varies from block to block. It may depend on the block's maximum capacity in terms of size, how big the transactions are (not in value but how many bytes) and the actual volume of transactions issued by the users. For example, a Bitcoin block can fit up to 1.3MB of data, and the transaction size is on average 500 bytes.

Timestamp: The timestamp is the exact time when the hashing of the block took place.

Transactions: depending on the protocol, transactions can be a transfer of value or any event, i.e. doesn't need necessarily to be a payment. It can instead be merely a transfer of data.

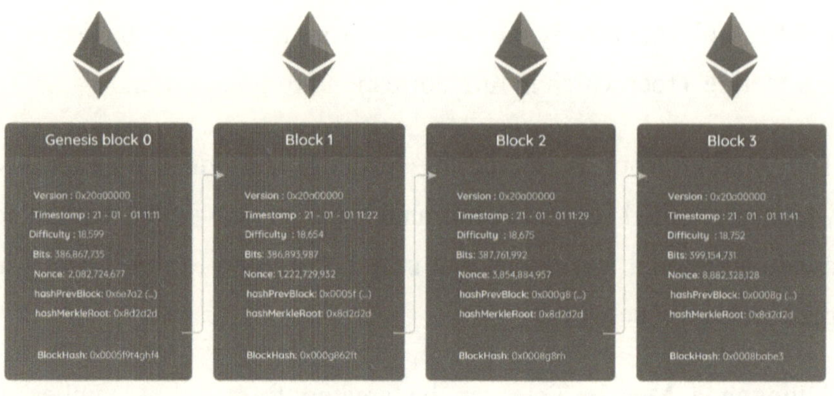

HashPrevBlock: each block contains the hash of the previous block. This is the way blocks are interconnected in an immutable way. Each block has the hash of the block that comes before. Data in previous blocks cannot be altered because that would change the already recorded block hash.

Bits: it represents the difficulty of the block. It's represented in hexadecimal notation, and it represents the current target for the difficulty in the block.

Difficulty: the difficulty is determined by the number of zeros that the hash needs to begin with when the hashing process occurs. The genesis block (the first block) had a difficulty=1. The block that we saw at the beginning of this chapter has a difficulty of 18,599,593,048,299.49. The difficulty is always in proportion to the number of miners (i.e. hashing power) in the network. It increases when more miners join the network and decreases when miners leave the network. Miners may join or leave the network according to the mining profitability, which is usually related to the Bitcoin price.

The Bitcoin mining difficulty is actually very similar to the gold mining difficulty. When the gold price goes up, usually more people and companies start mining gold, increasing the competition and consequently increasing the difficulty of actually finding gold. An excellent example of this was the California Gold Rush. San Francisco grew from barely 100 prospectors in 1846 to more than 30 000 in 1852, while the gold price was also rising. Most of the prospectors were not very luck in finding gold because the competition made it so difficult. During this period, the people who made most of the money were actually selling mining equipment. A shovel used to be sold for $36, which would be the equivalent to more than $1500 now.

Modern miners, the crypto miners, in this case, join mining pools in order to share efforts and increase profitability.

Let's go back to the present and dig more in-depth into the difficulty, shall we dear reader?

You have probably noticed that the block hash starts with several zeros. In the case of our block, it starts with 19 zeros but… why? Why does it need to start with 19 zeros? Where does this come from? Well, it comes from the Bits field and from the difficulty. Let's see how to calculate this in a simplified way.

D = expected/actual

D here would be the difficulty. What is the "expected" value? The Bitcoin protocol expects to add 2016 new blocks in 20160 minutes. This is an average of one block every 10 minutes.

The difficulty re-evaluation takes place every 20160 minutes (approximately 2 weeks), and the expected value is 20160 minutes. Actual = the time it took to mine the last 2016 blocks.

D = 20160/actual

If D > 1, it took less than 20160 min. for the miners to mine 2016 blocks the difficulty will increase. If D < 1, then it means that it took more than 20160 to mine 2016 blocks meaning that the difficulty needs to be decreased because it's a bit too difficult.

```
If D > 1

        Difficulty increase (0.25, 4)

If D < 1

        Difficulty decrease (0.25, 4)
```

The difficulty increases/decreases at least 0.25 or a maximum 4, depending on how the difficulty is adjusted.

Now the new difficulty that is going to be calculated every two weeks will be:

```
newDiff = oldDiff x 20160/actual
```

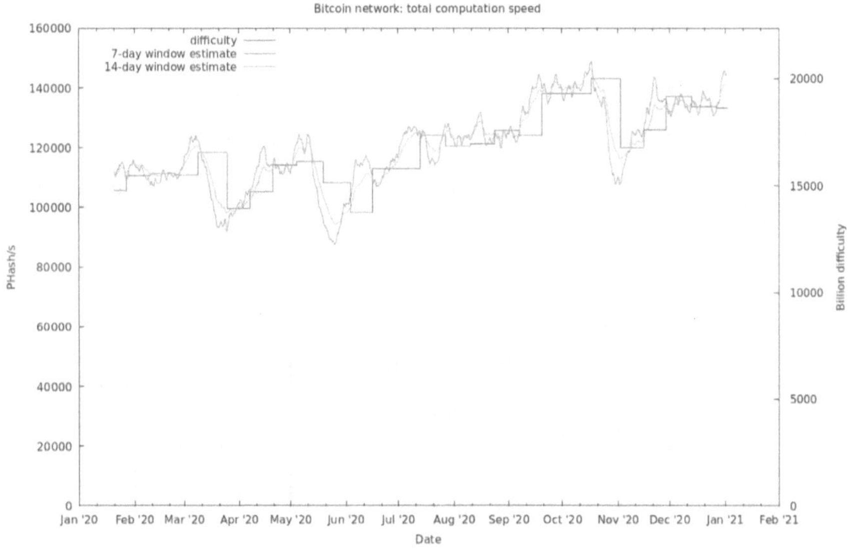

Bitcoin total hash rate and difficulty. Source: http://bitcoin.sipa.be

Mining difficulty increases according to the hash power in the network in order to keep the average time of 10 minutes to mine one block. As you can see in the chart, the difficulty will increase or decrease every two weeks based on the average time the blocks were added, and it's pretty much correlated with the mining power in the network (left y-axis).

Now that we have looked at the most important components a block, let's look at how a digital signature is created. We need them to sign transactions, documents and really use it every day!

Digital Signature

Let's look at digital signatures with some level of detail. Digital signatures are an important cryptographic component of blockchain transactions, where a transaction is digitally signed by the sender and verified by the receiver.

Digital signatures are way safer than handwritten signatures because they cannot be replicated or copied, while handwritten signatures are easily copied. Have you ever tried to copy your parents signature when you were a kid? Me neither.

Now we will be talking about signing transactions or documents and not encrypting the document. Encryption would be a separate process.

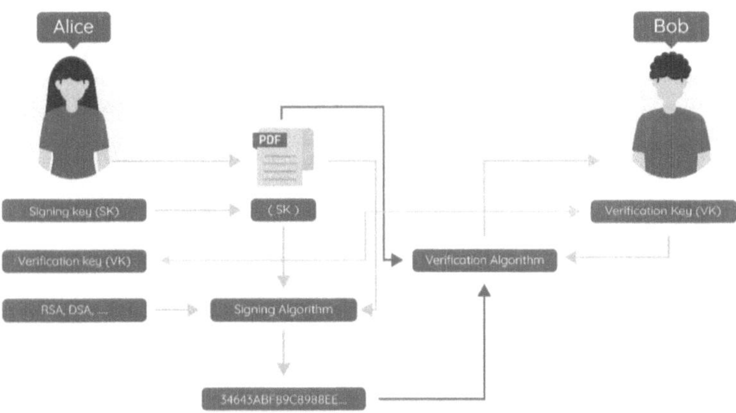

When Alice sends a transaction (or document) to Bob, she wants to ensure that the message will be not corrupted or hacked in transit. It's also important to make sure that Alice uniquely signs the transaction.

The transaction is parsed by the signing algorithm to sign the transaction, which creates a hash of the document plus the signing key (private key). If anything, even a single bit is changed, the hash would change, making it invalid. There's automated protection that ensures document integrity.

Alice will also send a verification key (public key) for Bob to validate the document signature. The verification key derives from the signing key. Bob can then verify the document's integrity and who signed the document with Alice's verification/public key and using the verification algorithm.

Let's perform the steps to sign a document digitally. We will need big prime numbers to do this. In real life, we would rely on code and existing algorithms and libraries instead of doing it manually but just for the sake of the example, let's take a look at who it works. Let's first look at the DSA – Digital Signature Algorithm:

1. Select a Prime number q

2. Select Prime number p

3. p-1 must be divisible by q

```
mod((p-1)/q=0
```

4. create L from g:{2...p-2}

```
L = (g^((p-1)/q) mod p)!= 1
```

5. Select a random integer in range

```
1=< d => q-1
```

6. Compute

```
B = (L^d mod p)
```

7. Generate public key

```
Kpub = (p, q, L, B)
```

8. Private key

```
Kpriv = d
```

9. Select a random integer in range

```
0 < Ke < q | Ke : Ephemeral Key
```

10. Compute the first part of the signature

```
R = (L^Ke mod p) mod q !=0
```

11. Compute the second part of the signature

```
S = ((SHA(m) + d * r)Ke^-1 mod q !=0
```

We will also need very long prime numbers. These are the recommended prime number length in bits. The bigger the length, the more secure the digital signature is.

L = 1024, N = 160
L = 2048, N = 224
L = 2048, N = 256
L = 3072, N = 256

Voila, we are now supposed to have a DSA digital signature! Hmmm…. But the reality is that we don't have it yet, right?

Later in we book, we will also see how to create programmatically a ECDSA signature and actually do most of these steps in the Python console, which will help a lot consolidate knowledge!

Consensus Mechanisms

There are many different consensus algorithms, and they all have advantages, disadvantages and security trade-offs. The blockchain trilemma well illustrates these trade-offs. When planning to use or deploy a new blockchain, we need to check what use case we are trying to address, the requirements in terms of scalability, security, and decentralization, and then ask a question…

…and the question is: How can we have good scalability without compromising the security and preserving good levels of network decentralization?

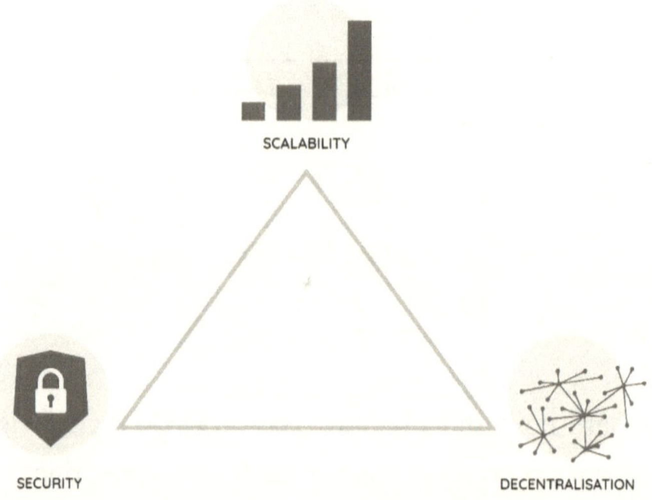

Do you want a very secure consensus mechanism? Fine, here you have proof of work, but it will consume electricity and make the blockchain slow and not very scalable.

Do you want a very fast consensus and scalable? Fine, here you have DPoS, but it will be more centralized and a bit less secure.

Do you want a scalable and costless consensus? Fine, here is PBFT but it will be less secure and a bit centralized.

Traditionally, when looking at security, scalability and decentralization, we can pick only two.

Generally speaking, what are the main consensus mechanisms?

There are several types of consensus mechanisms, but most of them fit into two groups: Byzantine fault-tolerance based and leader-based mechanisms. I'm sure you are asking, "WTF is this dude talking about?!"

Byzantine fault-tolerance consensus depends on how nodes are arranged to sign and broadcast transactions. When the majority of nodes agree with what was broadcasted, it can be said that consensus was reached. On the other hand, a leader-based consensus requires the nodes to compete between them in some kind of lottery where they have to guess certain values or take some action like staking coins in order to increase the odds of winning the lottery. The winning node is the one the commits the block to the blockchain. We can see Hyperledger Fabric as a Byzantine fault-tolerant based and Ethereum as a leader-based consensus.

Proof of work

Let's start by looking at proof of work, Bitcoin's consensus mechanism, and most first-generation blockchains. Proof of work is a leader-based consensus mechanism.

The miners need to calculate a challenging lottery or mathematical problem in the Bitcoin blockchain and other blockchains using a proof of work consensus mechanism. It's a bit like trying to guess the number of a lottery ticket. Once a node resolves the lottery, he broadcasts the result to the other nodes, and a new block is appended to the blockchain.

The lottery's difficulty is adjusted to make sure that all the miner's computing power generates one Bitcoin block on average every 10 minutes. Suppose the number of miners or computational power in the network increases, the difficulty of calculating the mathematical problem (aka nonce) will increase to keep the coin distribution/supply and the block production predictable. In that case, proof of work difficulty is adjusted when more people join or leave the network.

In other blockchains such as Ethereum, blocks may are added with different frequency. In Ethereum, for example, a new block is added every 15 seconds.

You can see proof of work as a string of data that is difficult to produce (it is time-consuming and resource-intensive) but once discovered, it is easy for others to verify it.

One of the reasons it requires some work to add a new block to the blockchain is to make it more secure. Each miner needs to solve a difficult lottery to add a new block, but if it was too easy, then any hacker could easily try to add new blocks or change the blockchain to his benefit.

The mathematical problem is nothing more than guessing a nonce, a long string of numbers with millions or billions of trial and error. In order words, brute-forcing the result. A miner must guess a nonce, add it to the hash of the current header, rehash the value, and compare the result to the target hash.

The mining difficulty is mostly a measure of how hard it is to find a new block in the blockchain or, in other words, how rare is the nonce is that miners needed to brute force to find a hash smaller than the target hash.

I always thought that is quite funny when people say that what miners are doing is to "solve a very complex mathematical problem" when what they are really doing is trying to guess a "lottery" number.

In most public/permissionless blockchain, miners will receive a block reward for their work. This reward will likely pay their expenses related to hardware and electricity, and it is an incentive to keep running the network. In 2021, the Bitcoin block reward is

6.25 BTC, and it will continue to be 6.25 until 2024 when it halves again (it halves approximately every 4 years or, to be more accurate, every 210 000 blocks). So in 2024, the Bitcoin block reward will be 3.125 BTC. In 2028 it will be 1.5625 BTC and so on.

Proof of work is used mainly by permissionless blockchains where any person can add a node to the blockchain, and the identities of nodes in the blockchain are not known. Thus, it is necessary to have a consensus mechanism that allows nodes to collaborate in a trustless way.

Other permissioned or private blockchains can choose other methods to add a block and reach consensus. They can have a different level of trust in the nodes in the network (because, for example, the nodes had to gain a certificate tied up to their real-world identity).

Proof of work accounts for 90% of the total market capitalization of existing cryptocurrencies. It requires work from the nodes that are participating in the validation of blocks to, well, do some difficult work. Nodes, aka miners, need a certain incentive to perform this work. We will also see that it takes many quadrillion calculations to mine one block in the Bitcoin network. That's why in all proof of work blockchains, miners receive a block reward incentive, transactions fees or both.

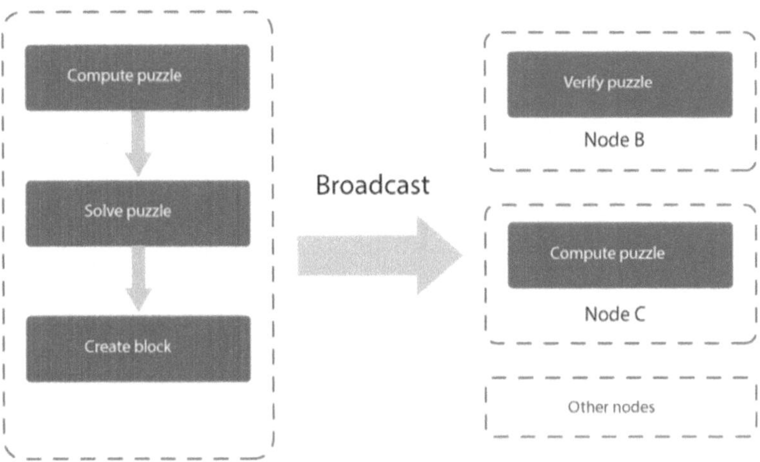

The economic incentive behind proof of work is a perfect example of how to keep the consensus in a completely decentralized network. To be a node/miner in a proof of work blockchain requires hardware resources, electricity and time, but if nodes play by the rules, i.e. according to the consensus mechanism, they receive a reward. If nodes try to attack the blockchain, tamper with data or perform double-spending, they will not get the reward, and they will be just wasting resources.

In 2020, miners received around 7 Billion dollars' worth of Bitcoin as a block reward and about 800 Million dollars in Bitcoin fees paid by the users. Not bad, huh? Being a miner is a rough job tho.

Pros of proof of work:

- Scalability of the network (in terms of node count)

- Security increases with node count, i.e. bigger the mining community, the more secure it is

- Miners receive an incentive in exchange for their computing power contribution to the network

- Very secure in most cases

Cons of proof of work:

- Vulnerable to 51% attacks (especially small proof of work blockchains)

- Mining difficulty usually gets harder, and mining hardware get obsolete quickly (profitability can go to zero in 3 years only)

- Mining is expensive and usually requires specialized hardware to be profitable

- It requires huge quantities of electricity

- Proof of work blockchains generally have low throughput (studies show that proof of work blockchains can achieve up to 60 transactions per second without compromising security) [xi]

- It takes time to have a transaction verified in the blockchain depending on the blockchain protocol being used - this is why it is recommended to wait 10 to 20 minutes until a transaction is verified/committed in the Bitcoin network (1 or 2 blocks) or 5 minutes in the Ethereum blockchain (around 20 blocks)

How the proof of work mining process works

```
8H1TTEF229033D4E7BE0EF62505E7ABBCC67959B2EC34D5B  ✕
Q1Q25FG8BA5B2C29DC3D064132C911FF37235903F729ADDE  ✕
7DE8569f1D2C2DFF7E3BB1D14FAC749406C252CD3A58FEFE  ✕
009R8G2fFE8B7CF2E4D2A515DB3193B377272F99FF9C1088  ✕
S6S6F8G85103D0D67B3647E2E12A9B5C706BDB085C69B20B  ✕
123456785668D2645282F5EC5583F9082FAB71553EA10E51  ✕
00092F5F21CD6DB1D3D74252D6E343BD7A0FCAC448EF01A5  💡
```

Mining Bitcoin is harder than mining gold. Imagine having to repeat hashes quadrillions of times until you find the correct one!

Different blockchains may have different mechanisms but let's look at our genesis blockchain, Bitcoin, as an example.

In bitcoin mining, miners need to come up with a block hash that meets a certain requirement. To come up with this hash, they need to change a piece of data inside the block called the nonce, and they need to do it a LOT of times. This is the lottery guessing process. Sounds complicated? No worries, let's make it simple.

How many hashes on average do bitcoin miners worldwide perform to mine one block? Well, as I said, a lot of times:

```
hashes per bitcoin
= (network hash rate) / (6.25 BTC per 10 minutes)
= (140 * Th / s) / (6.25 * BTC / (600 * s) )
= 140 * 600 / 6.25 * Th / s / BTC * s
= 13,440 Th / BTC
= 13,440,000,000,000,000 h/BTC
```

We divide the current network hashrate per second by 6.25 (BTC block reward per 10 minutes), and we get a VERY big number.

Miners need to calculate on average 13.44 Quadrillion hashes to generate one single Bitcoin as per January 2021. If we multiply this by 6.25, it takes 84 Quadrillion hashes to mine one single block! Miners need to repeat the calculation in the figure above literally quadrillions of times until a block is mined.

Imagine hypothetically that you are trying to find mine this Bitcoin block all by yourself and that all you have is the best CPU in the market, the AMD Ryzen 9 3900X 12-Core Processor. It would take you 225 730 years to mine one single Bitcoin block at the current difficulty.

Unfortunately, it's pretty useless to mine Bitcoin with a normal computer. This was possible back in 2009 and 2010 when the hash power in the network was still low, but currently, only very powerful hardware like specialized ASIC miners can do the job. Back then, not many people were interested in mining Bitcoin, and the BTC price was only a few cents.

The early believers in Bitcoin that mined it in the early days were able to buy the Lamborghinis.

But… why is that so difficult to mine Bitcoin?? And how is the mining process done?

As we saw before, the proof of work difficulty increases when more hashing power is added to the network. The difficulty and bits field of a block represents the number of zeros that the target hash has. This number of zeros at the beginning of the hash, is a condition that miners need to meet. To generate a hash that corresponds to this condition, miners will have to follow the process below, trying different nonces until they create the needed hash.

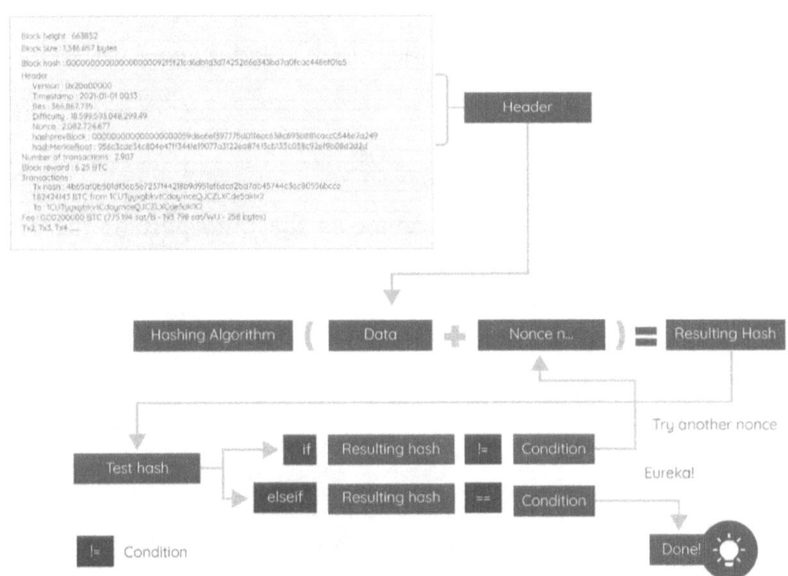

To create a block hash (i.e. to mine a block), you need to meet certain conditions in proof of work. Some small variations may apply depending on the algorithm used, but the condition is usually to find a hash whose value that is under a certain requirement. In other words, the hash needs to start with a number of zeros.

The process is quite simple yet very repetitive (miners repeat it billions or quadrillions of times, as we saw).

According to the diagram, to perform the necessary work to mine the block and get the block hash, the miner will perform the task. This is where the nonce, one of the fields in the block header, comes into play. A nonce is a 32-bit number, and the miner will need to guess so that it will create a hash according to the target.

1. The miner will create the block header, convert it into a string of data

2. The miner adds a nonce to the data and feeds that to a hashing algorithm (the nonce is the only part of the block that the miner can freely change)

3. Get the resulting hash

4. Run a test to check if the condition, i.e. the target hash, is met

5. If the condition is met, it means that the miner found the nonce that generates a hash according to the target

6. If the condition was not met (most likely) the miner will try a different nonce, i.e. he goes back to point 2, trying a new nonce until it produces a hash that meets the target

Miners will most likely have to perform these computations quadrillions of times until they get the correct value.

Once a miner finds the correct hash, he will broadcast the block to the network, and the other miners can easily verify that that nonce produces a hash according to the target. The miner that mined the block, will also include in the block the coinbase transaction. This transaction corresponds to the block reward that he will receive.

Bits and Target

In mining, the miners try to find hash values lower than the target value. The hash value must be lower than the value represented by the bits field in the block header. This will also mean that the target hash will have to start with a number of zeros. This number of zeros will increase with difficulty. The greater the difficulty, the harder it is to mine a block because it's harder to find a hash meeting the required target.

Why do these "zeros" in the hash impact so much the difficulty? If you think, the probability of hashing a block with, let's say, 20 straight zeros, it's extremely low. It's like trying to find a lottery thicket among quadrillions of lottery tickets, that starts with 20 zeros. Or the same as tossing a dice and get the same number 15 times in a row. It's a very very low probability, and that's why it is so hard.

To illustrate the probabilities and how hard it is to get a hash with a big number of zeros to be lower than the target hash, let's imagine that we are playing with dices. What's the probability of tossing 15 dices and get them all with the same value?

```
P = pⁿ = (1/s)ⁿ
```

$$P = p^n = (1/s)^n$$

```
Assuming that our dices are 6 sided dices:

1 dice: (1/6)^1 = 0.16 or 16% probability

2 dices: (1/6)^2 = 0.02(7) or 2.77% probability

4 dices: (1/6)^4 = 0.00077160493827 or
0.077160493827% probability

6 dices: (1/6)^6 = 0.00002143347050 or
0.002143347050% probability

15 dices: (1/6)^15 = 0.00000000000212682249 or
0.0000000000212682249%
```

This probability which means that you would need to toss the 15 dices on average 470 184 984 737 times to get them all facing the same value. That's 470 billion times!

You see now how it is harder than it looks to get all dices with the same value or a hash with so many "zeros".

Now that we understand the concept, let's look at it with the actual formulas and see how miners find the hash according to the difficulty.

```
Difficulty = MAX_TARGET / current_target
```

So MAX_TARGET is the difficulty that was set for the first block, and it's basically Difficulty = 1, and it's written as 1d00ffff hexadecimal value.

If we convert the bits value of our block of 386,867,735 to hexadecimal, we will get the value 0x170f2217. This value is divided into four bytes. The first is the index, followed by 3 bytes. In this case, bits are the index of 0x17 and the coefficient of 0x0f2217. Here, the 0x means that we are talking about a hexadecimal number, aka hex, a numerical system used in computing.

The target threshold is a 256-bit integer which the hash needs to be equal or below to meet the target hash. This is the target hash we were referring to in the mining process.

```
0x170f2217  →  0x0f2217        *  256     ^  (0x17      -  3)
nBits          Significand        Base        Exponent     Bytes            in
                                                            Significand

Result: 0xf221700000000000000000000000000000000000000000000000000000000000
```

We can also compare this target value with the hash value, following a simple equation:

Target = coefficient * 2 ^(8 * (index - 3))

We need first to convert our bits value to hex:

386,867,735 → 0x170f2217

Then, we substitute the equation with our values,

```
0x0f2217 * 2^(0x08 * (0x17 - 0x03))
```

You can use your Python calculator to help with the dec to hex and hex to dec conversions:

```
C:\Blockchainapp
λ python
Python 3.7.7 (tags/v3.7.7:d7c567b08f, Mar 10 2020, 10:41:24) [MSC v.1900 64
bit (AMD64)] on win32
Type "help", "copyright", "credits" or "license" for more information.
>>> int(0x0f2217)
991767
>>> int(0x17)
23
>>> 991767 * 2 ** (8 * (23 - 3))
1449469094350757594478113895488529861555105250349678592
>>> |
```

Converting from hexadecimal to decimal, we get,

$$991767 \times 2 \wedge (8 \times (23 - 3)) =$$
1449469094350757594478113895488529861555105250034967859
2

Which in hex is

0x**0000 0000 0000 0000**
00f22170000000000000000000000000000000000000000000000

Which when comparing to the hash of the block, we see that our hash of the block is lower:

0x**0000 0000 0000 0000**
00092f5f21cd6db1d3d74252d6e343bd7a0fcac448ef01a5

Easy right?

We could also use the Python calculator to go straight to the point and check if the hash is lower than the target.

Let's calculate the target using the equation:

Target = coefficient * 2 ^(8 * (index -3))

```
>>> 991767 * 2 ** (8 * (23 - 3))
14494690943507575944781138954885298615555105250349678592
>>> 0x0f2217*2**(0x08*(0x17-0x03))
14494690943507575944781138954885298615555105250349678592
>>> #now let's convert the result from decimat to hex
>>> hex(14494690943507575944781138954885298615555105250349678592)
'0xf2217000000000000000000000000000000000000000000000000'
>>> #and let's fill the space with zeros
>>> hex(14494690943507575944781138954885298615555105250349678592).zfill(64)
'000000000000000000xf2217000000000000000000000000000000000000000000000000'
```

As you can see, we get exactly the same result, which is a target value. If you want to try it by yourself, you can download python through your command prompt.

We can also check that the block hash is lower than the target:

```
>>> block_hash = 0x00000000000000000000092f5f21cd6db1d3d74252d6e343bd7a0fcac44
8ef01a5
>>> target = 0x00000000000000000000f2217000000000000000000000000000000000000000
00
>>> int(block_hash) < int(target)
True
```

int(block_hash) < int(target) = True

This last function shows that the block hash integer is lower than the target integer, meaning that the hash met the target, i.e. condition is true. YAY!

Proof of Stake

After proof of work, proof of stake is the second most well known and used consensus algorithm. A few cryptocurrencies use it, and it has a quite different mechanism compared to proof of work.

The mechanics and incentives of proof of state algorithms work differently. When creating a new block, the proof of stake algorithm chooses who is the block validator by checking how many coins a person is staking. The bigger the stake, the higher the probability of being chosen as a block validator. In proof of stake, we call the nodes doing the work block validators instead of miners, and we say that block validators mint new blocks instead of mining new blocks.

When a new transaction is issued, it is placed into a block with other transactions, and the block is limited to a certain size in MB. The validating node verifies the transactions' validity in a block and broadcasts the block to the other nodes in the blockchain. After validating the block and sharing it with the other nodes, the validating node will receive a reward if the other nodes agree with the content of the block.

Ethereum is moving to Ethereum 2.0, integrating Casper, a proof of stake consensus mechanism that will switch Ethereum from proof of work to proof of stake. The new Ethereum proof of stake protocol demands block validators to make a security deposit for the validator to be able to participate in the consensus. If they create a fraudulent block, their deposit will be forfeited, and the block validator loses the ability to participate.

Pros and cons of proof of stake

Pros

- It doesn't require much electricity when comparing to proof of work

- It's considered safe and resilient to 51% attacks when comparing to small proof of work cryptocurrencies

Cons

- Nothing at stake problem

- Fake stake attack and DDoS attacks – somebody can lie on how much stake do they own in order to connect to another node and flood him with connections (DoS attack)

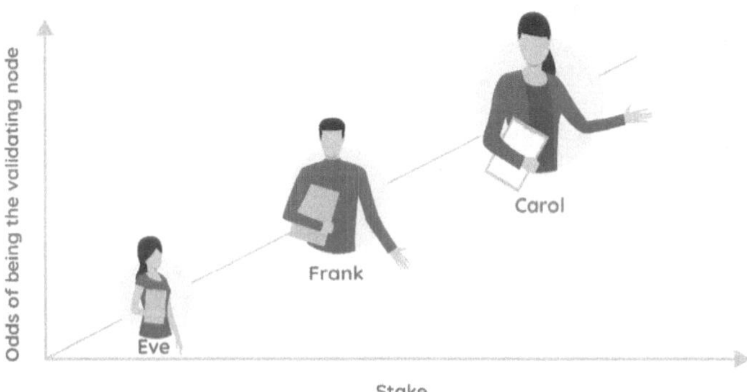

In proof of stake, block validators increase their chance of being selected to validate a block based on how much do they have at stake. Bigger the stake, the higher the odds of being selected to validate the block and win then reward. In other words, the more lottery tickets you buy, the higher the probability of winning the prize. Following the example of our chart, let's say Eve bought ten lottery tickets, Frank bought 20 lottery tickets, and Carol bought 30 lottery tickets, increasing this way her chance.

To perform a 51% attack, one's would need to buy at least 50% of the cryptocurrency available, which would be very expensive. Most of the proof of stake mechanisms have protections against this, but performing a 51% attack on a proof of stake cryptocurrency wouldn't be very smart anyway.

Although it would be very expensive for someone to acquire 51% of all the coins of a cryptocurrency, a person could indeed do it and try an attack. However, it wouldn't be in his is best interest to attack the network on which he holds a majority. This would harm the network and make the cryptocurrency value to fall, which means that the attacker's holdings would also fall. Consequently, someone who holds a majority in the network would be incentivized to maintain the network secure.

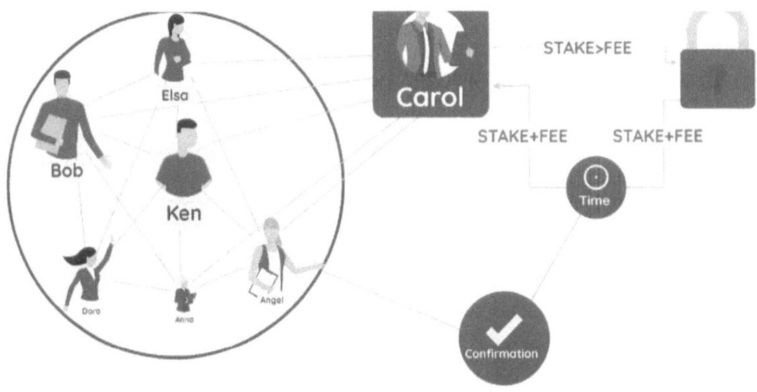

How does the proof of stake block validating or "mining" works?

The bigger the stake, the bigger the chances of being the chosen one for that specific round. In a network of nodes, Carol was selected to be the validating node of the round.

1. Carol is selected to validate the block for that round

2. Carol has to place a larger stake than the transaction fees and rewards that he may receive. This stake will be locked until the validation is completed

3. Carol produces a block with transactions

4. The new block is broadcasted to the other peer nodes on the network

5. A fixed amount of time needs to elapse in order to allow time for the peer nodes to confirm that Carol did a good job and that he validated the block correctly

6. If the validation is correct, the block is permanently appended to the blockchain

7. If the validation is incorrect (i.e. has incorrect data, incorrect transactions, or Carol tried to forge some fake coins for herself), Carol will lose the stake and reward and probably also get banned from the network

Delegated Proof of Stake of DPoS

Delegated Proof of Stake is something very similar to democracy. Let's call it only DPoS because the name is too long, and my fingers start to hurt from typing so much.

DPoS is a consensus mechanism where the stakeholders or hodlers of that cryptocurrency can elect a limited number of validating nodes in an election process. The validating nodes, also called witnesses or block producer in DPoS, validate transactions/blocks and are rewarded for the work.

Typically, elections for the validating nodes are real-time and ongoing, i.e. users/delegates can vote anytime. Stakeholders can vote on who they want to be delegates and block validators/witnesses. The voting power is defined according to the number of coins they own, i.e. more coins translate into more votes (just like a corporation's shareholder voting power). Stakeholders can also delegate their votes to other stakeholders who will vote on their behalf (again, very similar to a corporation shareholder proxy voting). DPoS is, therefore, a democratic process.

Similarly to proof of stake, block validators receive a reward for validating transactions. They may also be required to have a stake that may be forfeited in case of bad behaviour. Blocks with new transactions can be appended to the blockchain every few minutes. Because DPoS is more centralized in a small number of nodes – EOS, for example, has 21 block producers/witnesses – the network broadcasting is much faster and allows a much better throughput.

If a validating node fails to produce a block or shows some bad behaviour, he can lose his stake and be kicked out of the network. The stakeholders would then vote for a new validating node.

EOS, Steem and BitShares are some of the examples of DPoS blockchains.

Typically, to be a candidate as a validating node, node managers will present their proposal to the network and try to convince the community that they have all the requirements to be a validating node. Usually, some criteria such as the team behind the node, the hardware capacity, location, third-party audits, budget and community engagement are factors that favour a node being elected.

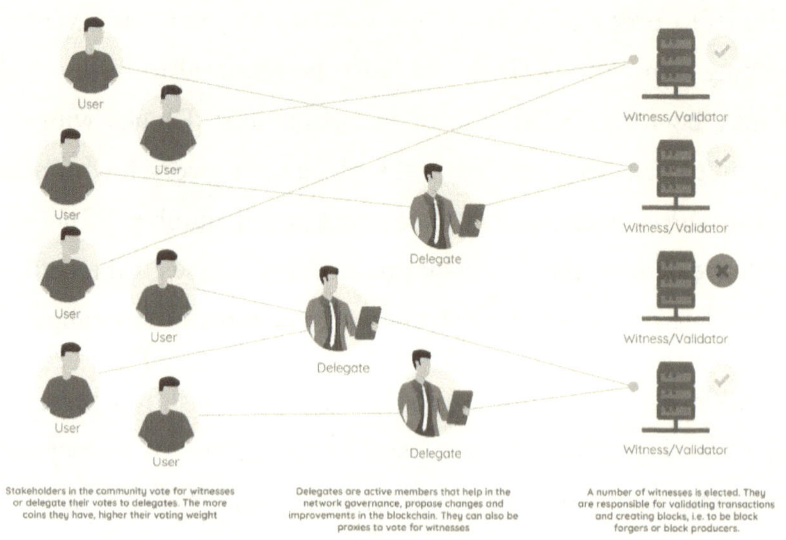

Stakeholders in the community vote for witnesses or delegate their votes to delegates. The more coins they have, higher their voting weight

Delegates are active members that help in the network governance, propose changes and improvements in the blockchain. They can also be proxies to vote for witnesses

A number of witnesses is elected. They are responsible for validating transactions and creating blocks, i.e. to be block forgers or block producers.

Similarly to proof of stake, in DPoS, the higher the stake, the higher the voting weight. Depending on the blockchain, users (or stakeholders) can usually delegate their vote in proxies or vote directly for witnesses. Delegates are active members in the community who improve the blockchain, develop new features, improve governance, and sometimes promote blockchain adoption.

The witnesses or block validators will be the "miners" in the network. Their work is to validate transactions, append blocks to the blockchains, maintain the consensus mechanism and preserve the network healthy. They are required to allocate computing resources (either on-premise servers or cloud-based) and must ensure high-availability, data integrity and high throughput. If a witness fails to keep the standards or acts in a malevolent way, she can easily be removed from the network.

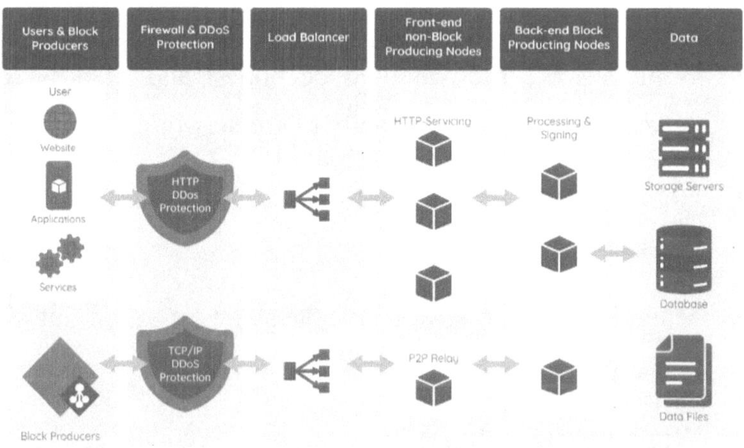

EOS block producers or witnesses need to invest in some infrastructure and architect the node in order to provide the necessary security, scalability and network requirements. In the above diagram, we can see a high-level diagram of the node architecture.

Although any person can be a candidate to be a block producer, some players in the market may have more advantage considering their engagement in the community and hardware capacity. As one of the biggest DPoS blockchains, EOS has partnered with Google Cloud to become an EOS blockchain block producer.

Cloud-based witnesses take advantage of cloud scalability, security, reliability and cost-efficiency. Cloud providers such as Google Cloud or AWS are in a great position to contribute as a witness.

Pros and cons of DPoS

Pros

- Witnesses are motivated to be honest and to provide the necessary computing capacity to the network

- High performance and better scalability with a good TPS – transactions per second

- Malevolent witnesses or delegates can be voted out almost real-time

- Witnesses can validate transactions in seconds

- Transactions fees are usually very low or inexistent

- Energy-efficient and cost-efficient because it doesn't require proof of work, and it can be cloud-based

- Semi-decentralized with a more robust governance system

Cons

- It can create some degree of centralization when big "whales" gain much power in the network and can vote for their cronies

- More susceptible to a 51% attack

- Stakeholders with small stakes may not have an incentive to vote

Proof of Burn

Proof of burn is an experimental consensus mechanism and a fascinating concept. Slimcoin, a defunct cryptocurrency used to use it. Proof of burn aims to provide a very different incentive mechanism for nodes to participate in validating transactions.

Proof of burn can be seen as precisely the opposite of what the Central Banks do: it destroys currency instead of printing it.

Instead of "burning" electricity and hardware like proof of work does, proof of burn just burns its own coins to provide an incentive for nodes to be good actors in the blockchain. Proof of burn miners need to send a number of coins to an unspendable address. The more coins they send to burn, the higher the probability of being chosen by the algorithm to mine a block. They receive a reward if they validate transactions and mine a block correctly. If not, they just simply burned the coins and wasted money.

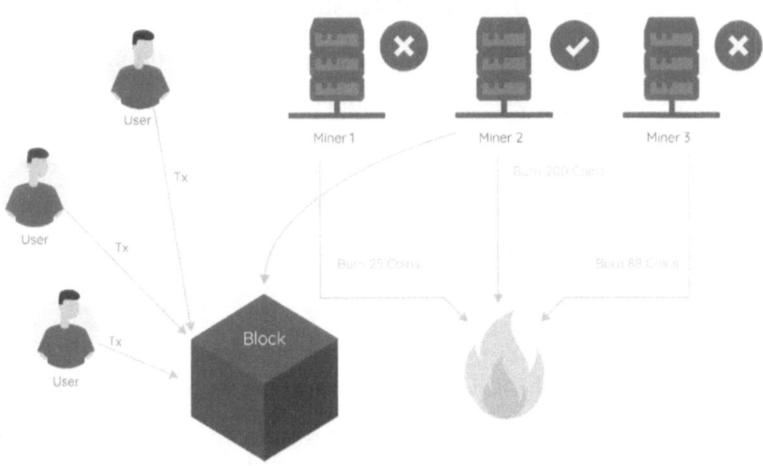

- Miners are randomly chosen according to the number of coins they sent to burning

- Burning more coins translates to more commitment, thus higher the chances of being selected as a miner (just like spending more electricity on proof of work increase the chances or mine a block)

- Burned coins are lost forever, locked in a burn address

An unspendable address or burn address is a blockchain address with no private keys, and consequently, the coins sent to this address are forever lost. The coins don't disappear from the blockchain; they are simply sent to a black hole and can't be used anymore.

Proof of burn is a deflationary concept where the supply of coins decreases over time, increasing the scarcity and more likely to increase the value of the coin holders. BNB (Binance coin) also burns BNB coins periodically, decreasing the supply in the market. On the other hand, coins that increase the supply over time tend to decrease value, i.e they are inflationary. Examples of inflationary currencies are the fiat currencies such as the USD and Dogecoin. Over time, these currencies decrease the value through printing, thus the number of coins necessary to buy certain good increases over time.

On a side note, 22% of the USD in circulation were printed in 2020. More than $ 9 Trillion flooded the market, making the USD cheaper. The USD lost a lot of its value in 2020, meaning that we can now buy less good with the same amount of USD. On the other hand, you can buy more goods with the same amount of Bitcoin because these currencies have a fixed and predictable supply.

Practical Byzantine Fault-tolerant

PBFT tries to solve the Byzantine General's problem. The Byzantine Generals Problem is a hypothetical situation where a number of generals leading their Byzantine army need to decide if they attack or retreat from the city they are surrounding.

They can only conquer the city if they all attack at the same time and no one retreats. To ensure the operation's success, the Generals need to reach a consensus: they need to wither attack or retreat altogether. They need to communicate horse messengers that carry the information between the generals. One of the problems is that the messenger can be a traitor or be killed halfway. One of the messengers can also change his mind or chicken out, which would compromise the entire army. This is why the Byzantine General's need to have a consensus mechanism to ensure that everyone is on the same page.

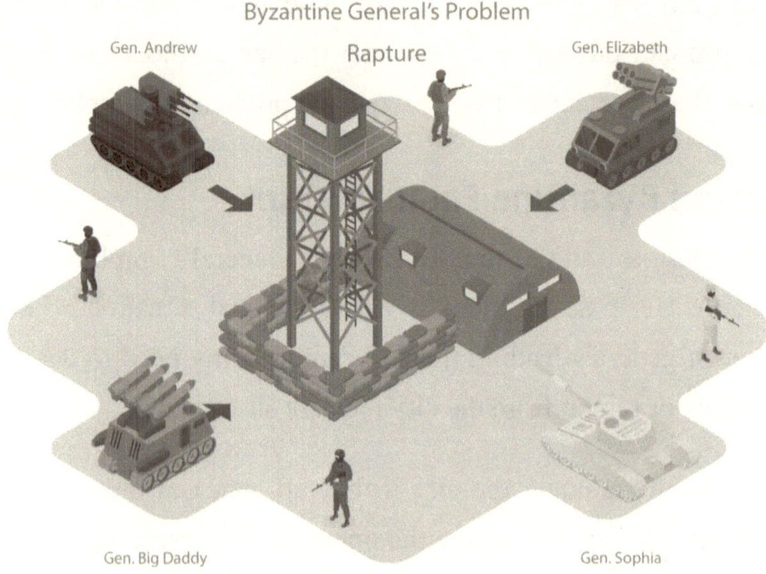

In the context of a blockchain network, the potential traitors may be the nodes, and the messengers may be the potentially corrupted communication channels between them. This problem was solved in 1999 by the PBFT algorithm, developed by two computer scientists, Miguel Castro and Barbara Liskov. PBFT can also be used in other distributed systems other than blockchains, such as peer-to-peer networks and IoT networks.

The **PBFT** enables decentralized systems to be resilient to failures and allows systems with multiple participants to work in consensus. PBFT systems are resilient, i.e. fault-tolerant, to nodes that are malicious or fail to communicate properly with the other nodes. PBFT can secure systems with multiple nodes and add some resiliency and fault-tolerance.

The Byzantine General's problems:

- *The communication channel may not be trusted*

- *The message could be altered or replaced*

- *Messenger can be killed*

- *Messenger can be delayed*

The solution:

- *Consensus algorithm that it's immune to the lack of trust*

- *Consensus mechanisms such as PBFT, PoW and PoS are Byzantine Fault Tolerant*

- *The "good" generals must have more power in the network than the faulty ones*

- *Cryptography integration to create consensus and data immutability*

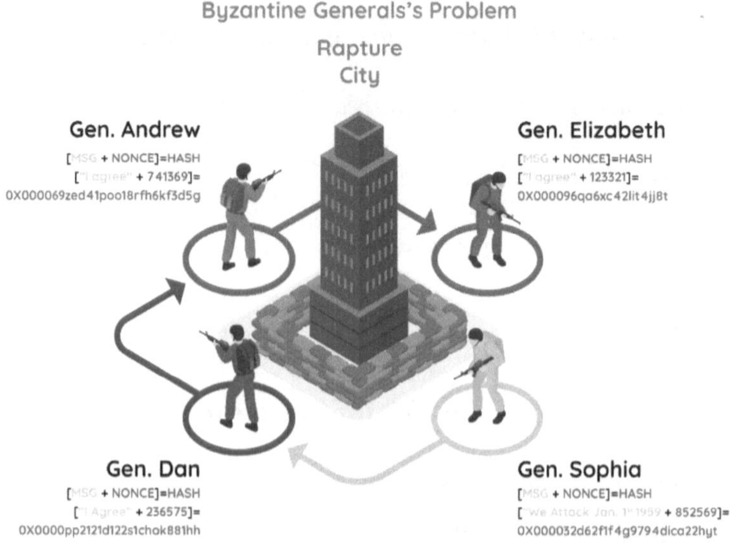

In Bitcoin and other proof of work blockchains, when General Andrew wants so send a message to General Big Daddy, he can take the message, and add a nonce, producing a certain unique hash. Then, he can send this to Big Daddy. Even if the messenger tries to change the message (men in the middle attack), he would have to change the hash of this message and the other messages sent by the other generals. This would require too much work, making it infeasible to make this attack.

Once General Big Daddy receives the message from General Andrew, he can easily verify that the message was not altered, and he will reply "I agree" to the group, adding a nonce and a hash for the others to see that the message is legitimate. The other generals will do the same and reach a consensus. Everyone has to perform this proof of work, making it hard for an attacker (insider or outsider attack) to change the generals' consensus.

If one of the generals decides to retreat instead of attacking, that decision will not bother the consensus because all the other 3 generals keep the consensus. This is why these consensus mechanisms are called "fault-tolerant" because they tolerate a number of nodes' failure. Once the generals reach consensus, they can attack Rapture and conquer the city!

Blockchains that don't have proof of work also apply Byzantine Fault Tolerant mechanisms. Hyperledger Sawtooth, for example, uses PBFT – Practical Byzantine Fault Tolerance.

We saw that Byzantine fault-tolerant systems are distributed systems that can tolerate faulty nodes to some extend. In PBFT, if f is the number of faulty nodes, then $2f + 1$ non-faulty nodes are required to reach consensus.

Let's look at how PBFT algorithms are resilient. Assume the following

n = **total of nodes**

f = **number of faulty nodes**

PBFT can tolerate up to $f = (n-1) / 3$

Or $n - f = (2n + 1) / 3$

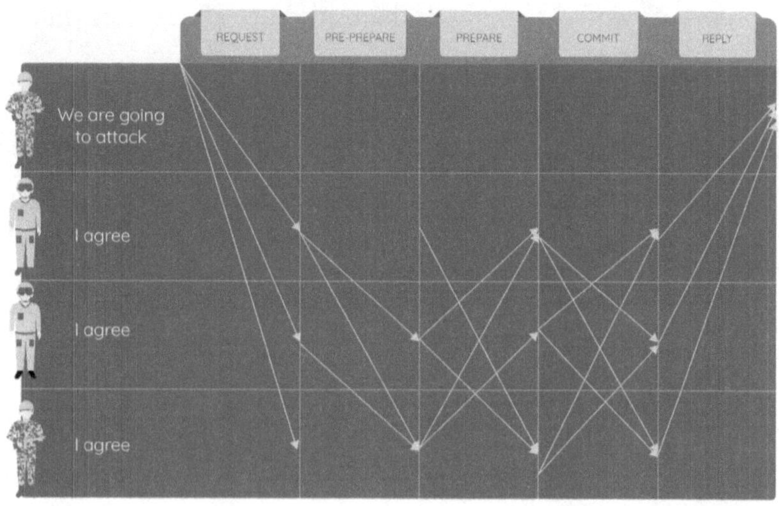

High-level illustration of the PBFT algorithm:

1. A client, in this case, our General Andrew, sends a message/request to one of the peer nodes – General Big Daddy

2. Both Andrew and Big Daddy multicast the message to the other nodes, sometimes also called replicas in PBFT (generals Sophia and Elizabeth)

3. The replicas execute the request and send a reply to the other nodes

4. The client waits for n + 1 replies from the generals with the same result. This will result in a positive consensus

5. Voilà, consensus is reached and the Byzantines General's problem solved! Let's conquer Rapture!

Proof of Elapsed Time

Also known as PoET, this consensus is everything but poetry! The algorithm is used mostly in permissioned blockchains like Hyperledger Sawtooth (in addition to PBFT). PoET uses a lottery-style random selection to select the node that is going to win the new block.

PoET started to be used in Hyperledger Sawtooth in 2016/2017, introduced by Intel. The "miners" must first join the network, gaining a membership certificate. Once they are in the network, the nodes need to wait a certain amount of time that is randomly decided. The miner must wait at least the amount of time that was defined before starting mining a new block into the blockchain. In PoET, the miner that has the shortest amount of time is elected to do the block mining that round. The system tends to be fair and choose miners with a good degree of randomness. It doesn't require much electricity consumption and miners can "go to sleep" while they wait for their turn.

POeT is based on special CPUs developed by Intel called SGX – Software Guard Extensions. SGX allows a logical separation of the CPU memory that cannot be accessed or changed. These parts are also called enclaves and can perform isolated commands and memory encryption. Only enclaves can access and changed stored in this compartment. The code is encrypted and cannot be accessed outside the enclave, making it very secure for the processes that happen inside the enclave.

The main use case for proof of elapsed time is Hyperledger Sawtooth, a permissioned blockchain designed for enterprises that mainly uses POeT as a consensus mechanism. Sawtooth it's used to develop and make smart contracts, as well as distributed ledgers. It can be deployed on-premise or on the cloud. The consensus mechanisms available for Sawtooth are RAFT, PBFT or POeT, and the interesting thing is that the consensus mechanism can be changed on the fly according to the needs or growth of the network. It is compatible with a wide range of use cases from healthcare, supply chain traceability, financial system, digital assets exchanges, asset settlement, similar to the other Hyperledger products, and its Open Source. Sawtooth's main use cases are to allow the creation and traceability of assets on the blockchain. Sawtooth's most well-known use cases are related to supply chain traceability and food traceability applications.

To participate as a node in Sawtooth's POeT consensus, the node needs to download the application software and gain a membership certificate. The code will then generate a key pair for the participating node. SGX uses an asymmetric key approach with the private/public key pair. The miner needs to send SGX's attestation to the network in order to be approved.

The POeT mechanism generates a random wait time for the miner, and the miner gets the signed timer from the SGX trusted code. After waiting for the time to elapse, the miner gets a certificate saying that he has waited the necessary amount of time. Once the block is mined, the miner broadcasts the block together with the certificate. Depending on how the blockchain was designed, the miner may receive a reward or not for the work.

Proof of importance

In the proof of importance consensus, nodes receive a rating according to the stake they have (i.e. the number of coins owned) plus for how long the node owned those coins. Additional metrics such as how many times they transact and net transfers - number and size of the transactions over the last x number of days are also included in the proof of importance calculation. Unlike proof of stake, in proof of importance the nodes not only need to stake, they also need to gain some importance in the network by owning the coins for a period of time, i.e. vesting, and actually using them for transactions.

In proof of stake, the rich nodes get richer just by accumulating coins. Proof of importance tries to solve this problem by adding other variables that will give "importance" to the node. This consensus mechanism was developed and implemented by the cryptocurrency NEM.

NEM started as a fork of the cryptocurrency NXT. It was launched in March 2015 as an energy-efficient blockchain, ready for enterprises. It proposed to solve some of the issues related to proof of stake, such as the drawback of the richer becoming richer. Proof of importance introduces a rating or score system based on additional variables. The higher the rating, the better the probability of a node to be selected as a block harvester (they call miners block harvesters). The variables included in calculating the score are vesting, transactions partners and the number and size of transactions.

In NEM proof of importance mechanism, nodes need to meet the following conditions as part of the conditions to get a higher rating and be selected as a harvesting node:

- Have a balance of at least 10 000 XEM (the NEM native cryptocurrency). This is also called the minimum vested stake, and it's an amount that needs to be in the node's account for a minimum period of time to start harvesting

- Have transferred at least 1 000 XEM

- Have happened within the last 43 200 blocks (approximately 30 days)

- Have transaction partners, i.e. make transactions with other nodes in the network. In this case, network theory is used to verify the importance of a node (it avoids, for example, someone creating two accounts to transact with each other only)

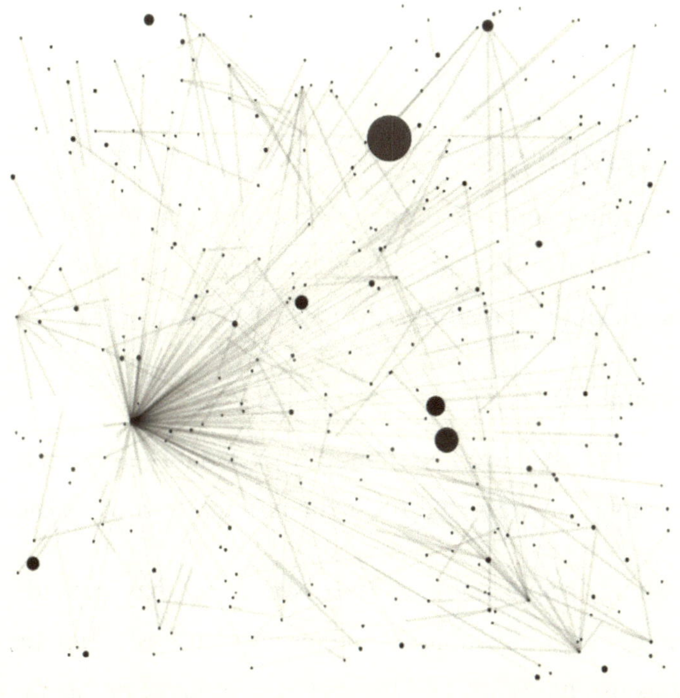

Nem's transaction graph as of 29th April 2015. Source: Nem's white paper

The algorithm then puts together the values and computes a rating for each node. According to the rating, the node will have a certain probability of being randomly selected for the next round of block harvesting. If the node selected is not online, the block harvesting can be delegated to another node, aka delegated harvesting.

Proof of importance doesn't require nodes to compute complex problems, and consequently, it doesn't spend much energy, and it doesn't need any specialized hardware.

Don't worry, you don't need to give any proof of importance. If made so far reading this book, I'm sure you are important!

Cryptography

Wow, cryptography! So what is cryptography? How do we use prime numbers and random numbers and all that stuff to encrypt a message? Continue reading, this is super duper cool!

Prime numbers

Prime numbers are extremely important in hashing and cryptography, so we will discuss them in this section of the book.

For hashing, prime numbers are used since they provide a better chance of creating unique values for a hash function. Hash functions use modulus, and the use of composite numbers (i.e. non-prime) increases the probability of hash collisions (i.e. different inputs to result in the same hash). Prime numbers will increase the chance of creating unique values when hashing by multiplying values by the prime number. This is just the nature of mathematics. For example, if you have a string "Unblockchain", multiplying each letter with a prime number and then adding those all up will give a very unique hash. Got it?

A prime number is a number that is only divisible by itself and divisible by 1. Some examples of prime numbers are: 1, 3, 5, 7, 11, 13, 17... and the 89, 97, 8191 and also the largest known prime number is $2^{82,589,933}$ which is a which is an astronomically big number 24,862,048 digits long when written.

The number of prime numbers decreases towards infinity. The higher the number is, the lower is the probability of finding it. For example, there are 25 prime numbers between 1 and 100, but only 21 prime numbers between 100 and 200, and 15 prime numbers between 200 and 300, and there are only 6 prime numbers between 10 000 and 10 100.

Euclid proved more than 2000 years ago that prime numbers are infinite. Although it's effortless to check if a small number is prime or not, the bigger the number it gets, the harder it is to check if it is a prime number which poses big challenges in mathematics and computer science. Also, the higher a range of numbers is, the less probability we have to find a prime and harder it is to verify if a number is prime. It's very hard to figure out an efficient computational formula to find big prime numbers.

Prime numbers can approximately be calculated by the formula *x/In(x)* and the density of prime numbers by *1/In(x)*. The bigger *X* is, the more accurate the formula is.

How can we find if a prime is a prime or not? Well, the most direct approach is to divide the number by every single number below it. If it is not divisible by any of them, then it's a prime. This is, however, very work intensively to perform.

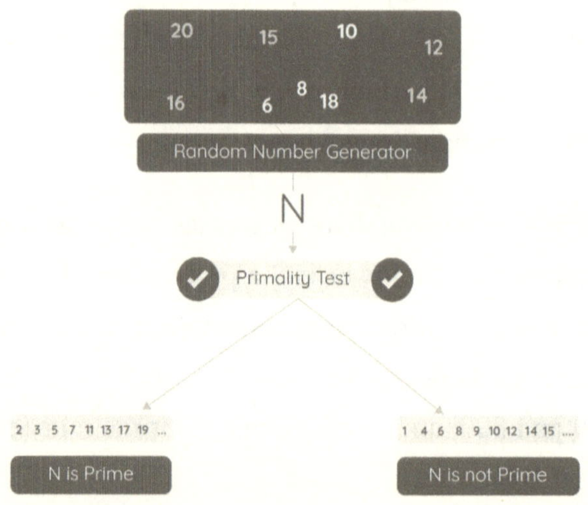

So we need to apply a test or algorithm to test if a prime number is a prime or not. Again, if we are looking for a small 6 digit prime, it is quite easy and fast to check if 100699 is a prime number. However, if we are searching large primes, say, that are more than 1000 digit long, the work starts to get a little bit more hardcore.

That's where the primality tests enter, and that's why we are going to talk about them as they are important for cryptography.

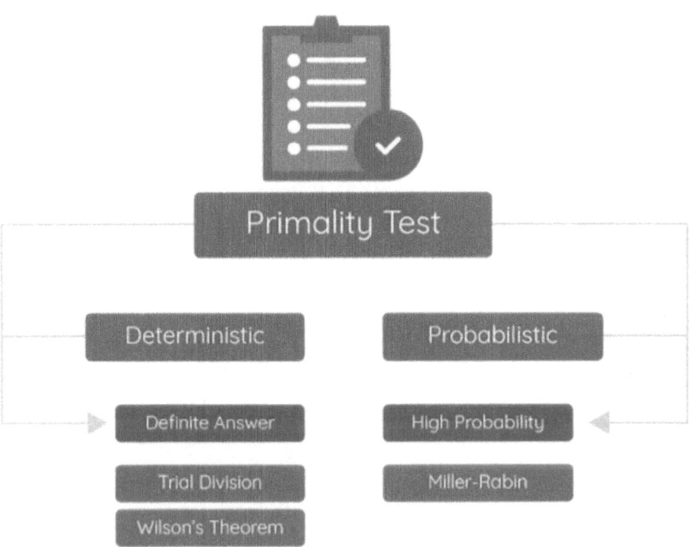

There are essentially two ways of calculating a prime. One is to use a deterministic algorithm like doing trial division (dividing the prime by all the numbers before it to check if it is possible to divide or not) or the Wilson's Theorem. Deterministic means that we will be able to say if the number is a prime with 100% accuracy. The deterministic algorithms are extremely computational inefficient.

The other alternative is the probabilistic way to get an answer faster, but it cannot tell us with 100% certainty that it is a prime number (although moderately accurate, it's not 100%).

The deterministic ways to test a prime number are very labour-intensive because they require a lot of calculations. The trial division requires that n (the integer to be factored) to be divided by any smaller number. Wilson's theorem also requires a lot of energy. It works the following way: given a natural number $n > 1$, it is a prime number if and only if the product of all positive integers less than n is one less than a multiple of n. i.e. *n prime* ➔ *(n – 1)! ≡ 1 (mod n)*

The Miller-Rabin is the probabilistic way, i.e. it's not 100% accurate, but it's accurate enough for most of the cryptography algorithms. Most cryptographic systems use the Miller-Rabin primality test to determine if a number is likely to be a prime or not.

Random numbers

Random numbers are also very important in cryptography. It may sound simple to generate a random number, but that's not true. At all. If you ask me to generate a random two-digit random number, I may say 87. Was my selection random? Or was I influenced by my culture and personal experiences? My selection of 87 may not be so random. 8 is a lucky number in Chinese culture, and 7 is Cristiano Ronaldo's number. Maybe the 87 pops up in my brain for this reasons.

In the same way, a computer also has a hard time to generate random numbers. Not that computers care about local culture or soccer starts, but everything is defined in a computer. There's no randomness in a computer code. Computers are deterministic, which means that they always produce the same output, given a certain initial state and input.

Cool fact on the importance of randomness: Germany lost World War II probably due to lack of randomness. The Enigma machine used by Nazi Germany to encrypt messages used in the war was cracked by the British Bombe, the machine developed by Alan Turing that exploited the Enigma machine's lack of randomness. After that, the British allies were able to listen to the messages and eventually made the necessary moves to defeat Nazi Germany.

This is why we need to have special methods and ways to generate random numbers which are important in cryptography. Random numbers are a cornerstone in cryptography because they allow generating unique keys. They also remove the reasoning and predictability of generating numbers, making it hard for an attacker to access the information. The attacker will have no way or mechanism to reason on how those numbers were generated, making it harder to hack and discover how the cryptographic keys were created.

Putting lava lamps in a blockchain book it's not that random!

So, how can we produce completely random numbers? There are different methods to generate random numbers, like hardware devices that can generate fairly random numbers based on some random data used as a seed. This is also called a random seed, and it's the data that is used to initialize a random number generation.

Choosing a good random seed is essential for cryptography security. If the random seed is not random enough, let's say the number 87, a hacker could easily discover the seed that was used to produce a pair of encryption keys. However, if the random seed has high entropy, it's much harder or impossible for a hacker to discover the seed. Let's look at some example of high entropy random seed sources that can be generated:

- Linux kernel can generate entropy from keystroke timing and mouse movement. Some Open-Source projects allow seed data from audio and video sources

- Linux systems have the */dev/urandom* pseudorandom number generator which generates randomness from noise collected from the computer hard drives. You can try it out by typing *cat /dev/urandom* in your command-line interface. This random seed comes from noise and random actions that you perform you're your computer which is very unique to each computer's activity

- Windows uses different entropy sources such as motherboard data, CPU, interrupt timings, mouse movement and keystroke timing

- Hardware generated random seeds generated by CPU modules

- Sound randomly collected from the computer microphone

- Sensor measuring air turbulence inside the computer's hard drive

- An image feed from 80 lava lamps is used by Cloudflare as a seed source of randomness and entropy. Oh, here come our lava lamps!

- DNA sequencing data

- The motion of electrons in subatomic particles

- Light variations

- How bacteria grow and multiplicate

…and you could list more potential seeds for our random number, but the most important is that it can create a random product out of it. Of course, some of these random seeds are more convenient than others, and most of us don't need to generate randomness from a group of 80 lava lamps.

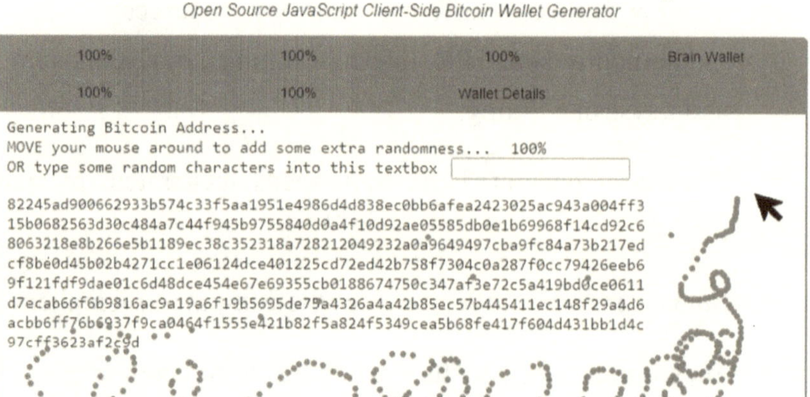

Bitcoin keys generated through random mouse movements

As you can see, generating random numbers is extremely important for all cryptographic activities, and computers can use multiple PRNG – pseudo-random-number generators – to generate fairly random numbers. I say fairly random and not 100% random because to achieve 100% randomness is almost impossible to achieve. Or it is?

The RSA algorithm

The RSA cryptographic algorithm was created by Ron Riverest, Adi Shamir and Leonard Adlema in 1978. RSA implements asymmetric encryption with public-key infrastructure and digital signatures. RSA is the most commonly used public-key algorithm in the world and the most copied software in human history. Every internet user uses RSA every time you make an online transaction or a payment, and we also use it every time we sing a blockchain transaction or send Bitcoin to someone.

As we saw before, in public-key encryption, two kinds of keys are generated: the public keys, which can be shared with anyone and the private keys that are only known to its owner. The public keys are used to encrypt the data, and the private keys can decrypt the data, which means that only users that own the corresponding private keys can decrypt the data or sign a transaction. In a transaction exchange, both users generate their public/private key pair used as digital signatures.

You can pretty much see this cryptography system in the following way: Alice has a lock and the respective key. She sends an open lock to Bob, Bob puts the message in the lock and sends it back to Alice. Then, Alice can then open the lock with her private key.

In this public key infrastructure, the users' digital signatures are used to validate a transaction signature's authenticity, providing a secure way to check that a user's transaction was signed by its owned private key. Anyone can send a message using the recipients public key, and only the recipient will be able to open the message with his private key.

This is the part where prime numbers and random numbers come into play.

The RSA signatures are very secure because they are generated from the multiplication of large prime numbers that are quite hard to factor. The RSA concept is composed of 4 steps: generating the keys, distributing the keys, encrypting data and decrypting data.

Why random numbers matter? Well, the random numbers we were looking at are going to help us to select the prime numbers that we will be using to generate the RSA keys. After getting the random number (a very large one) if this random number is not a prime number, the function will search for the next closest prime number.

Let's look at the steps to generate an RSA key pair:

1. Generate a random number. It needs to be large—something like 154 digits long or 10^154.

2. If the random number is not a prime number, pick the closest prime number using the function *nextprime()*. Pick another prime number. Let's call these two prime numbers p1 and p2.

3. Get the product of p1 and p2: N = p1 x p2, and as you can see, this composite number N will be more than 300 digits long

4. Get Φ or Phi: Φ (N) (Euler's theorem), replacing the prime numbers by p1-1 and p2-1 and multiply them: Φ(N) = (p1-1) x (p2-1). Note that Φ is the "breakability" of a number. Given n, Φ measures how many integers are less than or equal to n that do not share any common factor with n. Example Φ8 = 4. Calculating Φ is hard to expect in one case. The Φ of any prime number is always p1-1.

   Once you have Φ(N) = (p1-1) x (p2-1), if you have the factorization for N, then finding Φ(N) is easy. For example, the prime factorization of 77 =7x11.

5. Choose an exponent. Choose e:1 < e < Phi(N)

6. Lock: Lock (N,e)

7. Chose private key: choose d:d x e mod Phi(N) = 1

8. Key: your key result is (d, N), where d is the private key and N is the public key

In step 5, we connect the phi (Φ) function to modular exponentiation, exploring Euler's Theorem relationship between phi function and modular exponentiation: $m^{\Phi(n)} \equiv 1 \bmod n$.

This means that we can pick any two numbers with no common factor, let's say 5 and 8 and replace m and n in the equation:

$5^{\Phi(8)} \equiv 1 \bmod 8$

Which is $625 \equiv 1 \bmod 8$

Now we can shuffle things a bit, and we get

m^k*Φ(n)+1≡m mod n   OR   m^e*d ≡ m mod n which is also e*d=k* Φ(n)+1

now it's easy to calculate d, only if the factorization of n is known:

$$d = \frac{k * \Phi(n) + 1}{e}$$

Meaning that d is the private key!

Let's do a simple example to see the keys in action between Alice and Bob.

Alice is going to generate two prime numbers, the p1 and the p2 (for the sake of the example let's pick 2 small prime numbers) and multiply them to get n. Then, she calculates Φ easily since she knows the factorization of n, Φ turns out to 3016. Then, she picks a "public" exponent, which must be odd and not the same as Φ, let's say 3 in this case. Finally, she finds the value of her private key, *d*.

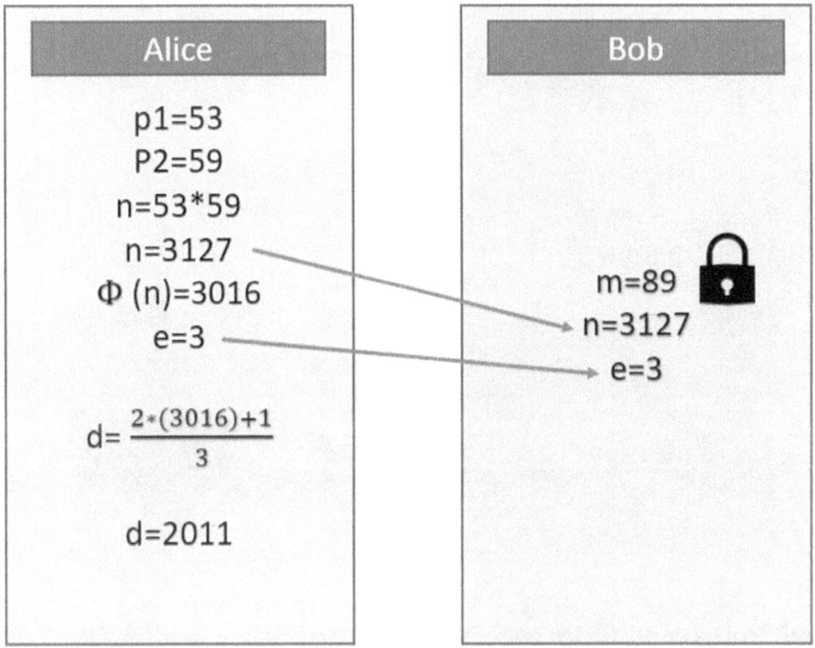

Now she has *d*, the private key and *n* and *e* are the public key. The *n* and the *e* is like an open lock that she can send to Bob! Now Bob can send a message, locking the message mathematically by calculating m to the power of e, mod n. Here, m is Bob's message and let's call this new "c" Bob's encrypted message. This way, Bob is encrypting is message with Alice's public key, n and e!

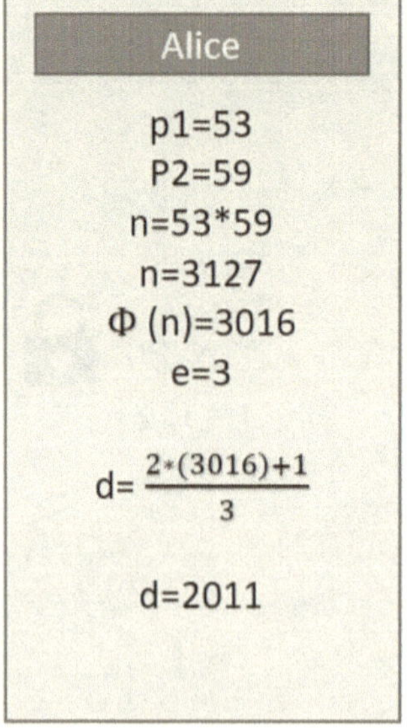

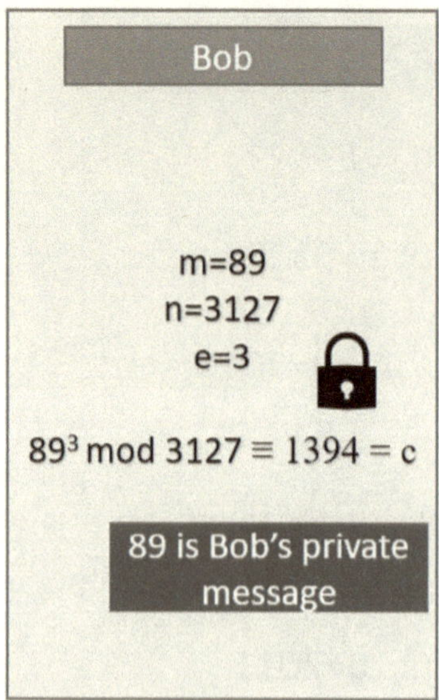

Now Bob sends C to back to Alice, and Alice will decrypt the message using her private key d. Easy!

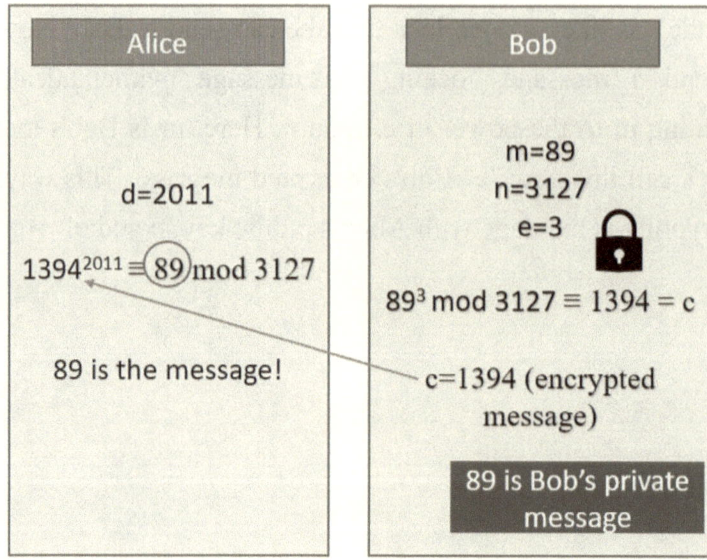

Notice that anyone else could be eventually listening to the messages that they have exchanged (men in the middle attack), but with no c, n or e, they cannot find the exponent d, which is the private key necessary to decrypt the message.

As you can see, it would also take someone many, many years do discover the two prime numbers that were multiplied to create N. To discover the factorization of such a large number – RSA is at least 200 decimal digits (663 bits) long – it would take a loooooooooooong time to do it, which is computationally infeasible. Even quantum computers would likely take a very long time to crack this.

Hashing algorithms

SHA – Secure Hashing Algorithm

Did I tell you that I love this hashing thing? We already took a brief look at hashing algorithms in this book but let's now take a deep dive on it.

SHA corresponds to several algorithms developed by the NIST – National Institute of Standards and Technology in the US. SHA hashing algorithms have the main characteristics that hashing need to have. They are pre-image resistant, meaning that it is extremely hard (or impossible) to reverse the hash's output into the original input. For example, the SHA1 hash of the sentence "I love dogs jumping in the park" is 03D6FD883EDC045071EFBF5E48F56811090FDAD4, but we can never get the input from the hash output alone. This n-bit hash always has the same length in each hashing algorithm, and it's a one-way collision resistant mechanism, meaning that it is extremely unlikely to get the same hash from 2 different inputs. SHA hashing algorithms are used to sign blockchain transactions, including Bitcoin, and for multiple uses in computer science, such as certificate signing. Some hashing algorithms may have a limit size for an input message, and all of them will always have the same size message digest, i.e. the hash result.

SHA-0

Sha-0 was the initial SHA series hashing algorithm. It has a digest size of 160-bits. It was soon replaced by SHA-1 that although also 160-bits, was more secure. SHA-0 is not used anymore in cryptographic keys

SHA-2

SHA-2 came very soon after the SHA-1 release and started standardizing different output sizes. From SHA-224, SHA-256, SHA-12 and others.

SHA-256

SHA-256 allows a bigger maximum message size which is 2^{64} bits, digest size of 256 bits, block size of 512 bits and word size of 32 bits. Don't worry, this is more than enough to hash thousands of books with the size of *Complete Works of Shakespeare, Atlas Shrugged* and *Les Miserables* combined. The SHA-256 hard limit allows inputs up to 2097152 Terabytes. SHA-256 has a 32-bits output. Normal computers use SHA-256 all the time, and this is also one of the foundational hashing algorithms behind Bitcoin and many other blockchains.

SHA-384 and SHA-513

These two SHA have a maximum message size of 2^{128} bits that is better than SHA-256, and requires more computing power. The maximum block size is 1024 bits, and the word size of 64 bits. They compute with 64-bits and use pretty much the same operations as SHA-256 and SHA-224, and they perform 80 rounds.

SHA-3

SHA-3 was created in 2015, and it allows different sizes from 224, 256, 384 and 512 bits. The Keccak algorithm used in Ethereum is part of the SHA-3 family. SHA-3 can provide an output in different sizes according to the needs, and block sizes vary based on the digest size, from 576 to 1152 bits. The SHA-3 performs 24 rounds.

Now let's look closer and break down SHA-256, probably the most widely used hashing algorithm in blockchains.

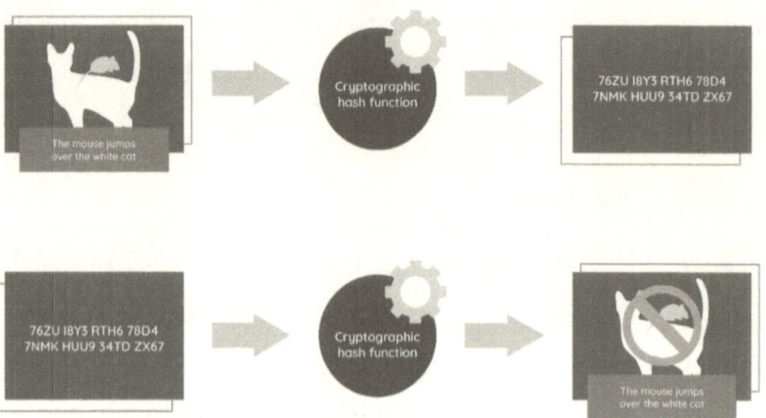

As we saw before, a hashing algorithm converts any input into a fixed-length string. This string cannot be converted back to the initial output, meaning that the hashing functions are pre-image resistant.

Cryptographic hash functions take arbitrary blocks of data and return fixed-size bit strings. We will see below how to transform M (the message) into the hash value, also called digest or simply hash.

Let's hash something manually, shall we? You can see below the steps that are required from the message processing to hash computation.

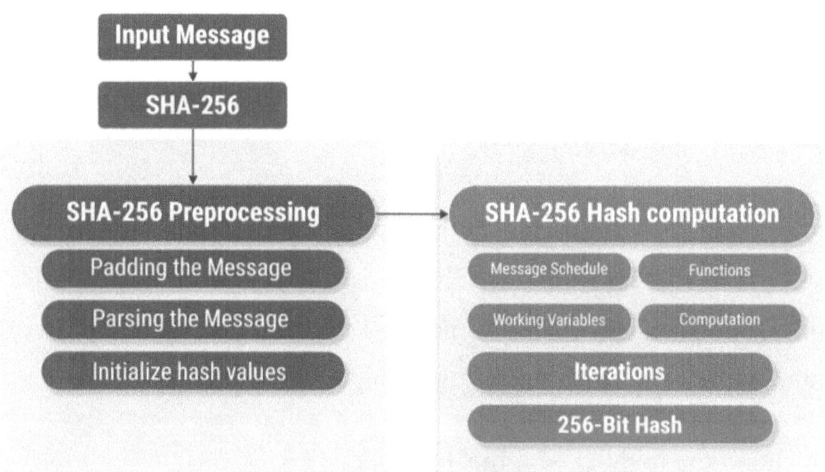

Let's take a look at what happens behind the scenes to produce an SHA-256 string.

Step 1: Padding the message

SHA-256 starts by converting the message to a binary number and get length l. The objective of this padding is to prepare the message before the hash computation begins. The padding ensures that the padded message is a multiple of 512 bits.

I want to convert the message "M = Moky" to 8 bit binary representation. Moky was the name of my dog and my best friend for 17 years.

M = 01001101 o = 01101111 k = 01101011 y = 01111001

Then, add 1 bit to the end of the message M

M = 01001101 01101111 01101011 01111001 + 1 bit

Length = l = 32 bits (i.e. the length of the original message)

Now append the message with K zero bits so that it becomes a multiple of 512 and add a 64-bit representation of the length I to the end of the string (we need to pad it with k number of zeros just to complete the desired bit size for the algorithm)

Calculate the number of 0 bits to append:

K = 512 - (l+1) - 64

Now convert 1 to a 64-bit representation of the input message length:

M = 01001101 01101111 01101011 01111001 + 1 bit + (k zero bits) + I as 64-bit bin newLenght = l + 1 + {k zero bits} + (64 bit i) = 512

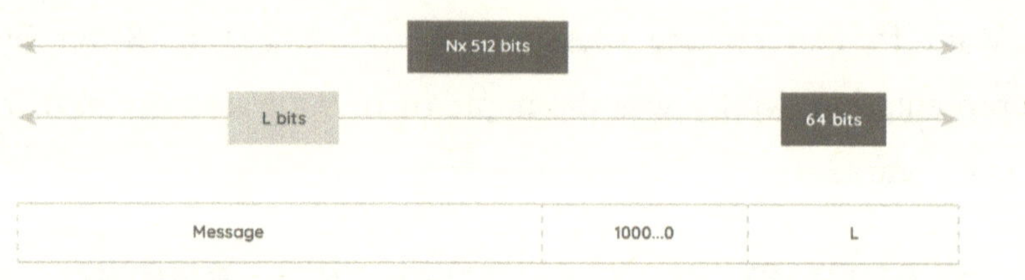

Graphical representation on how our padding should look like.

Our message looks like this after padding:

```
01001101  01101111  01101011  01111001  10000000  00000000  00000000
00000000  00000000  00000000  00000000  00000000  00000000  00000000
00000000  00000000  00000000  00000000  00000000  00000000  00000000
00000000  00000000  00000000  00000000  00000000  00000000  00000000
00000000  00000000  00000000  00000000  00000000  00000000  00000000
00000000  00000000  00000000  00000000  00000000  00000000  00000000
00000000  00000000  00000000  00000000  00000000  00000000  00000000
00000000  00000000  00000000  00000000  00000000  00000000  01100000
```

Step 2: Parsing the message

Now we are going to parse the padded message. After the message padding, we now need to parse the message into 512-bit blocks before the hash computation can begin.

To parse, we will take each set of 8 bits and convert the elements – i.e. each 4 set of 8 bits - into hexadecimal values. We will form a 512-bit W(0) field with 16 * 32 bit W, each W representing 4 sets of 8 bits. When you see "0x" it means that it is a hexadecimal value.

```
01001101 01101111 01101011 01111001  = W(0) 0 = 0x4D6F6B79

10000000 00000000 00000000 00000000 = W(0) 1 = 0x80000000

00000000 00000000 00000000 00000000 = W(0) 2...14 = 0x00000000

00000000 00000000 00000000 00000000 = W(0) 15 = 0x00000060
```

Step 3: Initialize hash values

Our SHA-256 will need a few additional initial values to work.

The initial hash values will be the following:

```
W(0) which represents our message. This is what
we have generated during the step 1 and 2:
```

```
W(0) 0 = 0x4D6F6B79

W(0) 1 = 0x80000000

W(0) 2...14 = 0x00000000

W(0) 15 = 0x00000060
```

$H(0)$ is the first 32 bits of the fractional parts of the first 8 prime numbers square rooted. These values are called the initial hash values and are constants that are provided with the SHA-256 algorithm. These will also be part of our working variables:

```
H0 = 0x6a09e667

H1 = 0xbb67ae85

H2 = 0x3c6ef372

H3 = 0xa54ff53a

H4 = 0x510e527f

H5 = 0x9b05688c

H6 = 0x1f83d9ab

H7 = 0x5be0cd19
```

$K(0)$ represents the first 32 bits of the first 64 prime numbers (i.e. from 2 to 311) to the cube root. These values are constants and are provided with SHA-256 code and are always the same, as they are part of cryptography standards:

```
k[0..63]    =    0x428a2f98,    0x71374491,    0xb5c0fbcf,    0xe9b5dba5,
0x3956c25b,    0x59f111f1,    0x923f82a4,    0xab1c5ed5,    0xd807aa98,
0x12835b01,    0x243185be,    0x550c7dc3,    0x72be5d74,    0x80deb1fe,
0x9bdc06a7,    0xc19bf174,    0xe49b69c1,    0xefbe4786,    0x0fc19dc6,
0x240ca1cc,    0x2de92c6f,    0x4a7484aa,    0x5cb0a9dc,    0x76f988da,
0x983e5152,    0xa831c66d,    0xb00327c8,    0xbf597fc7,    0xc6e00bf3,
0xd5a79147,    0x06ca6351,    0x14292967,    0x27b70a85,    0x2e1b2138,
0x4d2c6dfc,    0x53380d13,    0x650a7354,    0x766a0abb,    0x81c2c92e,
0x92722c85,    0xa2bfe8a1,    0xa81a664b,    0xc24b8b70,    0xc76c51a3,
0xd192e819,    0xd6990624,    0xf40e3585,    0x106aa070,    0x19a4c116,
0x1e376c08,    0x2748774c,    0x34b0bcb5,    0x391c0cb3,    0x4ed8aa4a,
0x5b9cca4f,    0x682e6ff3,    0x748f82ee,    0x78a5636f,    0x84c87814,
0x8cc70208,    0x90befffa,    0xa4506ceb,    0xbef9a3f7,    0xc67178f2
```

Step 4: SHA-256 hash computation

The hashing algorithm will then perform the necessary computations that include the iterations to create the hash. We now feed the initialize hash values that we have prepared before into the algorithms.

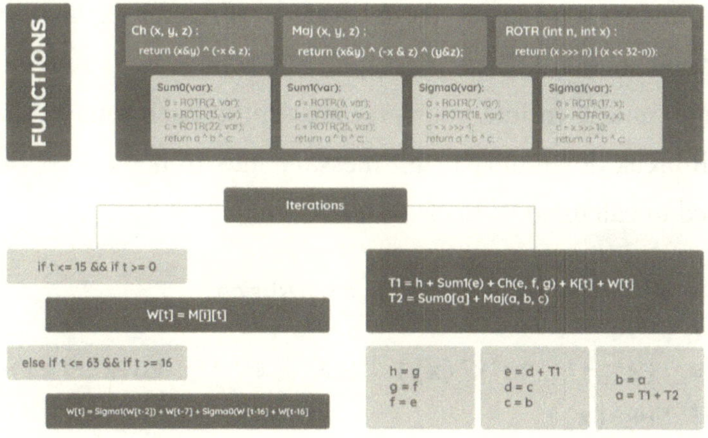

For the hash function computation, the algorithm will grab the message that was divided into chunks and put it through 64 rounds of operations. The output obtained in each round is fed as an input of the next computation round.

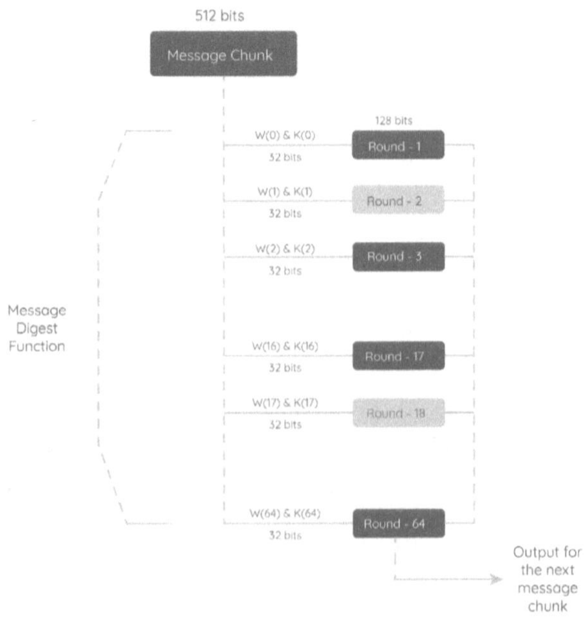

In this image, we can see the 64 rounds of operations that will be performed in the 512-bit message. The inputs W (chunks of the message) and K (prime numbers) are sent in each round. The first 16 will break down the 512-bit message into 16 parts of 32 bit, and we need to calculate W in each step.

$$W(i) = W^{i-16} + \sigma^0 + W^{i-7} + \sigma^1 \quad \text{where,}$$

$$\sigma^0 = (W^{i-15}\ ROTR^7(x))\ XOR\ (W^{i-15}\ ROTR^{18}(x))\ XOR\ (W^{i-15}\ SHR^3(x))$$

$$\sigma^1 = (W^{i-2}\ ROTR^{17}(x))\ XOR\ (W^{i-2}\ ROTR^{19}(x))\ XOR\ (W^{i-2}\ SHR^{10}(x))$$

$$ROTR^n(x) = \text{Circular right rotation of 'x' by 'n' bits}$$

$$SHR^n(x)\ =\ \text{Circular right shift of 'x' by 'n' bits}$$

Now we are able to create W(i) for all the 64 rounds

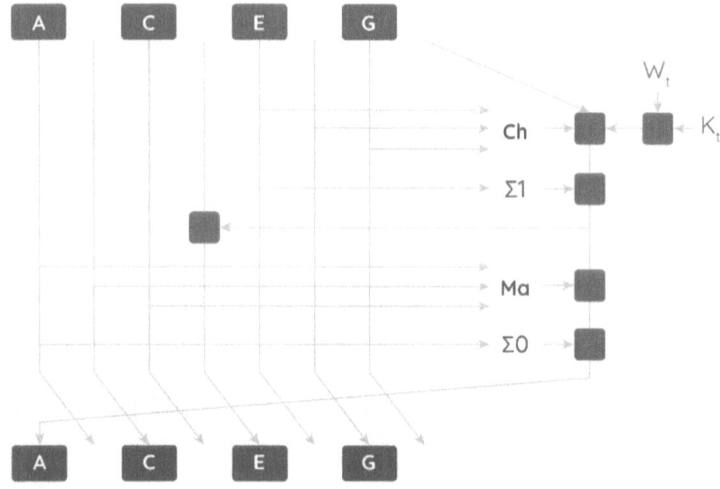

The image illustrates what happens in each round/iteration. Once that all the iterations are completed, we can complete the hashing process.

One iteration in a SHA-2 family compression function. The blue components perform the following operations:

$$Ch(E,\ F,\ G) = (E\ AND\ F)\ XOR\ ((NOT\ E)\ AND\ G)$$

$$Ma(A,\ B,\ C) = (A\ AND\ B)\ XOR\ (A\ AND\ C)\ XOR\ (B\ AND\ C)$$

```
Σ(A) = (A >>> 2) XOR (A >>> 13) XOR (A >>> 22)

Σ(E) = (E >>> 6) XOR (E >>> 11) XOR (E >>> 25)

+ = addition modulo 2³²
```

The red box is the addition modulo 2^32 for SHA-256.

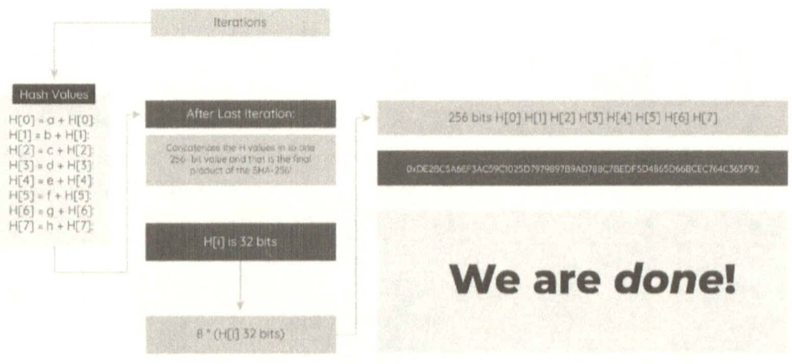

After all the iterations, we have all the hashes and get one 256-bit value which will finally translate into the final hash. Done!

The hash is:

278282C6C4FA7A2A3A3DCA4D6D08721E17E9B8CA491D5BB 1A5FBFC9E6ADFEFDE

SHA-256 is one of the most widely used algorithms and although infeasible to crack, it's very simple to calculate. I know it looks like it's a lot of steps, but for a computer, it's fairly simple to perform these calculations. Experts are still divided regarding SHA-256 safety, but the reality is that to crack a SHA-256… well, it's pretty much impossible as it would take billions of years to do it.

Chapter 5

Ethereum deep dive and node deployment

If Bitcoin is the new word's bank, Ethereum is the internet. These are big claims right? Stay with me.

Throughout the book, we have talked a bit about Ethereum, here and there but let's now do a deep dive on it. Ethereum is a pretty good blockchain case study to understand because most of the other blockchains have similar concepts. This will also give you some good background on how both public Ethereum and Enterprise Ethereum work.

The way the network is distributed, the blocks, the hashing, how transactions are processed, and the smart contracts, once understood, give you a good view of most of the technologies that are the backbone of most of the blockchains. There are many other blockchains, but to do a similar exercise with all the major blockchains, we would have to have a 20000 page book that would take me forever to read. For this reason, I want to focus on Ethereum, which will give you already a very good understanding of all the main concepts of most of the blockchains.

Ethereum was first described by Vitalik Buterin in 2013 in his white-paper, and it was described as a "next-generation smart contract and decentralized application platform".

Ethereum has its native currency, called Ether, ticker symbol ETH, which as a market cap of around 140 billion dollars as of January 2021. Ether is used both for transactions and used as currency to reward the miners for their work through transaction fees paid by the users and smart contracts. Per day, Ethereum processes more than one million transactions which are approximately four times more than Bitcoin.

It's important to say that Ethereum is completely free to read, i.e. the blockchain is completely public, but it's not free to write. To write on the blockchain any code, smart contract, data or transaction, payment in fees, also called gas, must be made. It's kinda this: you can see who is at the party, you can hear what music are they listening too, but to enter the party you will have to pay!

Ethereum is also described as a second-generation blockchain (being Bitcoin like blockchains, the first-generation), supporting for the first-time smart contracts and scripting functionality. Smart contracts allow a world of possibilities, and they can pretty much automate anything, being self-executing computer code that lives in a decentralized blockchain. Once conditions on a smart contract are met, an event (whatever the smart contract was designed for), is triggered, fulfilling the smart contract's purpose.

In Ethereum, the smart contracts are written in a programming language called Solidity and these programs are run in the EVM – Ethereum Virtual Machine. You can see the EVM as a giant Turing-complete, decentralized virtual machine that is distributed across all the Ethereum nodes, all around the world. In total, there are around 8500 nodes, and pretty much anyone can be a node in the network. The EVM is the core of smart contract execution. Due to its decentralized nature, it's also highly redundant, high fault-tolerant, and very resistant to attacks such as DDoS stacked and immutable. What's the catch? The trade-off is that Ethereum may have a bit low throughput and/or the transaction fees may be high sometimes.

Each Ethereum node stores the state of the blockchain and every smart contract, contributing to the blockchain's consensus mechanism. Ethereum's consensus mechanism is currently proof of work, but it's planned to switch to proof of stake sometime soon. The main difference between Bitcoin and Ethereum is that Ethereum can be seen as a supercomputer that runs a Turing-complete programing language, while Bitcoin can only be used to send transactions.

There are entire industries being built on the top of Ethereum. Hundreds of ICOs raised billions of dollars. Many NFTs marketplaces buy and sell non-fungible tokens for art, collectibles and cute criptokitties. Dozens of DeFi platforms are running on Ethereum, building entire banks on the platform.

Ethereum is a huge universe of possibilities, applications and creativity.

Ethereum block

The Ethereum block is composed of a number of fields represented below. We are going to break down all of them. Below, you can see a block that we retrieve from the Ethereum blockchain.

```
> eth.getBlock(888888)
{
  difficulty: 10128697710124,
  extraData: "0xd9830103028447657468867676f312e342e328777696e646f7773",
  gasLimit: 3141592,
  gasUsed: 0,
  hash: "0x3c7247429ede7c5ab18c55b92dc356860d4f11ab75c75efc87b729cae11b2842",
  logsBloom: "0x0000000000000000000000000000000000000000000000000000000000000000000000000000
00000000000000000000000000000000000000000000000000000000000000000000000000000000000000000000000000
00000000000000000000000000000000000000000000000000000000000000000000000000000000000000000000000000
00000000000000000000000000000000000000000000000000000000000000000000000000000000000000000000000000
00000000000000000000000000000000000000000000000000000000000000000000000000000000000000000000000000
0000000000000000000000000000000000000000",
  miner: "0xf8b483dba2c3b7176a3da549ad41a48bb3121069",
  mixHash: "0xa8cd021eeac59f8391f2eac3192477189b7c2ebd5c57e069e10a32c7e2359d0c",
  nonce: "0xeb9adf659012eb21",
  number: 888888,
  parentHash: "0x2c2da48b8633109b10586324ffb6856fc08649ce728cd06b180efc1086787a95",
  receiptsRoot: "0x56e81f171bcc55a6ff8345e692c0f86e5b48e01b996cadc001622fb5e363b421",
  sha3Uncles: "0x1dcc4de8dec75d7aab85b567b6ccd41ad312451b948a7413f0a142fd40d49347",
  size: 543,
  stateRoot: "0x8a620d697f7786ce4575b38102aaaa26144f107f176dd03bb54497a326883c03",
  timestamp: 1453494307,
  totalDifficulty: 5915885579893218276,
  transactions: [],
  transactionsRoot: "0x56e81f171bcc55a6ff8345e692c0f86e5b48e01b996cadc001622fb5e363b421",
  uncles: []
}
```

The Ethereum block is slightly different when comparing to Bitcoin, although some of the fields are identical. This is an actual block, more precisely the block 888888 that was mined with time timestamp 1453494307 which in human-readable time is January 22, 2016 8:25:07 PM GMT. This block sample illustrates well what any other Ethereum block looks like.

Deploying an Ethereum node on the cloud

Let's play around with Mr. Ethereum! For this section, we will need to use a Virtual Machine to deploy your Ethereum node. You can follow along (it's a fantastic way to learn) or just read it. If you get stuck for some reason, please don't hesitate to reach out to me and ask for help!

This section will have a lot of screenshots from the command line so that it is easier to follow along and check what is actually being done.

There are two main options: to deploy an Ubuntu Virtual Machine using Oracle VM VirtualBox (it's free to use), or you can use one of the major cloud providers – AWS, Google Cloud, Azure, Alibaba Cloud or IBM – to deploy an Ubuntu virtual machine. The second option is probably easier, more flexible and faster. Ubuntu is just a Linux operating system, just like Windows or macOS but it's really easy to use for this case.

Going back to deploying you Ubuntu VM, if you deploy a Virtual Machine on your laptop, it may consume a lot of resources from your computer and make it very slow. For this reason, deploying on the cloud is probably the best option. The book's purpose is not to teach how to deploy a virtual machine, but there is a lot of content online, or alternatively, you can ping me a message on LinkedIn, and I will reply as fast as possible.

A third alternative would be to eventually do it directly from your computer, but it's indeed safer if you connect from an isolated Virtual Machine which you can basically use as a playground. Also, suppose you connect with your personal computer. In that case, you will be exposing your IP to the Ethereum network and being a computer dealing with crypto, you become a honeypot for hackers.

Okay, let's get our Ubuntu machine ready on AWS!

I'm going to leave you here a quick step by step to deploy an Ubuntu VM on AWS. It's really simple. Just follow the steps below.

1. Assuming that you have an AWS account (it takes 3 minutes to open) go to the AWS console and search for EC2

2. Once your AWS account is ready, navigate to services and select EC2

3. Click instances → Launch instances

4. Choose AMI: scroll down until you find the first "Ubuntu Server" option. Click select

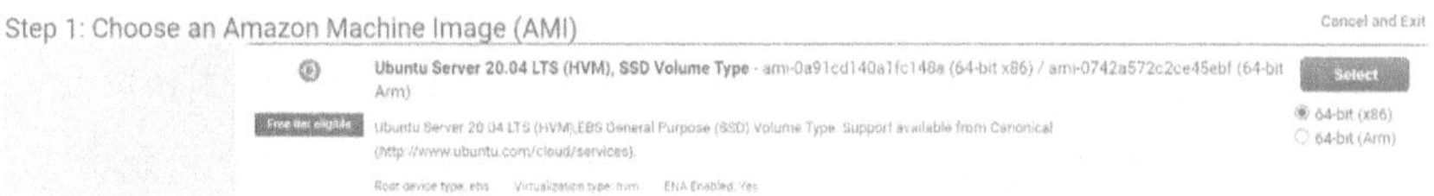

5. Select the instance type. Whatever is the free tier may be ok to play around for a bit but note that the instance on the "free tier" may become slow when running an Ethereum node. If that's the case, the alternative may be selecting a t2.large or t2.xlarge and stop the instance whenever you are not using it to avoid incurring additional costs. Click next

6. Configure instance details. You can leave most of it as it is. In "auto-assign public IP" select "enable". To save some money, you can also click "request spot instance". Spot

instances may allow you to save around 50% of the cost, but note AWS may terminate the instances if the spot price increases. You should not use a spot instance if you are running a production blockchain.

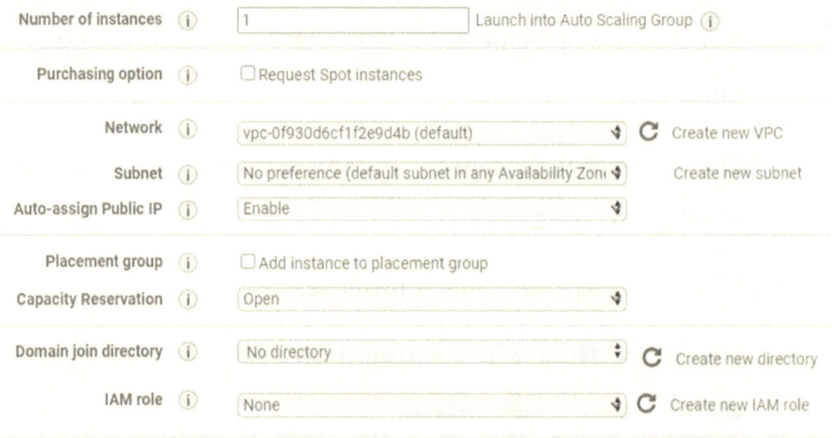

7. Add storage. We will need some storage for our node. To play around, 200GB to 300GB of general-purpose SDD should be enough. Click next

8. Tags. You can name your Ethereum node here. Type "Name" in the key field and "Ethereum node" in the Value field.

9. Configure security groups: make sure SSH port 22 is open to the IP range 0.0.0.0/0. This means that it is open to the world. Make sure you remove this once the playground is finished. Click review and launch

10. Select a key pair that you already use or create and download a new key pair

NOTE: if you are just testing and playing with your new Ethereum node, don't forget to terminate the EC2 instances, even if they are free tier. The free tier has a limit, for example, 750 hours, after which you will start paying. These EC2 instances may cost a few cents per hour, but if you leave them running for one full month, they may add up a quite expensive bill.

The best setup is to have a t2.xlarge which can run at around 60% of the CPU utilization to update an Ethereum light node:

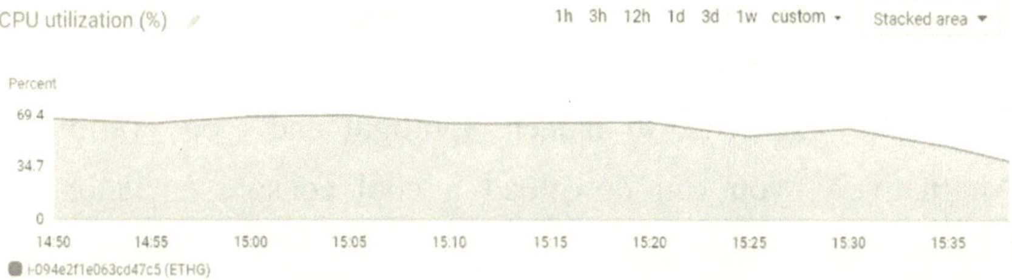

So if you can, you can request a t2.xlarge or equivalent to avoid having the node crashing all the time and generally having a better experience. The t2.xlarge will give you 4 vCPU, 16GB memory and better network performance. On AWS you can request the spot instances, which will have a better price.

Okay! Now that your Ubuntu EC2 instance is created, you need to SSH into it to interact with the VM and install the Ethereum software.

In the EC2 panel, select your new instance and click connect

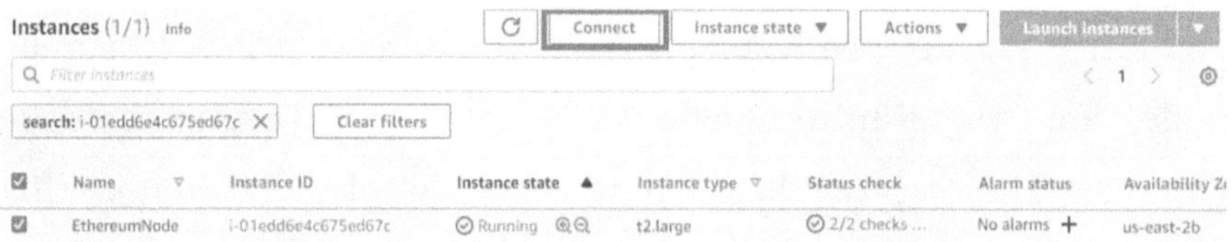

Follow one of the options. You can use EC2 Instance Connect option, a web-based command-line interface provided by AWS, or SSH into it, using any CLI – Command Line Interface. To SSH, follow the steps as shown you the SSH option. You can use the Command Prompt in your computer - for Windows, click the Windows menu and type cmd. For Mac, open the applications folder, then utilities and double-click on Terminal, or press Command - spacebar to launch Spotlight and type "Terminal". Alternatively, you can download a cool console emulator like Cmder, which is what I use.

```
C:\Users\henri
λ cd Downloads

C:\Users\henri\Downloads
λ chmod 400 19012021.pem

C:\Users\henri\Downloads
λ ssh -i "19012021.pem" ubuntu@ec2-3-140-208-132.us-east-2.compute.amazonaws.com
```

To follow along you need to locate the folder where your AWS key pair is stored and then follow the commands just like shown in the connect page for your instance.

Once you connect/SSH to your Ubuntu machine, run the following commands to install some packages and libraries that we will need

sudo apt-get install (to install APT - Advanced Package Tools)

sudo apt-get update (for updating a package)

sudo add-apt-repository ppa:ethereum/ethereum (to install the ethereym repository repository)

sudo apt-get update (to update the package)

sudo apt-get install ethereum (to install the latest version of Ethereum Go/Geth)

λ Cmder

```
Unpacking ethereum (1.9.25+build24398+focal) ...
Setting up rlpdump (1.9.25+build24398+focal) ...
Setting up puppeth (1.9.25+build24398+focal) ...
Setting up clef (1.9.25+build24398+focal) ...
Setting up bootnode (1.9.25+build24398+focal) ...
Setting up geth (1.9.25+build24398+focal) ...
Setting up evm (1.9.25+build24398+focal) ...
Setting up abigen (1.9.25+build24398+focal) ...
Setting up ethereum (1.9.25+build24398+focal) ...
```

We are now ready to go! Now that we have installed Geth, you can take a look at the help option by typing

geth –help.

You can also take a quick look at the folders inside your node to see what's inside the Ethereum folder. For this, type the command `ls -all` (this will list at the objects and folders store in the instance. You should be able to see .ethereum as per image below) and then,

cd .ethereum/ (to enter the .ethereum folder, note that it may take a few minutes to update)

```
ubuntu@ip-172-31-28-97:~$ ls -all
total 32
drwxr-xr-x 5 ubuntu ubuntu 4096 Feb  9 03:08 .
drwxr-xr-x 3 root   root   4096 Feb  9 02:51 ..
-rw-r--r-- 1 ubuntu ubuntu  220 Feb 25  2020 .bash_logout
-rw-r--r-- 1 ubuntu ubuntu 3771 Feb 25  2020 .bashrc
drwx------ 2 ubuntu ubuntu 4096 Feb  9 02:55 .cache
drwx------ 4 ubuntu ubuntu 4096 Feb  9 03:08 .ethereum
-rw-r--r-- 1 ubuntu ubuntu  807 Feb 25  2020 .profile
drwx------ 2 ubuntu ubuntu 4096 Feb  9 02:51 .ssh
-rw-r--r-- 1 ubuntu ubuntu    0 Feb  9 02:56 .sudo_as_admin_successful
```

.ethereum/ is our default path to call any functions in our Ethereum node, and we will use geth.ipc to later connect to the blockchain.

If you cant find your .ethereum folder for some reason, it may be related to the path to the .ethereum folder. You can probably try typing the following path to enter the .ethereum folder. This is your default path.

cd /home/ubuntu/.ethereum/

To start our node, the first step is to sync it with the blockchain. As a blockchain node, we need to be synchronized with the other nodes on the blockchain. However, to download the full blockchain to the node, it could take days and a lot of space.

According to Etherscan, the Ethereum blockchain is currently more than 600GB and growing every minute. Consequently, it requires a lot of space to be an Ethereum full node.

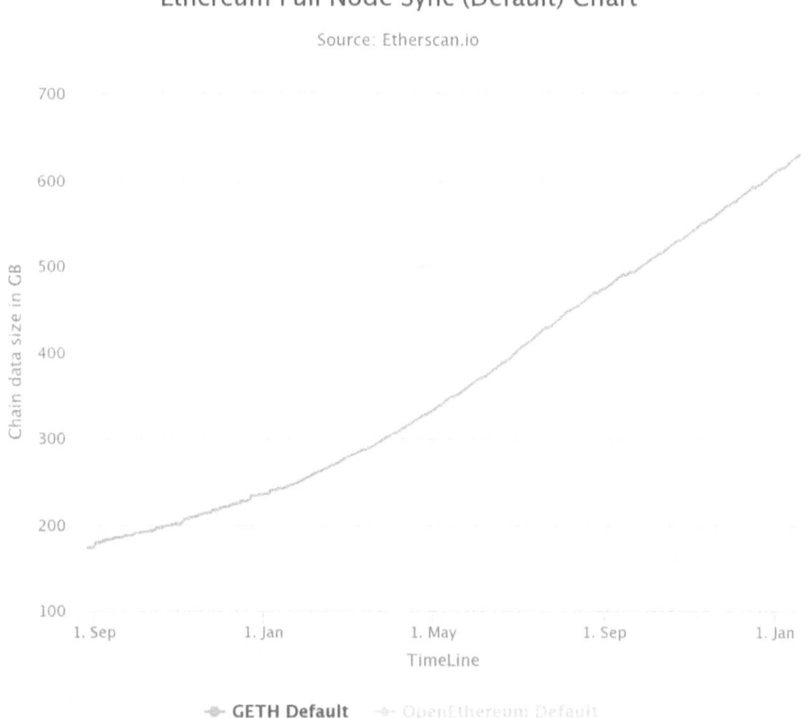

Considering the blockchain's size, we can allocate a maximum cache to our node (we are using an EC2 instance with only a few gigabytes available), and we want to select a synchronization mode that will allow doing a more lightweight synchronization. There are 3 modes for Ethereum node synchronization: fast, light and full.

`syncmode=fast` – it downloads block headers and s snapshot with the last 64 blocks. It does not replay transactions and reduces the amount of work that your machine needs to do

`syncmode=light` – it downloads only block headers and validates the data against the headers' hash. Complete updates on the go connecting to other peer full nodes. The syncmode light is not compatible with mining

`syncmode=full` – it runs a full node, downloading all the blockchain since the genesis block. It goes through all the transactions in the blockchain, one by one, replaying them all and providing a full validation of the blockchain. It requires a lot of resources in terms of computing power, broadband and storage

In this case, because we just want to play around with the network, we will use the syncmode=fast, where our node will only download the block headers and validate only the last 1000 blocks.

There's also another type of node: the archive node. This kind of node is like an expansion of the full node. Most people won't need an archive node, but this kind of node may give advantages to exchanges, block explorers, wallet vendors and other companies that need to quickly retrieve information. Archive nodes need much more space – between 2 and 3 terabytes, and they store all the historical data, allowing us to retrieve information much faster. Archive nodes allow to quickly retrieve all historical data, speeding up the process.

Let's get back to our node. The next step to connect to start our Ethereum node is to start synchronizing it. Let's start by typing:

```
geth --syncmode=fast
```

Once you run this command, the node will start synchronizing, and you should start seeing something like the screenshot below. Using --syncmode=fast or --syncmode=light, your node may take around 30 minutes to get synced with the network.

NOTE: to use the geth console or to use Python3 console to interact with the Ethereum network, you will need to be running the Ethereum node. Otherwise, it will just not work.

```
Cmder                                                                                    –  □  ×
INFO [02-09|03:25:05.539] Imported new block headers               count=576  elapsed=34.546ms     number=124416
hash="d1c1b9…2e76c6" age=5y6mo2w
INFO [02-09|03:25:05.779] Imported new state entries               count=2304 elapsed=11.560ms     processed=7706
30 pending=32550 trieretry=0   coderetry=0 duplicate=0 unexpected=0
INFO [02-09|03:25:06.117] Imported new state entries               count=2304 elapsed=12.484ms     processed=7729
34 pending=31070 trieretry=0   coderetry=0 duplicate=0 unexpected=0
INFO [02-09|03:25:06.358] Imported new state entries               count=1920 elapsed=10.105ms     processed=7748
54 pending=30952 trieretry=0   coderetry=0 duplicate=0 unexpected=0
INFO [02-09|03:25:06.419] Imported new state entries               count=768  elapsed=3.391ms      processed=7756
22 pending=33599 trieretry=0   coderetry=0 duplicate=0 unexpected=0
INFO [02-09|03:25:06.677] Imported new state entries               count=2304 elapsed=11.557ms     processed=7779
26 pending=32562 trieretry=0   coderetry=0 duplicate=0 unexpected=0
INFO [02-09|03:25:06.890] Imported new state entries               count=2304 elapsed=11.240ms     processed=7802
30 pending=31158 trieretry=0   coderetry=0 duplicate=0 unexpected=0
INFO [02-09|03:25:07.122] Imported new state entries               count=2304 elapsed=13.285ms     processed=7825
34 pending=29416 trieretry=0   coderetry=0 duplicate=0 unexpected=0
INFO [02-09|03:25:07.207] Imported new state entries               count=768  elapsed=3.292ms      processed=7833
02 pending=34121 trieretry=0   coderetry=0 duplicate=0 unexpected=0
INFO [02-09|03:25:07.224] Imported new state entries               count=384  elapsed=1.312ms      processed=7836
86 pending=37746 trieretry=0   coderetry=0 duplicate=0 unexpected=0
INFO [02-09|03:25:07.304] Imported new state entries               count=768  elapsed=2.125ms      processed=7844
54 pending=40628 trieretry=0   coderetry=0 duplicate=0 unexpected=0
INFO [02-09|03:25:07.392] Imported new state entries               count=768  elapsed=3.159ms      processed=7852
22 pending=43379 trieretry=0   coderetry=0 duplicate=0 unexpected=0
INFO [02-09|03:25:07.543] Imported new state entries               count=1536 elapsed=8.495ms      processed=7867
58 pending=43879 trieretry=0   coderetry=0 duplicate=0 unexpected=0
```

If instead of connecting to the Ethereum main network, you want to connect to one of the testnets, like Goerli, Rinkeby or Ropsten, you can use one of the following commands:

```
Geth --goerli
```

`Geth --rinkeby`

`Geth --ropsten`

Connecting to the test networks allow you to play around without the need to top up your account with real Ether. Testnets have faucets that allow you to get some free test Ether. Note that Goerli and Rinkeby are proof of authority blockchains and consequently may not replicate exactly the Ethereum main network. By the way, if you didn't guess yet what the testnet names have in common, these test networks were named after Swedish villages.

Now that the node is running, we can connect to the Geth Javascript console and start interacting with the blockchain.

Open a second command line in a new window and SSH into your instance

In your command line, type

`geth attach`

to start the Geth Javascript console

just like the screenshot below

```
ubuntu@ip-172-31-28-97:~$ geth attach
Welcome to the Geth JavaScript console!

instance: Geth/v1.9.25-stable-e7872729/linux-amd64/go1.
15.6
at block: 0 (Thu Jan 01 1970 00:00:00 GMT+0000 (UTC))
 datadir: /home/ubuntu/.ethereum
 modules: admin:1.0 debug:1.0 eth:1.0 ethash:1.0 miner:
1.0 net:1.0 personal:1.0 rpc:1.0 txpool:1.0 web3:1.0

To exit, press ctrl-d
```

☺ Welcome to the matrix!

Now we can start playing around. One of the first commands to learn in the Geth console is

eth. and press the tab key twice very fast.

You will see the list of API commands. These API commands are compatible with different programming languages like JavaScript and Python.

```
> eth.
eth._requestManager
eth.accounts
eth.blockNumber
eth.call
eth.chainId
eth.coinbase
eth.compile
eth.constructor
eth.contract
eth.defaultAccount
eth.defaultBlock
eth.estimateGas
eth.fillTransaction
eth.filter
eth.gasPrice
eth.getAccounts
eth.getBalance
eth.getBlock
eth.getBlockByHash
```

The command line auto-completes any commands that you start
writhing to facilitate writing commands if you press the tab key.
For example, you can type eth.syn and if you press tab it should
autocomplete to *eth.syncing*

Once we are in, we can check if our node is synchronizing using the
command

eth.syncing

```
> eth.syncing
{
  currentBlock: 1987367,
  highestBlock: 11819845,
  knownStates: 7905034,
  pulledStates: 7856209,
  startingBlock: 0
}
> eth.syncing.currentBlock
2006603
>
```

Here we can see that we are syncing with the network, what's the status, the current block in the blockchain, etc.

There are a few additional commands under "eth.syncing". To check the list, you can type eth.syncing. and press the tab key twice very fast.

With the syncing commands we can see that the node is synchronizing, and we can use the command eth.syncing or eth.syncing.currentBlock to see what's the current block that our node is synchronizing.

Exploring the Ethereum block

We can also take a look and explore any block in the Ethereum blockchain. Let's get for example the block 987654 using the following command:

eth.getBlock()

You can either search for a block number, for example

eth.getBlock(987654)

or search for a block hash, if you know the hash of the block you are looking for

eth.getBlock("0x4ca44f16a98a6bc8206c152057cf0d7a6 caeb0b287e845e21a1da2849bea4c8a")

```
> eth.getBlock(987654)
{
  difficulty: 11980586356475,
  extraData: "0xd783010302844765746887676f312e352e31856c696e7578",
  gasLimit: 3141592,
  gasUsed: 63000,
  hash: "0x4ca44f16a98a6bc8206c152057cf0d7a6caeb0b287e845e21a1da2849bea4c8a",
  logsBloom: "0x00000000000000000000000000000000000000000000000000000000000000000000000000000
0000000000000000000000000000000000000000000000000000000000000000000000000000000000000000000000000
0000000000000000000000000000000000000000000000000000000000000000000000000000000000000000000000000
0000000000000000000000000000000000000000000000000000000000000000000000000000000000000000000000000
0000000000000000000000000000000000000000000000000000000000000000000000000000000000000000000000000",
  miner: "0x738db714c08b8a32a29e0e68af00215079aa9c5c",
  mixHash: "0x63f23867bb4d9bc54feb9d919aeb6ed43c185ec84d0d94bb9ae6761a55436990",
  nonce: "0x6a93f90b5e6c2ab4",
  number: 987654,
  parentHash: "0x6fa3f88aeeed00b71cee91f227e297ad762cdb2fce9b48460e437396f034fd93",
  receiptsRoot: "0xf87b6ac7b5c39e4f9bb76a77b892299efd410fc919b10373abf3811b1fd714dd",
  sha3Uncles: "0x1dcc4de8dec75d7aab85b567b6ccd41ad312451b948a7413f0a142fd40d49347",
  size: 886,
  stateRoot: "0x72d5c5654c5128427ad273af9b67d1927e877367d53cd3f60131c9039700768a",
  timestamp: 1455192272,
  totalDifficulty: 6988739597105965522,
  transactions: ["0x45bf261f89328b83bc865acf94e471f084e61ea55fee9cb108a59df793f44443", "0x6fe2bf49ef36eff8d
fc7dded2df912a21a4d74c2f44bdf751c3dc4326cca3171", "0x45860257466e8cbade4c5e8c6f1bcb98d6a8a0f6adb7fc23fc65ac
0017e702cb"],
  transactionsRoot: "0x32038100a8d1838f1c4e9333083c29599a69e169aa27a515407c247dd057408f",
  uncles: []
}
```

Here you can see all the information about the block, including the difficulty, gasLimit and gasUsed, hash, the nonce in hexadecimal, timestamp in UNIX time, totalDifficulty and the hash of the transactions.

timestamp: the block timespamp is expressed in seconds since unix epoch time. Time is the time when the block was mined. The timestamp is set by the miner that mined that block. As such, the miner can somehow manipulate the timestamp of the blocks or transactions, as long as they respect some basic rules like a block's timestamp must be a time in the future and not in the past.

What is the Unix time or epoch Unix time? Unix time is basically the way computers measure time. The Unix time is the number of seconds since 1st January 1970. Unix time "0" means midnight 1st January 1970, and you may see this date, for example, when you reset an old mobile phone. 1455192272 means in human time GMT Thursday, February 11, 2016 12:04:32 PM.

stateRoot: the start root can be seen as a giant Merkle Tree of all the previous blocks, transactions and code in the Ethereum blockchain hashed into the stateRoot of this block.

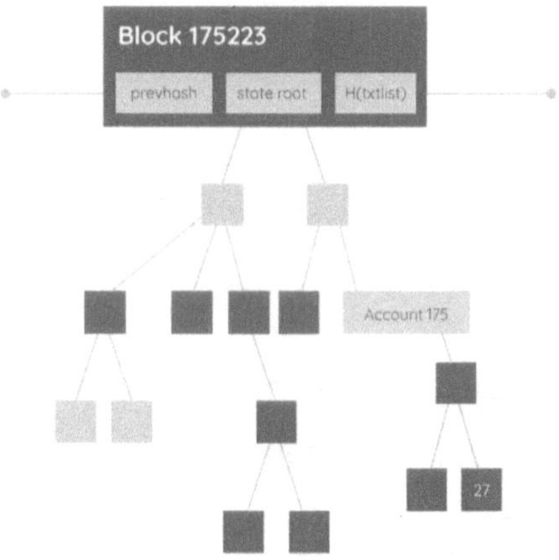

This state root has a very important purpose: it allows any node to easily validate with a very good degree of assurance that the block he has is correct without verifying all the blockchain blocks. He can instead verify only the hash tree from the other blocks. This is especially important when a node is a light node.

logsBloom: logsBloom is a 256 bytes string, and it's not really a log in the classical sense. It's the bloom filter for the logs of the block, and it allows to filter the hash of each element that is in the block. The objective is to minimize the number of queries that clients need to make by storing some events like historical transactions in the bloom. When there's a query "Is data z in the set?" the response can be "maybe" or "no". Thus is a probabilistic data structure.

receiptsRoot: this 32 bytes string is the root hash of the transactions receipts.

Transactions: here you see the hash of all the transactions in the block.

TransactionsRoot: a 32 bytes string is the root hash of the Merkle tree of all the transactions in the block.

We can also add a bit of magic to our eth.getBlock() and get the transaction details by using the command like this:

```
eth.getBlock(987654, true)
```

This will also retrieve all the transactions in that same block.

```
transactions: [{
    blockHash: "0x4ca44f16a98a6bc8206c152057cf0d7a6caeb0b287e845e21a1da2849bea4c8a",
    blockNumber: 987654,
    from: "0x2a65aca4d5fc5b5c859090a6c34d164135398226",
    gas: 90000,
    gasPrice: 50000000000,
    hash: "0x45bf261f89328b83bc865acf94e471f084e61ea55fee9cb108a59df793f44443",
    input: "0x",
    nonce: 164384,
    r: "0x6378ae10c227fde98885b878bdc60a319832001c628bfd46f42004bc223c239d",
    s: "0x2f8d5c1fafd04d66f450da5877b69e51969cc2fa92b73a9ee23e6ca09251bd28",
    to: "0xa0e9d5bea6464a16afc0f26a5fd706d37d5917d1",
    transactionIndex: 0,
    v: "0x1b",
    value: 1020334070000000000
}, {
```

Here are the details of one of the transactions in block 98764 that we retrieved using eth.getBlock(987654, true).

Let's now check our network status and check if our node is listening and connected to other peer nodes.

```
> net.
net._requestManager    net.getPeerCount    net.peerCount
net.constructor        net.getVersion      net.version
net.getListening       net.listening
> net.peerCount
16
```

Using the command net.listening we can see that our net.listening=true which is good and by running

net.peerCount

we see that we are connected to 16 peer nodes. Sweet!

Another interesting command to understand how is your network composed is

admin.peers

which will give you information about the peer nodes you are connected to.

```
> admin.peers
[{
    caps: ["eth/63", "eth/64", "eth/65"],
    enode: "enode://5de388c305ca6c16d8fd76c589906cf767c1455dc4c0
37108ac5bc32851596dc92055ff632c003a203f9f0a8d814e33d82a0f106320c
3e43f54ba32aab9d64a7@159.89.129.55:8888",
    id: "1888cec28574f0e4fecb176d4d331f6144e4820df0ae98bff3c3ffd
e7192ed34",
    name: "Geth/v1.9.25-stable-e7872729/linux-amd64/go1.15.6",
    network: {
      inbound: false,
      localAddress: "172.31.28.97:51194",
      remoteAddress: "159.89.129.55:8888",
      static: false,
      trusted: false
    },
    protocols: {
      eth: {
        difficulty: 2.0901451488381643e+22,
        head: "0x43d3d4cb7aa3b9c08dd1e82fbf1e8f139f970fa3b16aa52
9f9f15985549cf6b3",
        version: 65
      }
    }
}
```

In this screenshot, we can see some information about this node, including the version of his software – in this case, he is using Geth v1.9.25 – and we also see the IP address of the peer node. The IP address is exposed to the world, and that's why you shouldn't run a node from your personal laptop.

If you want to get the details of your node, you can run

`admin.nodeInfo`

and you will get similar information from your own node, including your version, the IP address, the blocks, consensus, and much more.

Playing with Python and eth serialization

Python is a great programming language to play around with blockchain and other technologies such as Machine Learning, AI and Data Analytics. It's great to have it in your toolkit, as a general-purpose programming language that is quite easy to read and to understand. Additionally, there are many Fintech applications in Python, making it very important if you are in this industry! And no, contrarian to the other pythons, Python code doesn't bite!

We now need to install Python in our Ubuntu instance and install the eth-rlp library to access a few additional functionalities.

From your Ubuntu command line, type

```
sudo apt install python3-pip
```

Once Python is installed, let's install the library that allow us to do the serialization

```
pip3 install eth-rlp
```

We will use this library to serialize block headers data and create a block hash. This will help us to process the data in order to fit it into the hashing algorithm.

Next, we need to install a Python hashing backend and cryptography library, the Cryptodome pysha3.

```
pip3 install pycryptodome pysha3
```

Then, Web3 is a JavaScript library that interacts with the Etherem blockchain. It's also called the next generation worldwide web, and it provides a decentralized web that allows us to interact with other Ethereum nodes using HTTP and IPC connections. It also enables to send transactions, retrieve user accounts and interact with smart contracts. Let's install it.

```
pip3 install web3
```

```
sudo pip3 install pyethash (later we will also
need pyethash for the ethash algorithm)
```

Now we have all that is needed installed, let's enter our Ethereum node path .ethereum/ and run python. Type the commands as per below:

```
cd .ethereum/
```

and then, type

```
python3
```

Welcome to Python3 console! Let's import some tools that we will need, starting with the IPC Provider from Web3. Every time you exit Python3, you will have to repeat the next 2 commands. NOTE: to make this work, you need to run in parallel the Ethereum node with the geth command you saw before.

```
from web3 import IPCProvider, Web3
```

The IPC provider will allow your node to connect via IPC connection. Ethereum Geth also allows HTTP and WebSocket connection, but IPC should be more secure.

Once this is done, we need to make sure that it works and that we can fetch the data. Let's call an object w3 (you can call it anything) with the following command to make calls. Type:

```
w3 = Web3(IPCProvider())
```

and now, if you type, for example, *w3.eth.* and press tab twice you will get the list of commands. Note that these 2 last commands may take a few seconds to take effect.

```
w3.eth.setContractFactory(
w3.eth.setGasPriceStrategy(
w3.eth.sign(
w3.eth.signTransaction(
w3.eth.signTypedData(
w3.eth.sign_munger(
w3.eth.submitHashrate(
w3.eth.submitWork(
w3.eth.syncing
w3.eth.uninstallFilter(
w3.eth.waitForTransactionReceipt(
w3.eth.web3
>>> w3.eth.|
```

After a few seconds (sometimes you may need to wait a minut to let it connect), you should also be able to type any command like

`w3.eth.getBlock(987654)`

And get the same block we saw before but in raw format:

```
>>> w3.eth.getBlock(987654)
AttributeDict({'difficulty': 11980586356475, 'extraData': HexBytes('0xd7830103028447657
46887676f312e352e31856c696e7578'), 'gasLimit': 3141592, 'gasUsed': 63000, 'hash': Hex
Bytes('0x4ca44f16a98a6bc8206c152057cf0d7a6caeb0b287e845e21a1da2849bea4c8a'), 'logsBloo
m': HexBytes('0x00000000000000000000000000000000000000000000000000000000000000000000000
00000000000000000000000000000000000000000000000000000000000000000000000000000000000000
00000000000000000000000000000000000000000000000000000000000000000000000000000000000000
00000000000000000000000000000000000000000000000000000000000000000000000000000000000000
00000000000000000000000000000000000000000000000000000000000000000000000000000000000000
00000000000000000000000000000000000000000000000000000000000000000000000000000000000000
000000000000'), 'miner': '0x738dB714c08B8A32A29e0e68Af00215079AA9c5c', 'mixHash': HexB
ytes('0x63f23867bb4d9bc54feb9d919aeb6ed43c185ec84d0d94bb9ae6761a55436990'), 'nonce': H
exBytes('0x6a93f90b5e6c2ab4'), 'number': 987654, 'parentHash': HexBytes('0x6fa3f88aeee
d00b71cee91f227e297ad762cdb2fce9b48460e437396f034fd93'), 'receiptsRoot': HexBytes('0xf
87b6ac7b5c39e4f9bb76a77b892299efd410fc919b10373abf3811b1fd714dd'), 'sha3Uncles': HexBy
tes('0x1dcc4de8dec75d7aab85b567b6ccd41ad312451b948a7413f0a142fd40d49347'), 'size': 886
, 'stateRoot': HexBytes('0x72d5c5654c5128427ad273af9b67d1927e877367d53cd3f60131c903970
0768a'), 'timestamp': 1455192272, 'totalDifficulty': 6988739597105965522, 'transaction
s': [HexBytes('0x45bf261f89328b83bc865acf94e471f084e61ea55fee9cb108a59df793f44443'), H
exBytes('0x6fe2bf49ef36eff8dfc7dded2df912a21a4d74c2f44bdf751c3dc4326cca3171'), HexByte
s('0x45860257466e8cbade4c5e8c6f1bcb98d6a8a0f6adb7fc23fc65ac0017e702cb')], 'transaction
sRoot': HexBytes('0x32038100a8d1838f1c4e9333083c29599a69e169aa27a515407c247dd057408f')
, 'uncles': []})
```

This is the exact same block we saw before but a bit less human-readable. It's raw dog data here. Cool right?

Calculating the difficulty

Now the reality is that this raw data is not very easy to read, but if we are looking for a specific piece of data, we can just ask for it:

```
>>> w3.eth.getBlock(987654)["difficulty"]
11980586356475
>>> w3.eth.getBlock(987654)["nonce"]
HexBytes('0x6a93f90b5e6c2ab4')
>>> w3.eth.getBlock(987654)["miner"]
'0x738dB714c08B8A32A29e0e68Af00215079AA9c5c'
```

Here you can see some examples where if you are looking for the difficulty, the nonce or the miner of a block, you can type the following commands respectively:

```
w3.eth.getBlock(987654)["difficulty"]
```

```
w3.eth.getBlock(987654)["nonce"]
```

```
w3.eth.getBlock(987654)["miner"]
```

Another thing you can do to improve the raw block's readability is to separate each value in a different line.

We can achieve this with the following:

```
myBlock = w3.eth.getBlock(987654)
```

```
print(*myBlock.items(), sep='\n')
```

```
('nonce', HexBytes('0x6a93f90b5e6c2ab4'))
('number', 987654)
('parentHash', HexBytes('0x6fa3f88aeeed00b71cee91f227e297ad762cdb2fce9b
48460e437396f034fd93'))
('receiptsRoot', HexBytes('0xf87b6ac7b5c39e4f9bb76a77b892299efd410fc919
b10373abf3811b1fd714dd'))
('sha3Uncles', HexBytes('0x1dcc4de8dec75d7aab85b567b6ccd41ad312451b948a
7413f0a142fd40d49347'))
```

Now it's more intelligible! I'm just showing a portion of the block here because you have already seen the rest of the block before.

How is the total difficulty value in the block calculated?

The total difficulty of a block is the total of the difficulty of all the previous blocks plus the previous blocks. How can we create a loop to calculate the difficulty of a certain block?

```
>>> totalDiff = 0
>>> limit = w3.eth.getBlock(1111)["number"]
>>> for i in range(0, limit+1):
...     totalDiff += w3.eth.getBlock(i)["difficulty"]
...     print("Block: [%d # %d] --- totalDifficulty: %d" % (i, limit,
totalDiff))
...
```

```
totalDiff = 0
limit = w3.eth.getBlock(1111)["number"]
for i in range(0, limit+1):
    totalDiff += w3.eth.getBlock(i)["difficulty"]
    print("Block: [%d # %d] --- totalDifficulty:
%d" % (i, limit, totalDiff))
```

and press enter twice

Soon enough, we get the totalDifficulty of the block 1111 but you can try to get the difficulty of any block really.

```
Block: [1103 # 1111] --- totalDifficulty: 24957205992620
Block: [1104 # 1111] --- totalDifficulty: 24986454638428
Block: [1105 # 1111] --- totalDifficulty: 25015717565801
Block: [1106 # 1111] --- totalDifficulty: 25044994781712
Block: [1107 # 1111] --- totalDifficulty: 25074286293138
Block: [1108 # 1111] --- totalDifficulty: 25103592107059
Block: [1109 # 1111] --- totalDifficulty: 25132912230459
Block: [1110 # 1111] --- totalDifficulty: 25162246670325
Block: [1111 # 1111] --- totalDifficulty: 25191595433647
>>>
```

This process has a problem right? This is a very intensive loop because it has to perform retrieval, addition and print out many times. There are more than 12 000 000 blocks in the Ethereum blockchain and a new block is added every 12 seconds. It was easy to calculate the difficulty of the block 1111 but it would take quite a lot of time and resources to calculate a higher block, like the block 11 111 111. Even if we want to calculate the difficulty of the block 987654, it will take at least 30 minutes.

This is, however, one of the key principles of a blockchain. You can always go back in the past and fully audit the values in the blockchain.

Transactions Receipts

Let's go over some additional functions on Geth, starting with the Transaction Receipt. If you are still on Python3 console, type exit() and enter the geth console by typing geth attach.

The function

```
eth.getTransactionReceipt()

eth.getTransactionReceipt("0xc280ab030e20bc9ef72c
87b420d58f598bda753ef80a53136a923848b0c89a5c")
(here with a hash)
```

Will give us additional info on the transactions. To retrieve the transaction receipt from any transaction we need its hash.

```
> eth.getTransactionReceipt("0xc280ab030e20bc9ef72c87b420d58f598bda753e
f80a53136a923848b0c89a5c")
{
  blockHash: "0xb4fbadf8ea452b139718e2700dc1135cfc81145031c84b7ab27cd71
0394f7b38",
  blockNumber: 999999,
  contractAddress: null,
  cumulativeGasUsed: 231000,
  from: "0x2a65aca4d5fc5b5c859090a6c34d164135398226",
  gasUsed: 21000,
  logs: [],
  logsBloom: "0x000000000000000000000000000000000000000000000000000000
00000000000000000000000000000000000000000000000000000000000000000000000
00000000000000000000000000000000000000000000000000000000000000000000000
00000000000000000000000000000000000000000000000000000000000000000000000
00000000000000000000000000000000000000000000000000000000000000000000000
00000000000000000000000000000000000000000000000000000000000000000000000
00000000000000000000000000000000000000000000000000000000000000000000000
0000000000000000000000000000000",
  root: "0x742df3094cb956938179464e090435508270cb85fa0d91698446cd8954c0
e606",
  to: "0x1c51bf013add0857c5d9cf2f71a7f15ca93d4816",
  transactionHash: "0xc280ab030e20bc9ef72c87b420d58f598bda753ef80a53136
a923848b0c89a5c",
  transactionIndex: 10
}
```

In a transaction receipt, we can see the blockNumber from which this transaction belongs to and the blockHash. In this TransactionReceipt, the contractAddress is null because the transaction doesn't involve a contract. The gasUsed is 21000, which is the fee paid, the root is the root hash of the rootState at the time of the transaction, and finally, we have also the transactionHash, which is obviously the hash of this transaction.

Gas and Gas Limit

Let's take a closer look at the gas. Gas corresponds to the transaction fees paid to the Ethereum Network. Gas it's basically fuel for the Ethereum blockchain.

The GasLimit is the maximum that a user is willing to pay to complete the transaction, and it's set by default to a minimum of

21000 Gwei. The GasLimit paid by the user contributes to the GasLimit of a block. Although Bitcoin blocks are limited by size in megabytes, Ethereum blocks can be limited by GasLimit. GasLimit is the maximum amount of gas consumed by all the transactions in a block; thus, the number of transactions is limited to the GasLimit. In the transaction shown above, the GasLimit was the same amount as the gasUsed.

How many transactions fit into a block depends on how much gas a transaction spends. For example, a more complex transaction may require more storage in the blockchain and consequently will require more gas. Miners will also prioritize transactions that pay more gas.

wei		1	1
kwei	ada, femtoether	1000	1,000
mwei	babbage, picoether	1000000	1,000,000
gwei	shannon, nanoether, nano	1000000000	1,000,000,000
szabo	microether, micro	1000000000000	1,000,000,000,000
finney	milliether, milli	1000000000000000	1,000,000,000,000,000
ether		1000000000000000000	1,000,000,000,000,000,000

The gas price is defined in Gwei, a fractional amount of Ether. 1 Gwei equals 0.000000001 Ether. Equally, 1 Ether equals 1 000 000 000 Gwei. This is basically the conversion. The smallest unit of Ether is the wei and 1 wei is 0.000000000000000001 Ether. So many zeros!

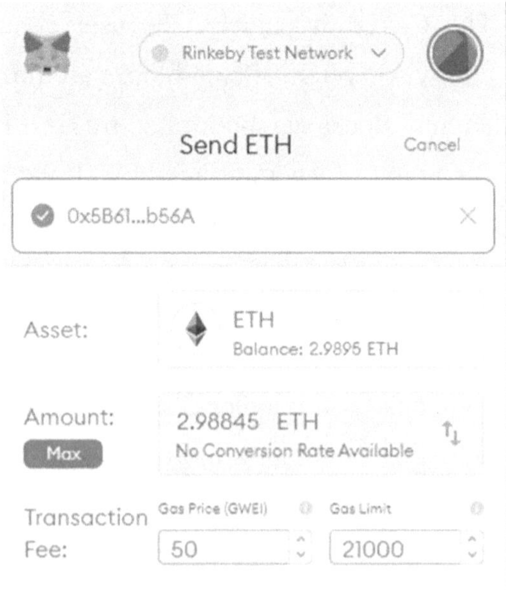

Using a wallet like Metamask we can define the gas price in Gwei and the gas limit to send a transaction.

In the example above, the user would pay a Fee = 50 * 21 000 = 1 050 000 Gwei, which converting to Ether is 0.000105 Ether. In USD this would be approximately 0.14 USD considering Ether prices in February 2021. Not too expensive.

Types of blocks in the Ethereum blockchain

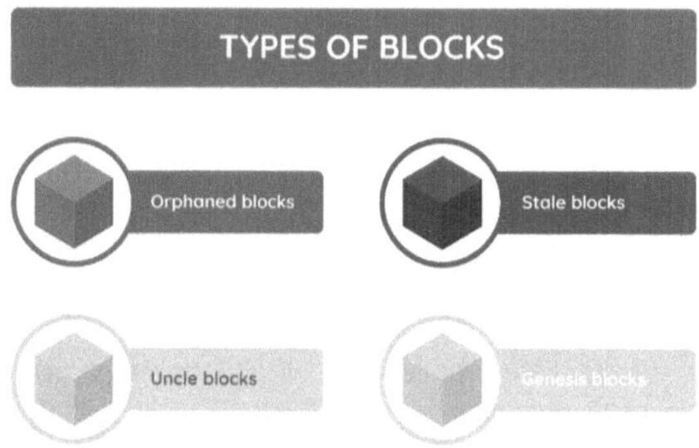

Huh? We have uncle blocks but not cousin blocks?

Orphan blocks

An orphan block is a block that looks pretty similar to any other block, and it has all the components of a block, but it will not belong to the blockchain.

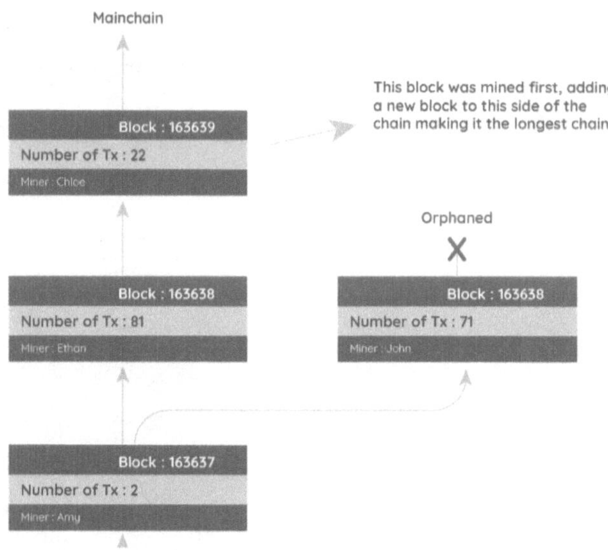

In the Bitcoin blockchain, orphan blocks are called orphan blocks, while in the Ethereum blockchain, they are called uncle blocks and are treated differently, but the reason they happen is quite similar.

Imagine that 2 different miners in different parts of the world, Ethan and John, mine the block height 163638 at the same time. Once they mine it, they will propagate it across the network. For a very brief period of time, there are 2 slightly different chains in the blockchain. However, Chloe, who is geographically closer to Ethan, received Ethan's block first, and she was also the miner mining the next block, adding it to Ethan's block. This means that the chain on the left will be the longest chain in the blockchain, and the block on the right will be orphaned. Chloe is then going to broadcast the new block 163639 to the network, and all the nodes will see that there's a longer chain that should be considered.

In the blockchain, the longest chain always wins. This is called the longest chain rule. What happens to the transactions? Well, some of the transactions on John's block were also included in Ethan's block. Additional transactions will probably be included in one of the upcoming blocks.

In the Bitcoin blockchain, the orphan block is totally discarded and the work performed by the miner that mined that block is just useless work. In the Ethereum blockchain, the orphan blocks are called uncles, and they are also listed in the next block mined in the blockchain. Miners that mine the orphan blocks receive a reward that is equivalent to 1/8 of the block reward. If you are curious to see how does a block with an uncle looks like you can run *eth.getBlock(987610)*. Yeah, I didn't have anything better to do with my free time, so I searched and found that block 987610 has one uncle.

The Ethereum blockchain rewards orphan blocks or uncle blocks to incentivize independent mining by giving these rewards. This way, small miners have a much lower risk of wasting resources if they mine orphan blocks, which is seen as more fair than other blockchains such as the Bitcoin blockchain.

Orphaned blocks are one of the reasons why users are advised to wait a couple of confirmations in the Bitcoin blockchain and around 12 confirmations in the Ethereum blockchain. Confirmations, in this case, means new blocks added to the blockchain. A bad actor may try to include a transaction in a block faster than the other miners, which may create a block with that transaction that will later be orphaned. To make sure that the block will not be orphaned, the receiver should wait to have a few confirmations.

Most of the exchanges and some wallets do this automatically. For examples, when you send an amount of Ethereum to an exchange, they will make you wait 5 minutes before making the amount available in your account.

How do exchanges and wallets check automatically for x amount of confirmations? Well, can run a little code that will compare that transaction block height with the current blockchain block height, but we can also do something similar in the command line:

```
eth.syncing.highestBlock - eth.getTransaction(" ").blockNumber
```

```
> eth.syncing.highestBlock - eth.getTransaction("0x62497f357906ca837cc3
1a25d37b55c100b38395840024bf50a03be333edae95").blockNumber
10832583
```

Because we are looking at an old transaction, the number of confirmations is 10 730 786, which means that many blocks have passed and the transaction is more than confirmed. Usually, in the Etehreum blockchain, you don't need to wait for 10 million confirmations. 12 confirmation will be enough.

Logs and Transaction details

We can look at all the details such as BlockHash, BlockNumber, from and to, gas, and much more of any given transaction by just using the transaction hash and the command

eth.getTransaction()

```
> eth.getTransaction("0x62497f357906ca837cc31a25d37b55c100b38395840024bf
50a03be333edae95")
{
  blockHash: "0x51abea3cf4db9eeb4bd7f8bd91b0b860aa80b8e3761dea04b7c1dfe3
0fd446ce",
  blockNumber: 987610,
  from: "0x2a65aca4d5fc5b5c859090a6c34d164135398226",
  gas: 90000,
  gasPrice: 50000000000,
  hash: "0x62497f357906ca837cc31a25d37b55c100b38395840024bf50a03be333eda
e95",
  input: "0x",
  nonce: 164330,
  r: "0x211a3978cae83e2adeae6fa4dad3a59467cdc06242da97ca418013c009549b59
",
  s: "0x557d0088eeb88a4486a3ec1074c5dc6066d1efa243b003e82fa0f2b704f66d37
",
  to: "0x414130c71d93c9baddb512cdd5a51ffdc0a497b0",
  transactionIndex: 0,
  v: "0x1b",
  value: 1124000400000000000
}
>
```

If we retrieve the transactionReceipt of the same transaction, we will get additional information: the logs and logsBloom.

Let's use the following command to check the transactionReceipt:

eth.getTransactionReceipt()

```
  blockHash: "0xb4fbadf8ea452b139718e2700dc1135cfc81145031c84b7ab27cd710
394f7b38",
  blockNumber: 999999,
  contractAddress: null,
  cumulativeGasUsed: 231000,
  from: "0x2a65aca4d5fc5b5c859090a6c34d164135398226",
  gasUsed: 21000,
  logs: [],
  logsBloom: "0x0000000000000000000000000000000000000000000000000000000
0000000000000000000000000000000000000000000000000000000000000000000000000
0000000000000000000000000000000000000000000000000000000000000000000000000
0000000000000000000000000000000000000000000000000000000000000000000000000
0000000000000000000000000000000000000000000000000000000000000000000000000
0000000000000000000000000000000000000000000000000000000000000000000000000
0000000000000000000000000000000000000000000000000000000000000000000000000
00000000000000000000000000",
  root: "0x742df3094cb956938179464e090435508270cb85fa0d91698446cd8954c0e
606",
  to: "0x1c51bf013add0857c5d9cf2f71a7f15ca93d4816",
  transactionHash: "0xc280ab030e20bc9ef72c87b420d58f598bda753ef80a53136a
923848b0c89a5c",
  transactionIndex: 10
},
```

We already saw before what are logsBloom used for, but now we can see in the transaction receipt that there is a field called logs that is directly correlated with the logsBloom. The logsBloom is like a search field for the logs.

The address is the address that generated the transaction in the logs, and it can be either someone's address or a smart contract. Then we have the blockHash, which is only the hash of the block from where this transaction belongs. We also have the blockNumber, again from the block where the transaction belongs to. Then we have the field data, topics it's searchable in the logsBloom and shows some information such as what kind of event was this, and it is part of the ERC20 standard. The field data is thus, the canonical signatures of one of the following type of events that were introduced by Ethereum EIP20:

```
function transfer(address _to, uint256 _value) public
returns (bool success)

function transferFrom(address _from, address _to,
uint256 _value) public returns (bool success)

function approve(address _spender, uint256 _value)
public returns (bool success)
```

This 256 byte is a bloom filter which means that it is a probabilistic data structure, that tells you if a certain set of that does not exist or that maybe it exists. logsBloom allows simplifying search queries, reducing the amount of work that nodes need to do when a query or a search is performed. For example, if I'm searching for if that transaction belongs to the block 4344444, the logsBloom can already tell us if that transaction does not belong to this block or if it maybe belongs and then the logs field is checked. This method reduces the necessary amount of computing power to complete searches.

Mining Ethereum

Let's continue to get our hands dirty! Now it's going to get even dirtier because we will be talking about mining!

This section will also be very useful if you wanna make some bucks by becoming an Ethereum miner! Well, you could do money mining by just installing one of those mining software, but it's much better if you understand the logic and that's what we are going to do.

We already went through proof of work mining and how mining works on Bitcoin, but now let's look at Ethereum mining and the differences.

Ethereum - Proof of Work Implementation

In Ethereum mining, the miner takes some data from the block header and a nonce and hash it, trying to get an input below a certain difficulty that is provided for each block. The Ethereum block difficulty is adjusted dynamically so that, on average, a new block is produced every 12 seconds.

For Ethereum mining, we also need to consider the DAG – Directed Acyclic Graph – which is a data set from which the data is hashed.

From the Ethereum wiki page, we can get the steps for Ethash mining but is all starts with the parameters from Ethash cache. Ethash cache depends on the block number, and the cache and dataset size grow linearly, but there are two ways to do it, either the cache size or the full size. The cash size allows block validation, but to mine, the get_full_size version is required.

```
def get_cache_size(block_number):
```

```
    sz   =    CACHE_BYTES_INIT   +   CACHE_BYTES_GROWTH   *
(block_number // EPOCH_LENGTH)
    sz -= HASH_BYTES
    while not isprime(sz / HASH_BYTES):
        sz -= 2 * HASH_BYTES
    return sz


def get_full_size(block_number):
    sz   =    DATASET_BYTES_INIT   +   DATASET_BYTES_GROWTH   *
(block_number // EPOCH_LENGTH)
    sz -= MIX_BYTES
    while not isprime(sz / MIX_BYTES):
        sz -= 2 * MIX_BYTES
    return sz
```

The mining process may be stalled by the bandwidth and/or by the memory. To mine Ethereum it's important to have a good memory cache, which is one reason why Ethereum miners frequently overclock GPUs memory.

The Dagger Hashimoto algorithm is the main loop that will then perform the required calculations to validate and mine Ethereum blocks. It will aggregate the data from the full dataset to produce a hash of the header plus a nonce. The nonce, is a 64 bit size integer that the miners need to brute force.

```
def hashimoto(header, nonce, full_size, dataset_lookup):
    n = full_size / HASH_BYTES
    w = MIX_BYTES // WORD_BYTES
    mixhashes = MIX_BYTES / HASH_BYTES
    # combine header+nonce into a 64 byte seed
    s = sha3_512(header + nonce[::-1])
    # start the mix with replicated s
```

```python
    mix = []
    for _ in range(MIX_BYTES / HASH_BYTES):
        mix.extend(s)
    # mix in random dataset nodes
    for i in range(ACCESSES):
        p = fnv(i ^ s[0], mix[i % w]) % (n // mixhashes) * mixhashes
        newdata = []
        for j in range(MIX_BYTES / HASH_BYTES):
            newdata.extend(dataset_lookup(p + j))
        mix = map(fnv, mix, newdata)
    # compress mix
    cmix = []
    for i in range(0, len(mix), 4):
        cmix.append(fnv(fnv(fnv(mix[i],   mix[i+1]),   mix[i+2]),
mix[i+3]))
    return {
        "mix digest": serialize_hash(cmix),
        "result": serialize_hash(sha3_256(s+cmix))
    }


def hashimoto_light(full_size, cache, header, nonce):
    return   hashimoto(header,   nonce,   full_size,   lambda   x:
calc_dataset_item(cache, x))


def hashimoto_full(full_size, dataset, header, nonce):
    return hashimoto(header, nonce, full_size, lambda x: dataset[x])
```

The algorithm maintains a 128 byes mix for each round, fetching it from the RAM. If the algorithm's output is below the desired target, the nonce is valid, and the miner wins the block. An extra sha3-256 is also applied. The Hashimoto function produces this hash from the mixHash (which comes from the header) and the hash.

The datasets to mine blocks are dynamically changed, and every 30 000 blocks, the DAG is regenerated. This means that considering that a new block is generated every 12 seconds on average, the DAG will regenerate every 100 hours approximately.

```python
def mine(full_size, dataset, header, difficulty):
    # zero-pad target to compare with hash on the same digit
    target = zpad(encode_int(2**256 // difficulty), 64)[::-1]
    from random import randint
    nonce = randint(0, 2**64)
    while hashimoto_full(full_size, dataset, header, nonce) > target:
        nonce = (nonce + 1) % 2**64
    return nonce
```

Then we have this mining algorithm. This is going to execute the Hashimoto function. We have in the mining algorithm a formulation of the difficulty that is placed into the target, and the target is set as a goal of the Hashimoto mining algorithm where we have

```python
while hashimoto_full(full_size, dataset, header, nonce) > target
```

The Hashimoto will try to generate a hash that is lower than the target. Else, it will repeat over and over again until it finds a hash that meets the condition. For this hash, he will apply the Hashimoto algorithm to the full_size dataset, header and a nonce. If the hash generated is bigger than the target, the mining algorithm needs to keep trying to guess the nonce which as you see is a number from 1 to 2^64: *nonce = (nonce + 1) % 2**64*

The miner will try all the nonce variations from 1 to 2^64 until finally the output is < target. When this happens, eureka! The proof of work is completed, and the nonce that meets the target is going to the block.

Block Mining – Proof of Work on Ethereum

We will now go implement a light mode of proof of work and understand what exactly is behind the scenes to mine a validate a block.

No worries, Mr. Ethereum is coming on the way to help us implementing this!

We will see how proof of work works from the programmatical point of view, understand how a block is mined and validated by other nodes. You can also check the code used for this section on the Ethereum wiki:

eth.wiki/en/concepts/ethash/ethash

So much wow!

We will be using the Hashimoto algorithm and experiment with the code, so I hope you enjoy it! The objective is to validate/mine a block using this algorithm and see the result. With the code below, our node will go through some checks and see if a block is valid and if it was correctly mined, i.e. if the miner met the difficulty condition.

To start, let's create a myetashtest.py file with some code that you can follow below.

You can either copy the code yourself by copying it to a text editor such as vim or nano, or import it to your Ubuntu machine using the following command:

git clone https://github.com/Bitatlas/etashpython

```
ubuntu@ip-172-31-28-97:~/b$ git clone https://github.com/Bitatlas/etash
python
Cloning into 'etashpython'...
remote: Enumerating objects: 8, done.
remote: Counting objects: 100% (8/8), done.
remote: Compressing objects: 100% (5/5), done.
remote: Total 8 (delta 1), reused 0 (delta 0), pack-reused 0
Unpacking objects: 100% (8/8), 4.16 KiB | 4.16 MiB/s, done.
ubuntu@ip-172-31-28-97:~/b$ ls
etashpython
ubuntu@ip-172-31-28-97:~/b$ cd etashpython
ubuntu@ip-172-31-28-97:~/b/etashpython$ ls
myethashtest1.py
ubuntu@ip-172-31-28-97:~/b/etashpython$ |
```

You can clone the code from the GitHub link, or if you are into BDSM, you can copy from below. No need to copy the #comments. If you think the next four pages are too boring for you, feel free to skip it, but I have provided comments throughout the code so that you can follow along.

```
#!/usr/bin/python3


import sys
from collections import OrderedDict
from eth_typing import Hash32
from eth_utils import big_endian_to_int


import rlp
from Crypto.Hash import keccak
```

```python
from rlp.sedes import BigEndianInt, big_endian_int, Binary, binary
from rlp import encode
from eth_utils import to_bytes, to_hex
from web3 import IPCProvider, Web3

_BYTES = 4                              # bytes in word
DATASET_BYTES_INIT = 2**30              # bytes in the dataset at
genesis
DATASET_BYTES_GROWTH = 2**23            # dataset growth per epoch
CACHE_BYTES_INIT = 2**24                # bytes in cache at genesis
CACHE_BYTES_GROWTH = 2**17              # cache growth per epoch
CACHE_MULTIPLIER=1024                   # Size of the DAG relative to
the cache
EPOCH_LENGTH = 30000                    # blocks per epoch
MIX_BYTES = 128                         # width of the mix
HASH_BYTES = 64                         # hash length in bytes
DATASET_PARENTS = 256                   # number of parents of each
dataset element
CACHE_ROUNDS = 3                        # number of rounds in cache
production
ACCESSES = 64                           # number of accesses in
hashimoto loop


address = Binary.fixed_length(20, allow_empty=True)
hash32 = Binary.fixed_length(32)
uint256 = BigEndianInt(256)
trie_root = Binary.fixed_length(32, allow_empty=True)

class MiningBlockHeader(rlp.Serializable):
    fields = [
        ('parent_hash', hash32),
        ('uncles_hash', hash32),
        ('coinbase', address),
        ('state_root', trie_root),
        ('transaction_root', trie_root),
        ('receipt_root', trie_root),
```

```python
        ('bloom', uint256),
        ('difficulty', big_endian_int),
        ('block_number', big_endian_int),
        ('gas_limit', big_endian_int),
        ('gas_used', big_endian_int),
        ('timestamp', big_endian_int),
        ('extra_data', binary),
        #('mix_hash', binary), we have removed these 2 fields
because we want a mining block header only
        #('nonce', Binary(8, allow_empty=True)
    ]


provider = Web3.IPCProvider('/home/ubuntu/.ethereum/geth.ipc')
w3 = Web3(provider)
print(w3.isConnected())


blockNumber = int(sys.argv[1], 10)


myHeader = MiningBlockHeader(
    parent_hash                                              =
to_bytes(int(w3.eth.getBlock(blockNumber).parentHash.hex(), 16)),
    uncles_hash                                              =
to_bytes(int(w3.eth.getBlock(blockNumber).sha3Uncles.hex(), 16)),
    coinbase   =   to_bytes(int(w3.eth.getBlock(blockNumber).miner,
16)),
    state_root                                               =
to_bytes(int(w3.eth.getBlock(blockNumber).stateRoot.hex(), 16)),
    transaction_root                                         =
to_bytes(int(w3.eth.getBlock(blockNumber).transactionsRoot.hex(),
16)),
    receipt_root                                             =
to_bytes(int(w3.eth.getBlock(blockNumber).receiptsRoot.hex(),
16)),
    bloom = int(w3.eth.getBlock(blockNumber).logsBloom.hex(), 16),
    difficulty = w3.eth.getBlock(blockNumber).difficulty,
    block_number = w3.eth.getBlock(blockNumber).number,
```

```python
    gas_limit = w3.eth.getBlock(blockNumber).gasLimit,
    gas_used = w3.eth.getBlock(blockNumber).gasUsed,
    timestamp = w3.eth.getBlock(blockNumber).timestamp,
    extra_data                                                       =
to_bytes(int(w3.eth.getBlock(blockNumber).extraData.hex(), 16)),
    #mix_hash                                                        =
to_bytes(int(w3.eth.getBlock(blockNumber).mixHash.hex(), 16)),
    #nonce                                                           =
to_bytes(int(w3.eth.getBlock(blockNumber).nonce.hex(), 16)),
)


from pyethash import hashimoto_light, mkcache_bytes


# Type annotation here is to ensure we don't accidentally use
strings instead of bytes.
cache_by_epoch: 'OrderedDict[int, bytearray]' = OrderedDict()
#here we cache by epoch order
CACHE_MAX_ITEMS = 10 #and limit the items to 10


def get_cache(block_number: int) -> bytes:
    epoch_index = block_number // EPOCH_LENGTH #this is where
we get the block number
    # Get the cache if already generated, marking it as
recently used
    if epoch_index in cache_by_epoch:
        c = cache_by_epoch.pop(epoch_index)  # pop and append
at end

        cache_by_epoch[epoch_index] = c
        return c
    # Generate the cache if it was not already in memory
    # Simulate requesting mkcache by block number: multiply index
by epoch length
    c = mkcache_bytes(epoch_index * EPOCH_LENGTH)
    cache_by_epoch[epoch_index] = c #stores the cash bytes
generated
    return c
```

```python
    # Limit memory usage for cache
        if len(cache_by_epoch) > CACHE_MAX_ITEMS: #this is related
to the lenght
            cache_by_epoch.popitem(last=False)    # remove last
recently accessed
            #ref line88
            return c
#now we will write the check proof of work funtion. We need here
to check if the data of the blocks is according to the
requirements
def check_pow(block_number: int,
              mining_hash: Hash32,
              mix_hash: Hash32,
              nonce: bytes,
              difficulty: int) -> None:
      cache = get_cache(block_number) #we get cache by block
number

      mining_output = hashimoto_light(block_number,
                                      cache,
                                      mining_hash,
                                      big_endian_to_int(nonce))
#not int_to_big_endian but the other way around

      #big_endian_to_int(nonce)
      #int_to_big_endian(nonce)) #this is the hashimoto light
mining output. It takes block_number, cache, mining_hash,
int_to_big_endian(nonce) and hash it

      print("MIX Digest: ", mining_output[b'mix digest'])
      print("MIX          HASH:                           ",
w3.eth.getBlock(block_number).mixHash.hex())

      print("RESULT:    ", mining_output[b'result'])
      print("CONDITION: ", (2**256) // difficulty)
```

```
        if mining_output[b'mix digest'] != mining_hash: #this is
to say that if the mining digest is not equal to the mix hash,
then...
            return False
        elif    int_to_big_endian(mining_output[b'result'])    <=
(2**256 // difficulty): #to convert the result int integer and
check if it meets the condition of being less or equal to 2^256
divided by the difficulty
            return False
        else:
            return True #if it returns true, then all good! We
could do more checks , but this is enough for now. For additional
checks        see        here        https://github.com/ethereum/py-
evm/blob/d553bd405bbf41a1da0c227a614baba7b43e9449/eth/consensus/po
w.py


#the next section's objective is tomake sure that data is
formatted correctly and make sure we can get the proper hash and
that the data is accurately formatted

block_number = blockNumber
myHash     =     "0x"     +     keccak.new(data=rlp.encode(myHeader),
digest_bits=256).hexdigest()
mining_hash = to_bytes(int(myHash, 16))


mix_hash                                                         =
to_bytes(int(w3.eth.getBlock(block_number).mixHash.hex(), 16))


nonce   =   to_bytes(int(w3.eth.getBlock(block_number).nonce.hex(),
16))


difficulty = myHeader.difficulty


check_pow(block_number, mining_hash, mix_hash, nonce, difficulty)
```

Now that I assume that you have this new file in your machine run it by typing

python3 "filename" "blockNumber"

which in my case would be;

python3 myethashtest1.py 999999

```
ubuntu@ip-172-31-28-97:~/b/etashpython$ python3 myethashtest1.py 999999
True
myethashtest1.py:93: DeprecationWarning: PY_SSIZE_T_CLEAN will be required for ':
' formats
  c = mkcache_bytes(epoch_index * EPOCH_LENGTH)
myethashtest1.py:109: DeprecationWarning: PY_SSIZE_T_CLEAN will be required for
#' formats
  mining_output = hashimoto_light(block_number,
MIX Digest:  b'[\x10\xf4\xa0\x8a1 \x9dBoaX\xbd$\xb5t\xf4\xf7\xb7\xaa\x00\x99\xc6
\x14\xa1\xf6\x93\xb4\xdd\x04\xd0'
MIX HASH:     0x5b10f4a08a6c209d426f6158bd24b574f4f7b7aa0099c67c14a1f693b4dd04d0
RESULT:       b'\x00\x00\x00\x00\x00\x08"N!W\xf10\x06\xbb\xdb\xb9\xcc%\x7f\x1a\x89
x8d\x9f\x1f\xe2\x8a\xe3]#\xb6\x14\x06'
CONDITION:  922244669575184768587843230036655612599434920450967216522220062840
```

Whoa! The block 999999 is valid! Here we can see that the condition is satisfied and that the block is valid, and although the result is not legible, the result is lower than the condition because it returns "true" from this condition on the code:

```
(mining_output[b'result']) <= (2**256 // difficulty)
```

Super blockchain geek stuff, right?! This way, we can see that the block was mined properly and that meets the difficulty condition. For the block to be in the blockchain, he obviously needs to meet the condition, but this is the work that a full node actually does. He needs to go through all the blocks and validate them.

Exploring blocks and transactions

Although we have looked at blocks, transactions inside blocks and transaction receipts, we didn't look at transactions individualistically and how are they structured. Wait, there's more? Yes, there's much more about transactions on Ethereum! We now need to see how to find a transaction and how to sign and verify a transaction.

```
> eth.getTransaction("0x22879e0bc9602fef59dc0602f9bc385f12632da5cb4eee4b813a0c271
59c4d24")
{
  blockHash:  "0xb4fbadf8ea452b139718e2700dc1135cfc81145031c84b7ab27cd710394f7b38"
,
  blockNumber: 999999,
  from: "0xc3665b8a9224ba8da9a20322f31d599cafa52c5c",
  gas: 21000,
  gasPrice: 60000000000,
  hash: "0x22879e0bc9602fef59dc0602f9bc385f12632da5cb4eee4b813a0c27159c4d24",
  input: "0x",
  nonce: 467,
  r: "0x43531017f1569ec692c0bf1ad710ddb5158b60505ea33fb7a21245738539e2d5",
  s: "0x3856c6a1117ff71e9b769ccb6960674038a3326c3dd84c152fc83ada28145a07",
  to:  "0x32be343b94f860124dc4fee278fdcbd38c102d88",
  transactionIndex: 0,
  v: "0x1c",
  value: 1162882720000000000
} .
```

Let's now look at this transaction that I "randomly" selected from the blockNumber 999999.

We can see here the blockHash, the "from" address, the gas used and the gasPrice, the hash of the transaction and the input data field. This "input" field, can be used for different purposes, including putting some smart contract data or miner name, but it's empty most of the times. Then we have the r, s and v fields which are related to the digital ECDSA signature, which we are going to look at in detail.

We also have the value, in this case 1162882720000000000 wei, which converted to Ether is 1.16288272 ETH (approximately USD 1500 in February 2021). Note that when you see the "0x", it means that the values are displayed in hexadecimal, but you can easily convert it to decimal. The ECDSA parameter used is the secp256k1: parameters of the ECDSA elliptic curve used in Bitcoin and Ethereum public-key cryptography.

Retrieving block data

Let's now look at our geth command line to understand how do we retrieve some of the block and transaction data:

If we want to check an individual transaction from a block, we can run the command

eth.getBlock().transactions[]

```
> eth.getBlock(999999).transactions[0]
"0x22879e0bc9602fef59dc0602f9bc385f12632da5cb4eee4b813a0c27159c4d24"
```

As you can see here, we retrieve the same transaction as before, as this is the first transaction of the block 999999. We can retrieve the first transaction of this block using

eth.getBlock(999999).transactions[0],

the second transaction with

eth.getBlock(999999).transactions[1]

and so on.

Without wanting to repeat the same info, you could also retrieve the data in that transactions using the command below, adding "true" after the block number.

eth.getBlock(999999, true).transactions[0]

```
> eth.getBlock(999999, true).transactions[0]
{
  blockHash: "0xb4fbadf8ea452b139718e2700dc1135cfc81145031c84b7ab27cd710394f7b38"

  blockNumber: 999999,
  from: "0xc3665b8a9224ba8da9a20322f31d599cafa52c5c",
  gas: 21000,
  gasPrice: 60000000000,
  hash: "0x22879e0bc9602fef59dc0602f9bc385f12632da5cb4eee4b813a0c27159c4d24",
  input: "0x",
  nonce: 467,
  r: "0x43531017f1569ec692c0bf1ad710ddb5158b60505ea33fb7a21245738539e2d5",
  s: "0x3856c6a1117ff71e9b769ccb6960674038a3326c3dd84c152fc83ada28145a07",
  to: "0x32be343b94f860124dc4fee278fdcbd38c102d88",
  transactionIndex: 0,
  v: "0x1c",
  value: 1162882720000000000
},
```

What we are doing here is basically to get the printout of the transaction from the first transaction of the block, i.e. The transaction [0].

Now, if I want to know only the "from" address of that transaction, I could use the command below. In this case, we only need to add "from":

eth.getBlock(999999, true).transactions[0].from

```
> eth.getBlock(999999, true).transactions[0].from
"0xc3665b8a9224ba8da9a20322f31d599cafa52c5c"
```

So as you see, you can narrow down a search to any specific field that you may be looking for.

Now we can do some comparations that may help us. For example, checking is a given transaction in a block comes from a specific address.

```
> eth.getBlock(999999, true).transactions[0].from == "0xc3665b8a9224ba8da9a20322f
31d599cafa52c5c"
true
> |
```

We can then use the command

eth.getBlock(999999, true).transactions[0].from == "0x32be343b94f860124dc4fee278fdcbd38c102d88"

to check if a specific transaction comes from a specific address. The result in the screenshot above was obviously false but this is anyways an interesting command to search for transactions from a specific address.

You can, of course, try different combinations of the command and try to get creative. If you know what transaction are you looking for, you could use eth.getTransaction and compare the "from" result with a specific address.

eth.getTransaction("0x22879e0bc9602fef59dc0602f9bc385f 12632da5cb4eee4b813a0c27159c4d24").from == "0xc3665b8a9224ba8da9a20322f31d599cafa52c5c"

```
> eth.getTransaction("0x22879e0bc9602fef59dc0602f9bc385f12632da5cb4eee4b813a0c271
59c4d24").from == "0xc3665b8a9224ba8da9a20322f31d599cafa52c5c"
true
>
```

We can check all the single transactions from this address, putting it on a loop to check all the blocks' transactions.

Now let's go back to our python command line and see how we would execute them. Note that the commands, although very similar, may have some syntax differences.

To start our python3 command line so please type python3 to enter your python CLI and start typing the following commands in order to be able to connect to the network:

```
from web3 import IPCProvider, Web3
from web3.middleware import geth_poa_middleware
w3 = Web3(IPCProvider('/home/ubuntu/.ethereum/geth.ipc'))
w3.middleware_onion.inject(geth_poa_middleware, layer=0)
w3.clientVersion (to verify the connection and client
version)
```

Note: every time you get disconnected, you need to rerun these commands to connect to w3 and interact with the Ethereum blockchain using python.

```
>>> from web3 import IPCProvider, Web3
>>> from web3.middleware import geth_poa_middleware
>>> w3 = Web3(IPCProvider('/home/ubuntu/.ethereum/geth.ipc'))
>>> w3.middleware_onion.inject(geth_poa_middleware, layer=0)
>>> w3.clientVersion
'Geth/v1.9.25-stable-e7872729/linux-amd64/go1.15.6'
```

To retrieve the same transaction from a block, we would use:

```
w3.eth.getBlock(999999, True).transactions[0]
```

```
>>> w3.eth.getBlock(999999, True).transactions[0]
AttributeDict({'blockHash': HexBytes('0xb4fbadf8ea452b139718e2700dc1135cfc8114503
1c84b7ab27cd710394f7b38'), 'blockNumber': 999999, 'from': '0xc3665b8a9224ba8DA9a2
0322F31D599CAFA52C5C', 'gas': 21000, 'gasPrice': 60000000000, 'hash': HexBytes('0
x22879e0bc9602fef59dc0602f9bc385f12632da5cb4eee4b813a0c27159c4d24'), 'input': '0x
', 'nonce': 467, 'to': '0x32Be343B94f860124dC4fEe278FDCBD38C102D88', 'transaction
Index': 0, 'value': 1162882720000000000, 'v': 28, 'r': HexBytes('0x43531017f1569e
c692c0bf1ad710ddb5158b60505ea33fb7a21245738539e2d5'), 's': HexBytes('0x3856c6a111
7ff71e9b769ccb6960674038a3326c3dd84c152fc83ada28145a07')})
```

As you see, we have the same data as this is the same block, just organized (or disorganized) in a different way.

Similarly to what we have done before, if we run

w3.eth.getBlock(999999, True).transactions[0]['from']

we get the same address as this is the from the address of the first transaction of the block 999999

```
>>> w3.eth.getBlock(999999, True).transactions[0]['from']
'0xc3665b8a9224ba8DA9a20322F31D599CAFA52C5C'
```

As you can see, there are some small but important differences when we get these results in python. The address is, for example, printout in capital letters only. Python makes the distinction between capital letters and non-capital letters.

And in python, we can use an alias to facilitate our checks. In this case, I have transformed the "from" address into "myAdd" and then compare it to the from the address in the transaction. Not surprisingly, the result came "True":

```
>>> myAddress = '0xc3665b8a9224ba8DA9a20322F31D599CAFA52C5C'
>>> w3.eth.getBlock(999999, True).transactions[0]['from'] == myAddress
True
```

This may seem fairly basic, but I wanted to show how it works in python because you can develop anything in python from here.

Running a script to find a transaction from a specific address

Now let's use a script to run this automatically in a loop. You can ignore the text after #. These are comments to help to understand the script.

```python
def find(addr):
    for i in range(999000, 1000000): #here we define a range of blocks to search
        txLen = len(w3.eth.getBlock(i).transactions) #to get the transactions and lenght of the transactions
        for j in range(txLen): #this loop will go through all the transactions to check the transactions in the blocks
            print("Block: %d/%d ---Transaction: %d/%d" % (i, 1000000, j, txLen)) #will print the transaction in the block
            if addr == w3.eth.getBlock(i, True).transactions[j]["from"]: #if we get a transaction with the adress that we are looking for, it will print the transaction hash
                print("FOUND Block : %d\nTX: %s" % (i, w3.eth.getBlock(i).transactions[j].hex()))
                return
```

You can also find this script here:
https://gist.github.com/Bitatlas/88a4061e6c466c37537695ab5004d7fb

And now paste it to the python command line. Note that python is very sensitive to having the code well aligned and with the correct indentations. If the code indentations is not right, python will throw an error.

```
>>> def find(addr):
...     for i in range(999000, 1000000):
...             txLen = len(w3.eth.getBlock(i).transactions)
...             for j in range(txLen):
...                     print("Block: %d/%d --- Transaction: %d/%d" % (i, highes
tBlock, j, txLen))
...                     if addr == w3.eth.getBlock(i, True).transactions[j]["fro
m"]:
...                             print("FOUND BABIBlock: %d\nTX: %s" % (i, w3.eth
.getBlock(i).transactions[j].hex()))
...                             return
... |
```

We have previously defined a value for "myAddr" which is the
"from" address from the first transaction in the block 999999. After
pasting the code, let's run

find(myAddr)

Note: if you get an error saying that "highestBlock" is undefined,
you can replace "highestBlock" with "100000! Or whatever is the
number of the highestBlock.

```
Block: 999997/1000000 --- Transaction: 8/9
Block: 999998/1000000 --- Transaction: 0/12
Block: 999998/1000000 --- Transaction: 1/12
Block: 999998/1000000 --- Transaction: 2/12
Block: 999998/1000000 --- Transaction: 3/12
Block: 999998/1000000 --- Transaction: 4/12
Block: 999998/1000000 --- Transaction: 5/12
Block: 999998/1000000 --- Transaction: 6/12
Block: 999998/1000000 --- Transaction: 7/12
Block: 999998/1000000 --- Transaction: 8/12
Block: 999998/1000000 --- Transaction: 9/12
Block: 999998/1000000 --- Transaction: 10/12
Block: 999998/1000000 --- Transaction: 11/12
Block: 999999/1000000 --- Transaction: 0/11
FOUND BABIBlock: 999999
TX: 0x22879e0bc9602fef59dc0602f9bc385f12632da5cb4eee4b813a0c27159c4d24
```

The script is going to run through all the transaction in all the
blocks until it finds a transaction that has the address that we are

looking for. He indeed found the block we were looking for, which contains the transaction we have defined. YAY!

This is how we can find a transaction associate with an address.

Signing a transaction with ECDSA

You are getting closer to become a blockchain guru! Stick a bit more with me to navigate through transaction signing with ECDSA. This is an essential function in blockchain and cryptography. Not as critical as chocolate is critical for my survival but… still essential.

Do you remember the previous chapter where we were talking about RSA, Alice and Bob share and sign a message? Now we will do it programmatically.

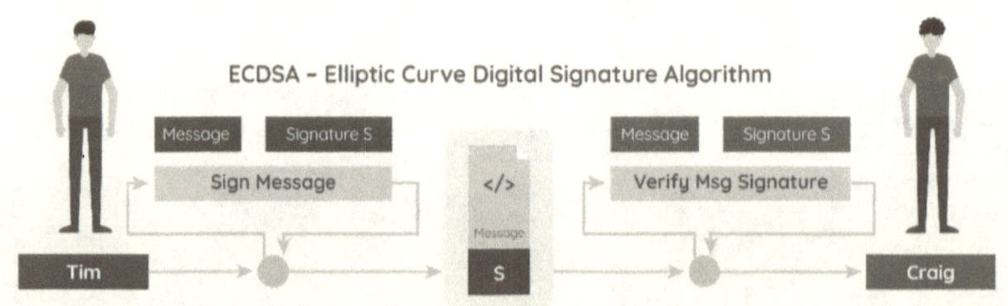

To sign a transaction, the users need to follow a few steps. To be more precise, the user's wallet or software needs to do it and not really the user. Thankfully, this complex process of signing a transaction is pretty much seamless and automatic. From the user experience point of view, all it takes is to press a button. However, we want to learn what's behind the scenes and how transactions are actually signed and verified.

Any transaction that is sent must be signed, and we can always check the validity of that signature and who has signed it.

In our case, the sender will sign a message with a signing key, pack the message with the signature and send it to the recipient. Then the recipient will take the signature and verify the message with the verification key.

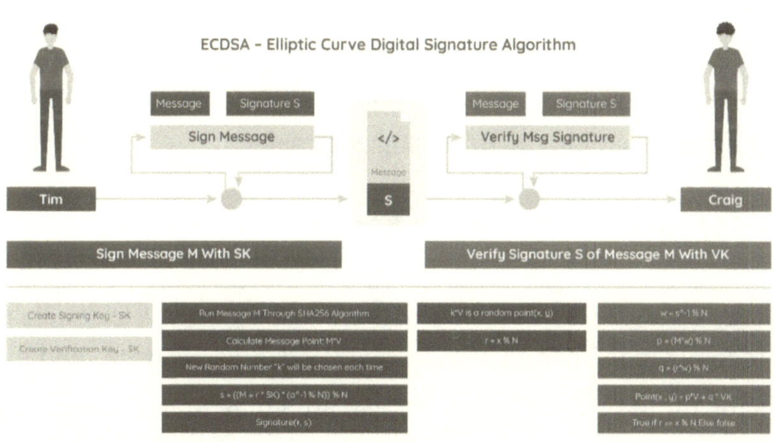

To sign a transaction with ECDSA, we will be using the recommended 192-bit elliptic curve domain parameters, more specifically the parameters for secp192k1 which can be found in Daniel R. L. Brown's "SEC 2: Recommended Elliptic Curve Domain Parameters" which are part of the industry standards developed by the SECG – Standards for Efficient Cryptography Group.

Let's start 😊

Let's go through the steps of signing, sending a message and verify the message. To start, let's use the Python3 command prompt to import Keccak. Keccak-256 is a variation of the SHA3 algorithm adopted in Ethereum.

Note: from your ubuntu machine, make sure you have the libgmb3 and fastecdsa libraries by running the commands

```
sudo apt install gcc python-dev libgmp3-dev
```

```
pip3 install fastecdsa
```

First, we are going to import Keccak from Crypto. Hash library. Let's do this running the following command:

```
from Crypto.Hash import keccak
```

and let's add the elliptic curve domain parameters extracted from the recommended parameters for secp192k1, as "Pcurve" and the N cofactor for the elliptic curve that we are going to use to sign. They are both big prime numbers, and they are part of the conditions for the private key. From your python3 console, type:

```
Pcurve = 2**256-2**32-2**9-2**8-2**7-2**6-2**4-1
```

Which is the same as the hexadecimal notation below

Then add

N =
0xFFFFFFFFFFFFFFFFFFFFFFFFFFFFFFFEBAAEDCE6AF48A03BBFD25E8CD0364141

Our private key will be within the range from 1 to N.

Also, add the following:

```
Ac = 0

Bc = 7

Gx =
0x79BE667EF9DCBBAC55A06295CE870B07029BFCDB2DCE28D959F2815B16F81798

Gy =
0x483ADA7726A3C4655DA4FBFC0E1108A8FD17B448A68554199C47D08FFB10D4B8
```

```
>>> Pcurve = 2**256-2**32-2**9-2**8-2**7-2**6-2**4-1
>>> N = 0xFFFFFFFFFFFFFFFFFFFFFFFFFFFFFFFEBAAEDCE6AF48A03BBFD25E8CD0364141
>>> Ac = 0
>>> Bc = 7
>>> Gx = 0x79BE667EF9DCBBAC55A06295CE870B07029BFCDB2DCE28D959F2815B16F81798
>>> Gy = 0x483ADA7726A3C4655DA4FBFC0E1108A8FD17B448A68554199C47D08FFB10D4B8
>>> |
```

These are the parameters that we will use to generate the public and private key.

There are also 2 functions that we will need to import, the egcd (greatest common divider function from the extended Euclidean algorithm) and the modular inverse:

```python
def egcd(a, b):
    if a == 0:
        return (b, 0, 1)
    else:
        g, y, x = egcd(b % a, a)
        return (g, x - (b // a) * y, y)


def modinv(a, m):
    g, x, y = egcd(a, m)
    if g != 1:
        raise Exemption('modular inverse does not exist')
    else:
```

```
      return x % m
```

You can also find the scripts here:

https://gist.github.com/Bitatlas/4a6fa3742713f50c07ed6aa6ae78bd94

```
>>> def egcd(a, b):
...         if a == 0:
...                 return (b, 0, 1)
...         else:
...                 g, y, x = egcd(b % a, a)
...                 return (g, x - (b // a) * y, y)
...
>>> def modinv(a, m):
...         g, x, y = egcd(a, m)
...         if g != 1:
...                 raise Exemption('modular inverse does not exist')
...         else:
...                 return x % m
...
>>> |
```

Once you have imported these two functions, we will need to add the following imports:

```
from fastecdsa.curve import Curve

from fastecdsa.point import Point

from fastecdsa.curve import secp256k1
```

```
>>> from fastecdsa.curve import Curve
>>> from fastecdsa.point import Point
>>> from fastecdsa.curve import secp256k1
```

These are all the libraries and recommended values for the parameters that we will need to use to sign a message!

Let's start by signing the message "I LOVE BLOCKCHAIN", doing as it follows:

```
keccak.new(data=b'I LOVE BLOCKCHAIN', digest_bits=256).hexdigest()
```

```
>>> keccak.new(data=b'I LOVE BLOCKCHAIN', digest_bits=256).hexdigest()
'e764eaba4076662680cf3dfcd8b50b2952610bb46f51e3e55ffb20a2b4ef7daa'
>>> msgHash = '0x' + keccak.new(data=b'I LOVE BLOCKCHAIN', digest_bits=256).hexdigest()
>>> msgHash
'0xe764eaba4076662680cf3dfcd8b50b2952610bb46f51e3e55ffb20a2b4ef7daa'
```

Let's also create a variable msgHash by using the command below. Note that we are adding "0x" just to represent the value in hexadecimal

```
msgHash = '0x' + keccak.new(data=b'I LOVE BLOCKCHAIN',
digest_bits=256).hexdigest()
```

The next thing we have to do is create a generator point that will help create the verifying key. The verifying key will be created by the multiplication of the signing key with the generator point.

```
GenPoint = Point(Gx, Gy, curve=secp256k1)
```

```
>>> GenPoint = Point(Gx, Gy, curve=secp256k1)
>>> GenPoint
X: 0x79be667ef9dcbbac55a06295ce870b07029bfcdb2dce28d959f2815b16f81798
Y: 0x483ada7726a3c4655da4fbfc0e1108a8fd17b448a68554199c47d08ffb10d4b8
(On curve <secp256k1>)
```

If we printout GenPoint, we will see the X and Y of our elliptic curve, which is the same curve used in Ethereum and Bitcoin.

Now we need to create a signing key and the verification key. The signing key is generated by creating a random number (this is why it's important to create truly random numbers), so we can just randomly create a smaller number than N. Then, we create the verification key by multiplying the signing key with the GenPoint. We will then have this:

```
>>> N
115792089237316195423570985008687907852837564279074904382605163141518161494337
>>> SK = 9998887776666555444333222111
>>> VK = SK * GenPoint
>>> VK
X: 0xa9ed8e36feb2d77b726b421907d8fd3d9d5f0b9c97d8ae90f4c859471915135e
Y: 0x16ce4f3ad14b34b74ab7d8b8f25653f164707a7894ffa032619326c5ad1bee60
(On curve <secp256k1>)
```

Next we need X and Y, another point, and it needs to be a random number. The more random a number is, the more secure it is. We could just type a "random" number on the keyboard, but let's try to do something that will generate a number a little more random than that:

```
import random

random.randint(99999, 999999999999)

randNum = random.randint(99999, 999999999999)
```

```
>>> import random
>>> random.randint(99999, 999999999999)
936462993105
>>> randNum = random.randint(99999, 999999999999)
```

And finally, create the XY1 point and r:

```
>>> XY1 = randNum * GenPoint
>>> r = XY1.x % N
>>> r
72491896197645640013875686547387356513753136180397244032341905707887100997589
```

Now let's create our "s". Note that we will need to use the msgHash value as an integer without the quote marks, for this, I called msgHash and copy-paste the value without the quote marks again to msgHash.

Then we can create s:

```
s = ((msgHash + r * SK) * modinv(randNum, N)) % N
```

```
>>> msgHash
'0xe764eaba4076662680cf3dfcd8b50b2952610bb46f51e3e55ffb20a2b4ef7daa'
>>> msgHash = 0xe764eaba4076662680cf3dfcd8b50b2952610bb46f51e3e55ffb20a2b4ef7daa
>>> msgHash
104662572759196296429738888904654853281163299501449923697008233877009714871722
>>> s = ((msgHash + r * SK) * modinv(randNum, N)) % N
```

And voila!!! We have our signature r and s. Signature(r, s)

```
>>> r
72491896197645640013875686547387356513753136180397244032341905707887100997589
>>> s
39783600229381686799503424716301635369690385392071726248944900464119340062780
```

Now we can go through the verification process. The condition to the verification process is r = x % N and every time we want to conduct a new signature we need to create a new k from a random point k*V as a random point(x, y) in our elliptic curve.

Let's go for the verification:

```
w = modinv(s, N)
```

```
u1 = msgHash * w % N
```

```
u2 = r * w % N
```

```
XY2 = u1 * GenPoint + u2 * VK
```

```
>>> u1 = msgHash * W % N
>>> u1
20564663811983266605459181249352207369687052693326681068079138552808520967808
>>> w = modinv(s, N)
>>> w
31895189114607610543285594184770253641607738669959779118017851990908358823385
>>> u1 = msgHash * w % N
>>> u1
20564663811983266605459181249352207369687052693326681068079138552808520967808
>>> u2 = r * w % N
>>> u2
16003415875730789388448256071959188762951232594758189986244786974650173033159
>>> XY2 = u1 * GenPoint + u2 * VK
```

And we can go lastly to the final verification:

r == XY2.x % N

```
>>> r == XY2.x % N
True
```

We get True! We have successfully signed and verified a transaction! Weeeee! Is it just me or this is super exceiting stuff to do?

When we look again at a transaction, the r, s and the v, it makes more sense why they exist and their role in signing and verifying a transaction.

```
> eth.getBlock(999999, true).transactions[0]
{
  blockHash: "0xb4fbadf8ea452b139718e2700dc1135cfc81145031c84b7ab27cd710394f7b3
8",
  blockNumber: 999999,
  from: "0xc3665b8a9224ba8da9a20322f31d599cafa52c5c",
  gas: 21000,
  gasPrice: 60000000000,
  hash: "0x22879e0bc9602fef59dc0602f9bc385f12632da5cb4eee4b813a0c27159c4d24",
  input: "0x",
  nonce: 467,
  r: "0x43531017f1569ec692c0bf1ad710ddb5158b60505ea33fb7a21245738539e2d5",
  s: "0x3856c6a1117ff71e9b769ccb6960674038a3326c3dd84c152fc83ada28145a07",
  to: "0x32be343b94f860124dc4fee278fdcbd38c102d88",
  transactionIndex: 0,
  v: "0x1c",
  value: 1162882720000000000
}
```

Ethereum addresses and public key

An Ethereum address is not the same as the public key. It's rather a hash of the public key plus some additional calculations. Let's check how to get an address out of the public key.

We will be using the keys that we have previously generated to sign and verify the message.

We will need to hash the public key (our VK), create a string of 24 characters out of our 64 character string and make it hex.

Let's start by retrieving our VK and merge the X and Y together in one single string and call it PubK as per below:

```
>>> VK
X: 0xa9ed8e36feb2d77b726b421907d8fd3d9d5f0b9c97d8ae90f4c859471915135e
Y: 0x16ce4f3ad14b34b74ab7d8b8f25653f164707a7894ffa032619326c5ad1bee60
(On curve <secp256k1>)
>>> PubK = 0xa9ed8e36feb2d77b726b421907d8fd3d9d5f0b9c97d8ae90f4c859471915135e16ce4f3ad14b34b74
ab7d8b8f25
653f164707a7894ffa032619326c5ad1bee60
>>> keccak.new(data=b'a9ed8e36feb2d77b726b421907d8fd3d9d5f0b9c97d8ae90f4c859471915135e16ce4f3
ad14b34b74ab7d8b8f25', digest_bits=256).hexdigest()
'be8d5bbfa171171f128a7fc76e9d6c0b98e0c4c863dabde47082ae461f09983d'
>>> pubHash = keccak.new(data=b'a9ed8e36feb2d77b726b421907d8fd3d9d5f0b9c97d8ae90f4c8594719151
35e16ce4f3ad14b34b74ab7d8b8f25', digest_bits=256).hexdigest()
>>> pubHash
'be8d5bbfa171171f128a7fc76e9d6c0b98e0c4c863dabde47082ae461f09983d'
>>> addr = 0x6e9d6c0b98e0c4c863dabde47082ae461f09983d
```

We then do the following in order to get the hash of the public key

```
keccak.new(data=b'a9ed8e36feb2d77b726b421907d8fd3d9d5f0b9c9
7d8ae90f4c859471915135e16ce4f3 ad14b34b74ab7d8b8f25',
digest_bits=256).hexdigest()
```

The hash in this case will be as per below. From this hash, we need to remove the first 24 characters of the 64 character string, ad we are left with the public address!

be8d5bbfa171171f128a7fc76e9d6c0b98e0c4c863dabde47082ae461f09983d

This is the process through the public address is created.

Writing an input or message into the blockchain

Now that we saw how transactions are signed and how a public address is created let's see how to read a message on the Ethereum blockchain. With a message, I mean really any message.

In the transaction data, the field "input" is where we can find a message. These messages are used for different purposes. They can be used to provide any additional information on a transaction. They can be used by smart contracts as an additional field to allow the smart contract to execute some function or be used to send tokens on the Ethereum blockchain. Let's see a few examples:

I have created a transaction "0x813850ba423fe4a7e38d89c0c4a1d0a166f58f9d369778086b3b1 a28edf92bc0" on the block 11792873 containing a message written by myself and you can also do it. Let's look at the transaction:

```
> eth.getTransaction("0x813850ba423fe4a7e38d89c0c4a1d0a166f58f9d369778086b3b1a28edf92bc0")
{
  blockHash: "0xbf4a5f0084ca1732a79576debb5ee0b237db1edc29f215a5be84b8c4b063a29e",
  blockNumber: 11792873,
  from: "0x5b61f379a48fac31be96a20b9f0463d0291ab56a",
  gas: 21304,
  gasPrice: 160000000000,
  hash: "0x813850ba423fe4a7e38d89c0c4a1d0a166f58f9d369778086b3b1a28edf92bc0",
  input: "0x49204c4f564520554e424c4f434b434841494e",
  nonce: 0,
  r: "0xb006730362d6bea4fdb92d684bd058ed78e713835909279241cd8462503d8268",
  s: "0xf5c7004de764e52627f7cc1c7c7553d088472f531c8c27f49d957d9c79e4d6c",
  to: "0x5b61f379a48fac31be96a20b9f0463d0291ab56a",
  transactionIndex: 131,
  v: "0x26",
  value: 0
}
```

You can notice that the transaction value is zero. The sender only had to pay gas in order to process a transaction, but he doesn't need to actually send any value.

The message is in the input field. The message is written in hex and not human-readable, but we can easily convert it. It's pretty easy. From you python command prompt, try the following commands to convert a hex string to UTF-8 text:

```
import codecs

codecs.decode("hex string", "hex").decode('utf-8')
```

We could write a few code lines to automate this but simply copy the input field without the 0x and run the command for the sake of the example. Let's decode the input of the above block:

```
>>> import codecs
>>> codecs.decode("49204c4f564520554e424c4f434b434841494e", "hex").decode('utf-8')
'I LOVE BLOCKCHAIN,'
```

Messages in the Ethereum blockchain are immutable, meaning that no one can ever change it, and it is censorship-resistant. People have been writing love messages, marriage proposals and political messages all over the Ethereum blockchain.

To write a message on the Ethereum blockchain, you need to have an Ethereum wallet with some Ether to pay the gas fee, and you need to connect to a wallet interface such as MEW – My Ether Wallet:

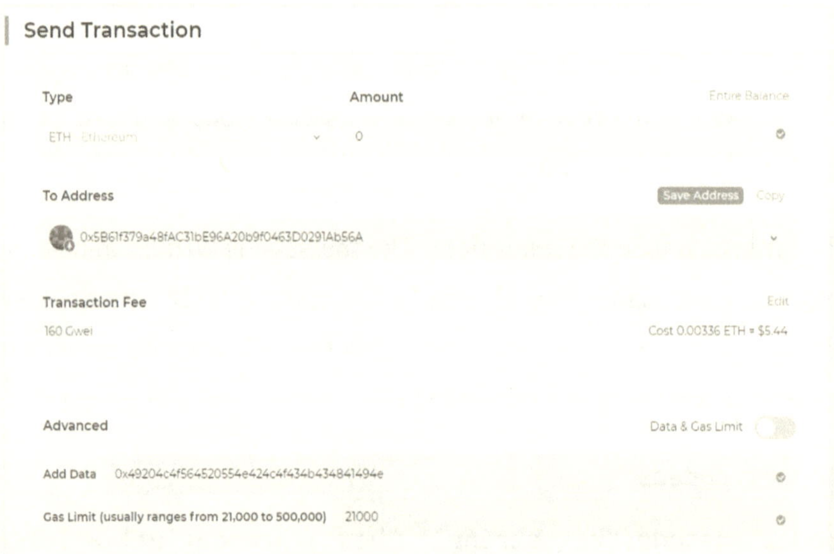

Then, you need to insert your message in hexadecimal value starting with 0x (you can convert your text message to hex in one of the many online converters). Then, just click send, and your message will live forever in the blockchain. To check this message, you could also visit a block explorer such as Etherscan.io and check the message:

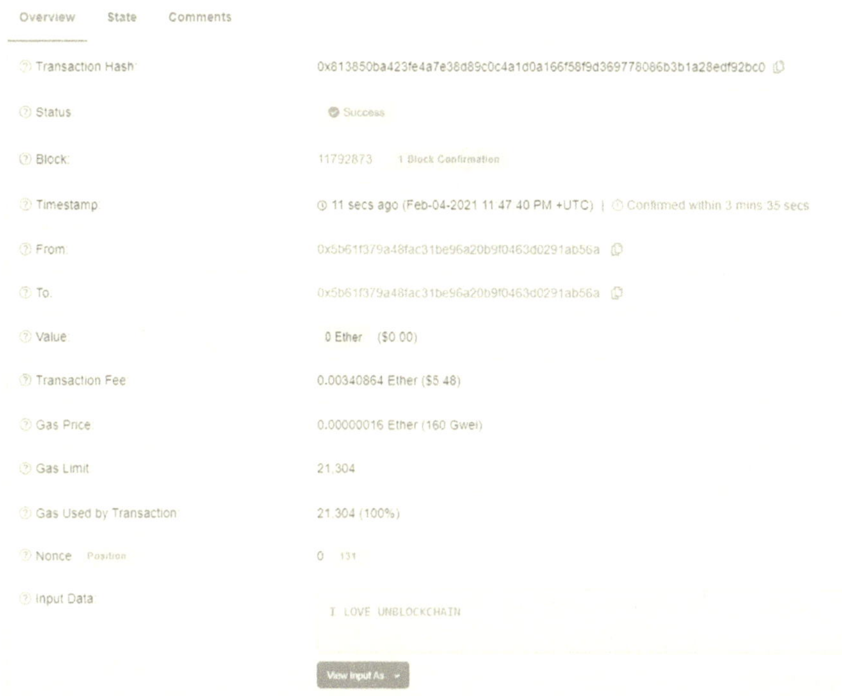

I randomly selected another transaction that has an ERC20 token transfer to a smart contract. This kind of message looks something like this:

{
  blockHash: "0x6d08ba853e887506b6d28ab13719950301f800bbca630d1d1af32affc131dfd9",
  blockNumber: ,
  from: "0x59a5208b32e627891c389ebafc644145224006e8",
  gas: ,
  gasPrice: ,
  hash: "0x238b5adb47481a490f575280a994dbd40748add21b8d939657492b2346fe5b5f",
  input: "0xa9059cbb000000000000000000000000a440e021f3f18294595489292987e0dc273c1fc50000000000000000000000000000000000000000000000001047ab243800",
  nonce: ,
  r: "0xf30f7023c2c420f9b19bbffb333e0d4eb90c9a7ad5e0af8fd032368de2fd110b",
  s: "0x4a191c57102474c964eb3de2ff2bf9997e6e976db6df1e49b799f3437b45a5ee",
  to: "0xc80c5e40220172b36adee2c951f26f2a577810c5",
  transactionIndex: ,
  v: "0x25",
  value:

To read this hexadecimal message, we would have to break it into smaller groups. The 0x, as we already know, means that this is a hex message. The subsequent 8 bytes "a9059cbb" is the function identifier. After that, every 32 bytes is a section of the message, corresponding to the address and to the amount. This message would be interpreted by a smart contract as transfer(address,uint256)

The message would look something like

MethodID: a9059cbb

Address:
000000000000000000000000a440e021f3f182945954489292987e0dc273c1fc5

Amount:
00000000000000000000000000000000000000000000000000000001047ab243800

Mining on Ethereum geth

There are different types of mining, and we could off course, explore the most profitable ways, how to connect to a mining pool, how to set up the necessary mining equipment (for Ethereum the GPU mining is usually more efficient, and miners assemble GPU mining rigs with for example 6 GPU cards). However, we sill be focusing on what's happening behind the scenes.

To start mining using your ubuntu machine, let's begin by creating an Ethereum wallet. Wallet creation is an important step to ensure that you have a public address that can receive mining rewards.

geth account new

```
ubuntu@ip-172-31-28-97:~$ geth account new
INFO [02-09|11:15:30.360] Maximum peer count                       ETH=50 LES=0 total=50
INFO [02-09|11:15:30.361] Smartcard socket not found, disabling    err="stat /run/pcscd/pcsc
d.comm: no such file or directory"
Your new account is locked with a password. Please give a password. Do not forget this passw
ord.
Password:
Repeat password:

Your new key was generated

Public address of the key:   0x910731875EfC9434de212a60f151a794fF0fabCB
Path of the secret key file: /home/ubuntu/.ethereum/keystore/UTC--2021-02-09T11-15-34.471130
827Z--910731875efc9434de212a60f151a794ff0fabcb

- You can share your public address with anyone. Others need it to interact with you.
- You must NEVER share the secret key with anyone! The key controls access to your funds!
- You must BACKUP your key file! Without the key, it's impossible to access account funds!
- You must REMEMBER your password! Without the password, it's impossible to decrypt the key!
```

Yes, never too much to say, create a strong password and never share your private key! You could also use an existing wallet to mine.

Now let's start our node and put our wallet for the tendies:

```
geth --rpc --etherbase 0x104Ac2177Cd8A744258ab83b17d2c0ded0245695
```

And you will be mining by now! Any rewards from the mining activity will be deposited into your account. Note that if you are serious about mining, you should configure a node with a mining pool. Mining pools increase the chance of receiving rewards, and for sure, they are likely to increase your mining profitability.

To check your existing accounts, you can run

eth.accounts

```
> eth.accounts
["0x104ac2177cd8a744258ab83b17d2c0ded0245695", "0x10f91aada6fff338d6e2703f28a4fe94f356aca2"]
>
```

To check your address, you can run

```
web3.fromWei(eth.getBalance("0x104ac2177cd8a744258ab83
b17d2c0ded0245695"), "ether")
```

If you have Ether in your account you can use the command to send it to another account:

```
eth.sendTransaction({from:"<ADDRESS_0>",to:"<ADDRESS_1
>", value: web3.toWei(0.01,"ether")})
```

Mining - Additional considerations

Mining pools

Miners in the pool!

Agriculture cooperatives were created to allow small farmers to contribute with their grapes and get a percentage of the cooperative wine sales.

A mining pool is a very similar concept, but instead of distributing earning proceedings from wine sale, they distribute proof of work mining earnings. Miners contribute with their computing power and get rewarded according to their contribution to the pool.

Every time the pool finds a block, the block reward is distributed proportionally through the participants. Because the pool puts together many people's efforts, it increases the chance of finding blocks and getting rewards that is good for everyone. If a pool accounts for 20% of the hash power in the Bitcoin blockchain, the pool will mine an average of 1.2 blocks per hour and distribute the reward through the miners. On the other hand, if a miner is doing "solo mining", i.e. not using a pool, he may need to wait months until he is lucky enough to mine a block.

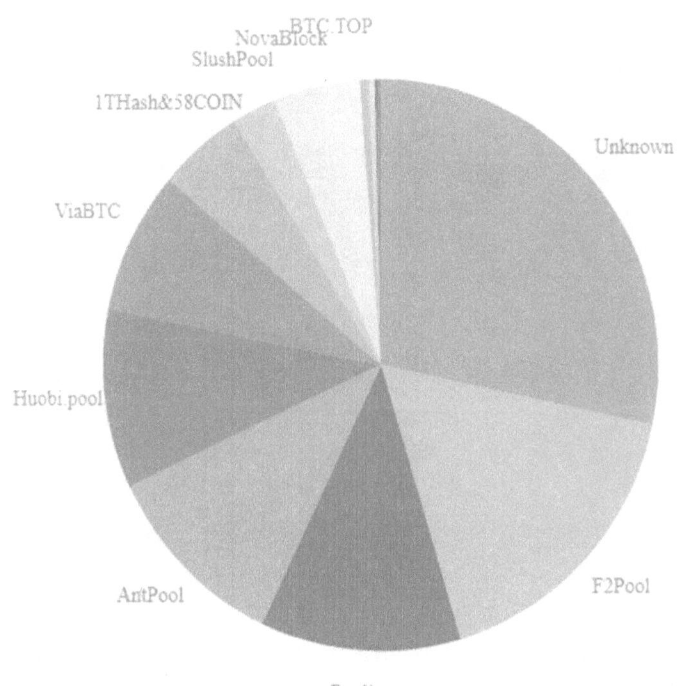

The issue with mining pools is when mining pools get too big, they can also be a threat to the blockchain. For example: although very unlikely, if the four biggest mining pools in China decide to come together, they could perform a 51% attack and jam the entire Bitcoin network.

In July 2014, the mining pool GHash.IO exceeded for a brief period of time 51% of the Bitcoin hash rate, which was enough to carry a 51% attack. This issue generated a lot of discussion in the Bitcoin community. The mining pool released a statement declaring that it would prevent its mining power from exceeding 40% of Bitcoin's total hash rate. GHash.IO is not operational anymore.

The ASIC issue

ASIC stands for Application-Specific Integrated Circuit. It's a chip that is built to be more efficient for a specific purpose rather than a general-purpose chip like the CPU in your computer. ASICS can be designed with some built-in logic and programmed for specific tasks like AI, image rendering, voice recognition, or mine cryptocurrencies with particular algorithms.

In theory, this hardware specialization makes it difficult for people to mine with their normal computers because ASIC miners take most of the mining hash power share. This could lead to less decentralization because more wealthy people/organizations can buy thousands of these ASIC devices and put them in gigantic mining farms, making people like you and me irrelevant in regard to participating as a miner node. To level down the playfield, some cryptocurrency developers create ASIC resistance features to block the usage of ASIC miners and avoid the alleged centralization that they may bring.

i Amazon Web Services – The biggest cloud provider in 2020.

ii BitTorrent protocol – Communication protocol for peer-to-peer networks. Used mainly for file sharing, it was launched in 2001. It's estimated the BitTorrent and similar networks account for more than 50% of the internet traffic.

iii RegTech – Regulatory Technology. Technology that enhances regulatory processes.

iv Decentralised Applications- Usually applications that run on the top of blockchain virtual machines such as EVM – Ethereum Virtual Machine.

v Open Account – When a seller ships the goods to the buyer that agrees to pay the seller's invoice in a future date

vi Bill of Lading – Document issued by a carrier as receipt for shipped goods. The document represents ownership of the goods

vii API – Application Programming Interface – Interface for system-to-system communication

viii RFID - Radio-frequency identification

ix SLA – Service Level Agreement – An agreement between an IT service provide or software provider and a client. It is usually related to metrics such as availability of the service, recovery time, throughput and security.

x PBFT – Practical Byzantine Fault Tolerance – It's the blockchain algorithm that allows nodes to reach consensus even if a percentage of nodes is faulty

xi https://eprint.iacr.org/2016/555.pdf

Wow, you sure covered a lot of ground in this book! Now take a look at what may interest you the blockchain world and keep drilling the technologies that you found the most interesting!

Don't hesitate reaching out to me on LinkedIn, drop me a message and ask me anything. Also, please let me know if you find any error in the book.

Cheers

www.ingramcontent.com/pod-product-compliance
Lightning Source LLC
Chambersburg PA
CBHW060518160726
47991CB00001B/92